AUSTRALIA'S FORGOTTEN PRISONERS

Civilians Interned by the Japanese in
World War Two

Christina Twomey

CAMBRIDGE
UNIVERSITY PRESS
OCM 72354340

CAMBRIDGE UNIVERSITY PRESS
Cambridge, New York, Melbourne, Madrid, Cape Town, Singapore, São Paulo

Cambridge University Press
477 Williamstown Road, Port Melbourne, VIC 3207, Australia

Published in the United States of America by Cambridge University Press, New York

www.cambridge.org
Information on this title: www.cambridge.org/9780521612890

© Christina Twomey 2007

First published 2007

Printed in China by Everbest

A catalogue record for this publication is available from the British Library

National Library of Australia Cataloguing in Publication data
 Twomey, Christina Louise.
 Australia's forgotten prisoners: Australian civilians interned by the Japanese in
  World War Two.
 Bibliography.
 Includes index.
 ISBN-13 978-0-52161-289-0 paperback
 ISBN-10 0-52161-289-6 paperback
 1. World War, 1939–1945 – Prisoners and prisons, Japanese – Personal narratives, Australian.
 2. World War, 1939–1945 – Personal narratives, Australian. I. Title.
 940.5472520922

ISBN-13 978-0-52161-289-0
ISBN-10 0-52161-289-6

CONTENTS

ILLUSTRATIONS

ACKNOWLEDGEMENTS

Writing and researching history has never been a solitary endeavour for me. Spending time alone is an inevitable and cherished part of the process, but it also involves many hours spent in archives, in seminars, and in conversations with friends and colleagues. It is therefore a wonderful moment when I have an opportunity to thank, publicly, the people and institutions whose support has been essential to the production and writing of this book.

The research has received funding from a number of sources. The most important came in 2004, when I was privileged to receive the National Archives of Australia Margaret George Award. The Award provided essential funding for research trips to Canberra, and I am grateful to the family of Margaret George and the Archives for providing that opportunity. My thanks also go to the Faculty of Arts at Monash University, the Faculty of Humanities and Social Sciences at the University of Adelaide and the Australian Research Council, via their Small Grants scheme, for providing funding towards the completion of research.

The archival material at the National Archives of Australia, the Australian War Memorial and the Mitchell Library in Sydney in relation to civilian internees was so rich, and untapped, that I decided to make it the focus of this work. Thank you to the archivists and librarians at those institutions. My understanding of internment was also enhanced by interviews I undertook with former internees Mrs Nelma Davies and Mr Ian Begley, and their generosity was greatly appreciated. Mrs Jean Langmead (nee Walker), whose parents and siblings were interned in China, also welcomed me into her home and shared her family's experiences with me.

I began work on this book many years ago now, during my time in the late 1990s as a Postdoctoral Fellow at Deakin University. Joan Beaumont provided much assistance during my time there, and has been an excellent travelling companion to World War II conferences in the years since. Glenda Lynch and Loes Westerbeek provided expert research assistance. My thanks to Margaret Allen, Vesna Drapac, Robert Foster, Susan Magarey and Amanda Nettlebeck who provided encouragement during my time at the University of Adelaide. In 2003, I was appointed to the School of Historical Studies at Monash University, and my colleagues there make teaching and writing history a daily pleasure. I have particularly benefited from discussions with Barbara Caine, Maria Nugent, Michael Hau and David Garrioch. Thanks also to Jo Lindsay, JaneMaree Maher and Vicki Peel, who helped make my first study leave a productive and enjoyable time. I also appreciated advice and research tips from David Walker, Bridget Griffin-Foley and Andrea Gaynor, who alerted me to the existence of Dorothy Jenner's diaries. Thanks to Kara Valle, from the School of Geography and Environmental Science, Monash University, for drawing the map. The support and intellectual companionship of Mark Peel, Joy Damousi and Andrew Brown-May, each of whom read and commented on the manuscript, has been essential. The friendship of Sarah Tomasetti, Clare Wright, Deborah Rechter, Elizabeth Knowles, Annalisa Giudici, Marina Henley and Cathy Coleborne is invaluable.

Researching and writing the book has relied on the understanding of my family. My parents, Peter and Sandra Twomey, have helped to look after the children during research trips and on school holidays, and I am very grateful to them. Patrick O'Shannessy has offered profound support and I will always be grateful to him.

Our children, Grace, Isobel and Maeve, were born during the years I have worked on this book. I think it is better because of them. They have each made comment on the process recently. When asked what I did for a job, the youngest replied that I hung clothes on the line then went inside and got some more. My middle daughter enquired what school-level reader the book will be. The eldest wants to know if it will be for sale at the shops. While my role model theory may not be working, it seems the oldest two already know that the book needs to be accessible and I hope that it is.

INTRODUCTION

Words about war might, in the end, tell us more than graphic images of it. In the last book she published before her death, Susan Sontag speculated about images of suffering in Western culture. *Regarding the Pain of Others* considers art, but photographic images of other people's suffering, particularly in war, are its focus. Sontag suggests that we have a 'camera-mediated knowledge of war'.[1] If there is no visual aid, no well-known photograph to accompany a particular war crime or atrocity, it has tended to be forgotten outside the circle of the people immediately affected and their descendants. Iconic images mark memory in ways that words do not, even if it is narrative that ultimately provides a more profound form of understanding.

Photographs of the emaciated and semi-naked bodies of POWs have become emblematic images of the experience of Allied soldiers captured by the Japanese in World War II. In Australia, the Burma–Thailand railway has become its defining story. The hold that the POW story has on popular memories of Australia's participation in the Pacific war, if we follow Sontag's logic, stems as much from the shocking nature of its images, from rib-cages and loincloths, as it does from the testimony of survivors. There are no equally famous images of Australian *civilians* – approximately 1500 men, women and children – who were also taken prisoner and interned by the Japanese during the war. This is one reason that their stories have been almost forgotten.[2]

How can a group's history be 'almost' forgotten? It can be almost forgotten or, more precisely, remembered only in particular ways, if there are influential forms of fiction dealing with the issue but no iconic

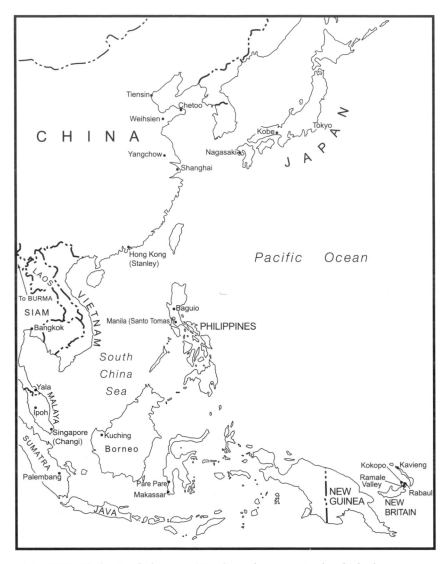

Asia, 1939–45, showing the location of significant places mentioned in this book.

photographs, no coherent public narrative and no prominent memorial. Australian cultural memory of life for civilians interned by the Japanese has resided largely in the realm of fictional re-enactment – films, television mini-series and plays – and not in the arena of national commemoration. Films about internment camp life have appeared in a steady stream since the end of the war. *Three Came Home* (1950), based on American woman Agnes Keith's memoir of her experiences on Borneo, was the earliest; the most recent is Bruce Beresford's 1997 film *Paradise Road*. The most familiar to Australian audiences is probably *A Town Like Alice*, based on Nevil Shute's 1950 novel and the subject of a 1956 film and a television mini-series in 1981. Except for *A Town Like Alice*, where an Australian POW is one of the main characters, Australians are usually incidental or minor characters in these productions. Nevertheless, such fictions remain the most influential source of information in Australia about the experiences of civilians interned by the Japanese in World War II. Recent generations of schoolchildren in New South Wales have learnt about internment by studying John Misto's play, *The Shoe-Horn Sonata*. Film-makers and playwrights like Misto have been most interested in the fate of interned women and children, and even the Australian War Memorial's display cabinets on civilian internment reflect this focus, despite the fact that more than two-thirds of Australian civilian internees were adult men. Notwithstanding the War Memorial's relatively recent and welcome acknowledgement of civilian internment in World War II, public awareness remains piecemeal and sketchy.

'Australian nationals abroad', which is how the Department of External Affairs referred to them in the 1940s, had formed part of the broader colonial and imperial presence in Asia in the period before World War II. They had never imagined a future in which some of the world's major colonial powers would be defeated by Japan, nor could they foresee that war in the Pacific would mean years of living in internment camps under the control of Japanese, Korean, Formosan, Sikh or Indonesian guards. On the eve of the conflict, large portions of the Asia–Pacific region were controlled by Western powers. Hong Kong, Malaya, Singapore and north Borneo were British territories; the Philippines was a US possession and the archipelago that formed the Netherlands East Indies was, as its name suggests, a Dutch colony. China was not itself a colony, although parts of it had been occupied by the Japanese, an Asian power with its own colonial ambitions, since the 1930s. Shanghai was a treaty port which had been divided into a French

Concession and an International Settlement, governed by a municipal council elected by foreign residents.

Immediately before the outbreak of war with Japan in December 1941, the majority of Australian civilians living in the Asia–Pacific region were located in the Australian external territory of New Guinea, in Singapore and Malaya, and in China. There were smaller concentrations of Australians in Hong Kong, the Philippines, the Netherlands East Indies and Siam (later known as Thailand). Most of the expatriates had not lived in Australia for many years, and had created a relatively prosperous and comfortable life for themselves in their adopted homes. Many had taken advantage of the increasing mobility that was to become such a defining feature of the twentieth-century world. Some achieved a standard of living beyond their wildest dreams. One young man, who had grown up in an orphanage as a ward of the state in Western Australia and had supported himself by working as a station hand since his early teens, arrived in China in the early 1920s on the advice of members of a freighter crew who suggested he might find a good living there. By the 1930s Roy Fernandez was a senior member of the Shanghai Municipal Police, lived in an apartment with servants, and took his wife and two children on holidays to the United States, England and South America.[3] Westerners who lived as part of expatriate communities in Asia enjoyed the benefits of a high standard of living, even as their home countries smarted from the effects of the Great Depression. Large trading, agricultural and commercial enterprises profited from cheap local labour; so too did members of the white community, who routinely employed cooks, housekeepers and nannies for their children. Even single foreign residents, free from the demands of running a family and large household, employed local domestic servants.

Career and conversion were the two major motives that lured Australians further north. Membership of the British imperial family provided opportunities for Australians so inclined to work in colonial health, education and welfare organisations. The tin, tea and rubber industries also attracted Australian men to the region. Most were based in Malaya, but a proportion were stationed in Siam, the Netherlands East Indies and the Philippines. There were well-rewarded careers on offer as a mine or plantation manager, or as an accountant, mining engineer or dredge-master in such enterprises. Others – men and women both – arrived as representatives of large commercial, insurance or trading firms, such as Jardine's, Burns Philp and Cable & Wireless Ltd, and worked in an administrative capacity for them or sought to establish their own businesses and livelihoods. Doctors, teachers and nurses were drawn to places like Singapore and Malaya in the hope of a successful and perhaps more lucrative career than was on offer in Australia.

Less motivated by commerce, and more by the prospect of converting indigenous peoples to Christianity, Australian missionaries had a long-standing presence in the region. Many of the countries invaded and occupied by the Japanese did not have strong Christian traditions and had been field targets for missionary societies since the great evangelical revivals of the nineteenth century. Japan itself was home to missionary societies and orders of missionary nuns. China was another scene of intensive Christian missionary activity in the period leading up to World War II. Australian missionary couples and their families, as well as single men and women, worked for various organisations including the China Inland Mission, the Church Missionary Society, the Methodist Mission Society and the Salvation Army. Many of these missionaries had lived in China for much of their adult lives, had reared their children there, and returned to Australia only on furlough every four or five years. Descendants of the original Salvation Army missionaries, who had travelled to China in the 1920s, refer to themselves to this day as part of 'The China Family'.[4]

In most parts of the region, Australians were a national minority in expatriate communities dominated by the British, Americans or Dutch, depending on the location. The situation was different in New Guinea. Formally from 1921, Australia had administered, on behalf of the League of Nations, most of the Pacific island territories that had been controlled by Germany before World War I, although the Australian military had in fact been in control since 1914.[5] This 'mandated territory' included the north-eastern part of the main island of New Guinea and the islands of New Britain and New Ireland; Ocean Island (Banaba, now part of Kiribati), administered on behalf of the United Kingdom as a British colony of the British Western Pacific Territories; and Nauru, by the joint mandate of Australia, New Zealand and the UK. Rabaul, a northern coastal township on the island of New Britain, was the administrative capital of the Australian external territory and home to a colonial community dominated by Australians. Most of the men worked in concerns linked to the trade in copra and gold, but at least 100 men and women were officers of the New Guinea Public Service. Colonial public service ran the gamut of occupations, from sawmilling, mechanical work and health care to more eminent appointments in the judiciary. There was also a significant missionary population in New Guinea. Hundreds of predominantly European missionaries worked there, a legacy of the time when the islands had come within the German sphere of influence. Missionary nuns, such as the Australian sisters of the order of Our Lady of the Sacred Heart, who lived as part of an international convent community of nuns at Vunapope, near Rabaul, were a visible and prominent presence in the islands. They were known as the 'white sisters' for the colour of their habits more than their skin; the Germans were the 'blue sisters'. There was also a group of Australian Methodist missionary men on the island of New Britain and four Methodist mission nurses. In the Pacific, missionaries were an influential presence, particularly given the isolated nature of many communities and relatively weak and under-financed colonial governments.[6]

Growing tension with the Japanese brought a host of new arrivals to New Guinea and elsewhere in the early 1940s. A number of journalists and war correspondents were present in the region by late 1941, reporting back to Australia on developments. One was the well-known Jack 'Jet' Percival. Once described as a 'buccaneering type' by his newspaper colleagues, Jack Percival was the *Sydney Morning Herald*'s representative in the Philippines. In the 1930s Percival had accompanied Charles Kingsford-Smith on his trans-Tasman flights, and became a noted aviation correspondent but by 1941 he and his wife, Joyce, were living in Manila and expecting their first child.[7] Recent arrivals like Percival felt no particular loyalty to the region and made desperate efforts to escape after war had been declared. Percival and his wife did not succeed but many women and children had already taken heed of evacuation orders and left before the Japanese occupied their homes. Those who stayed included some women who did not wish to leave their husbands and medical professionals who were required to remain behind. Long-standing residents with careers and commercial interests to defend, men and women both, were not interested in leaving; neither were missionaries, most of whom considered that abandoning their posts in the hour of need would destroy any credibility they had gained with the people whom they hoped to convert. Very few imagined that Japan would declare war on the United Kingdom and the United States and that, at least initially, it would defeat them both.[8] In a matter of months, between December 1941 and March 1942, the Japanese controlled all the Dutch, American and British territories in the south-west Pacific area, giving the lie to centuries of Western imperialism and domination based on doctrines of racial superiority. Expatriate communities in the colonies were as surprised as the imperial powers upon whom they had depended for their defence. They were also terrified.

Events had moved with frightening speed. Hong Kong had fallen in December 1941, Singapore surrendered the following February and the Netherlands East Indies fell to the Japanese in March 1942. What type of masters would the Japanese prove to be for the now-vanquished colonials? Many whites imagined the terror of rape, pillage and massacre. There were grounds for fearing the behaviour of victorious Japanese troops, as events at Nanking had attested so clearly in the 1930s, but in those early days of defeat every stereotype of Asian barbarity that the West had manufactured tormented defeated colonials as much as any hard evidence of brutality. As we will see, in the mess and violence of invasion such horrors did sometimes occur, but most foreign nationals were subject, at least in the first instance, to the more mundane treatment considered appropriate for 'enemy aliens' in a time of war. They were identified, separated from the rest of the population, and detained in prison-like facilities.

The Dutch in the Netherlands East Indies were the most numerous of approximately 130 000 Allied civilians interned by the Japanese in hundreds of camps that dotted the map between Shanghai and Rabaul.[9] The Allied powers, whose treatment of their own enemy aliens is certainly not an unblemished or uncontroversial record, at least followed international protocols and informed the International Red Cross of the whereabouts of interned persons.[10] The Japanese in most cases did not, and almost no information was available about civilian internees, as they became known, for the duration of the war.

Photojournalists recorded the liberation and homecoming of civilian internees in 1945. We now know that photographs at once reproduce and interpret reality. If any image were to sum up the sense of isolation and difference that many former internees felt in the immediate post-war years, the image reproduced in Figure 1 of Frank Merritt might be it. Frank Merritt was among the first group of internees liberated in February 1945, when the Philippines was reclaimed from Japanese occupation by forces led by General Douglas MacArthur. The following month, Merritt was photographed at Sydney's Central Station. Contrast Merritt's expression with that of the woman beside him, who positively beams. This is a man who appears sad, resigned and perhaps, given the trace of a forced smile, relieved. His cardigan is shabby and ill-fitting

Figure 1: *Frank Merritt, a Gallipoli veteran who was detained at Santo Tomas internment camp in the Philippines with his wife and their daughter. This photograph was taken on Merritt's homecoming to Australia in March 1945. Within months, he would criticise the Australian government for the mean treatment of its citizens who had 'suffered horribly'.*

Figure 2: *Jean Merritt, photographed in Sydney on her return from Santo Tomas internment camp. She was eighteen years old. After the breakdown of her parents' marriage in the early post-war years, she went to live in Canada with her father.*

compared to the schoolboy's tie and woollen jacket, and the fur collars that adorn the women's coats.

Frank Merritt's daughter, Jean, was also photographed that day. She carried a blanket tied with string and a small hessian bag, belongings crucial in an internment camp but out of place in metropolitan Sydney. The wrists that emerge from her cardigan are thin and the vertical stripes of her cotton pants draw the eye to her wisp-thin waist. Although she was eighteen, Jean appears to be a much younger girl.

The photographs are of homecoming, and they express displacement, but they do not tell of its context. For that we require words, and we need to turn to the archival record. After knowing so little for so long, the Australian government now watched and counted this first group of liberated internees very carefully. Frank, Mary and Jean Merritt had sailed from Manila to Townsville in northern Queensland, where they disembarked and transferred to a train bound for Sydney. During the journey south, officers from the US and Australian armies walked through the train and demanded that Frank Merritt and his fellow passengers sign a promissory note guaranteeing repayment of their repatriation costs.[11]

It was a homecoming in stark contrast to Frank Merritt's experience of returning from World War I. A member of the Light Horse Regiment who had exaggerated his mere seventeen years of age to nineteen in order to enlist, Merritt, a country boy from Gippsland in southern Victoria, had been wounded in the stomach at Gallipoli. After the war Frank had married and spent much of his adult life in the Philippines, enjoying a successful career and the comforts of an expatriate lifestyle in a house complete with servants.[12] His experience of war a second time around, by then a man in his forties who did not enlist in the military, was very different. This time, the battlefield came to him. In January 1942, the victorious Japanese forces who had occupied Manila commandeered Santo Tomas University and transformed it into an internment camp for the thousands of Allied nationals living in the area. The Merritt family spent more than three years detained at Santo Tomas, as civilian internees of the Japanese.

As Frank Merritt and members of his family would learn, there was a world of difference between returning to Australia as a war veteran, and repatriation as a liberated civilian internee. Frank Merritt was a man in a position to make a meaningful contrast between the civilian and military experiences of war. Mary Merritt was not, but she always resented – perhaps even more than her husband – the distinction that the Australian government drew between service personnel and citizens affected by war who had no actual service to the nation. In 1945, she informed the Australian Minister for Information that despite her civilian status, General MacArthur had 'regarded us as soldiers in the front line and commended us for maintaining faith and refusing to cooperate with the enemy'.[13] But civilian internees were not soldiers and it was a distinction the Australian government was keen to maintain. Returning POWs, for instance, would never be asked to pay for their journey home.

Dorothy Jenner looked a little happier than Frank Merritt when she was photographed on her journey back to Australia from internment in Hong Kong. She and five other Australian women and their children appear on the deck of their repatriation ship, wearing printed cotton dresses, smiling and waving for the camera. The original caption in the *Argus* newspaper noted that Dorothy Jenner was better known in Australia as 'Andrea', a columnist for Sydney's *Sun* newspaper. In her luggage, Jenner had extensive notes that she had made during her time in Hong Kong's Stanley internment camp, written on any available scraps of paper she could find. Words, stories and wry observations of human nature were Jenner's stock in trade, and a practice she maintained throughout her captivity.

A worldly, twice-divorced and childless woman who had just turned fifty, Jenner arrived in Singapore in late 1941 to work as a war correspondent for her newspaper. Initially thrilled at the prospect of joining the action, it was an attitude Jenner later considered naive, reflecting that she went off to war as if it were a trip to Manly on the ferry.[14] By December 1941 she had made her way to Hong Kong, and witnessed the siege and eventual surrender of the colony to the Japanese on Christmas Day. Uninterested in battlefield tactics or stories that would bolster a preconceived image of military valour, Jenner instead documented the shock of defeat for Hong Kong's colonial population. Two weeks before surrender, the impending sense of doom felt by those caught on the island was reflected in their ever-increasing consumption of alcohol. Jenner also thought terrified civilians, herself included, found release in sex. She described the atmosphere as an 'orgy of "forgetfulness"', in which lust and fear circulated throughout the colony.[15] When the rumour of surrender had been confirmed, Jenner confessed to her diary that the words 'tore with jagged edges at my brain'.[16]

Figure 3: *Dorothy Jenner (1891–1985), far right, aboard her repatriation ship. Jenner, a journalist better known in Australia as 'Andrea', spent the war at Stanley internment camp on Hong Kong. Flamboyant to a fault, she later claimed that the camp was a 'hotbed of immorality'.*

Throughout the period of her internment in Stanley, Jenner continued to observe men and women under duress, retained an acute eye for sexual tension, and admitted to periods of fear and doubt. Hers is not an account of imprisonment that constructs it as a steady rehearsal of the familiar qualities of Anzac. There is not much bravery, egalitarianism or mateship. Jenner's diary and a later memoir reveal as many instances of conflict as they do of community, of struggle and strain in equal measure to stoicism. 'During the almost four years I spent in camp,' Jenner later remarked, 'I saw friendships come and go. In the end everybody hated everybody else'.[17]

When he was liberated from internment on the island of New Britain, Gordon Thomas was photographed with the three other men with whom he had spent most of the war. He always considered this group to be the only Australian survivors of the Japanese occupation of Rabaul.[18] Like Jenner, Thomas was a journalist who has left behind

Figure 4: *The remains of a devastated community. Four Australian men liberated at Rabaul in September 1945: (left to right) Arthur Creswick, Gordon Thomas, George McKechnie, James Ellis. Almost 200 other civilian men from the prewar white community in New Guinea had perished aboard the* Montevideo Maru, *along with over 800 Australian servicemen. A further eleven are believed to have been executed at Kavieng in 1944.*

a valuable eyewitness account of internment by the Japanese but, unlike Jenner, he was no recent arrival to colonial life. Thomas had spent most of his adult life in New Guinea. He considered himself 'Australian by adoption', as he put it, having arrived from North America when he was barely twenty. Perhaps as a declaration of his loyalty to the new nation, he served with the First AIF in France during World War I.[19] Between the wars Thomas lived and worked in New Guinea, eventually achieving social prominence there as editor of the *Rabaul Times*.

In some respects Thomas was right about his status as one of the few who had survived Japanese occupation. In mid-1942, almost 200 men from Rabaul's pre-war white community, by then civilian internees under the control of the Japanese, boarded the *Montevideo Maru* for transportation to Japan. Over 800 Australian service personnel were also on board that ship. En route, American submarines torpedoed the ship, which was not marked as prisoner transport, and all the Australians on board were lost. A group of sixty Australian army officers and eighteen Australian women, including army, government hospital and mission nurses, had boarded another ship bound for Japan, which had arrived safely. The women spent the rest of the war interned at Yokohama and Totsuka.[20] There were also executions of civilians in the islands to Australia's north. War crimes investigators believed that another party of Australians, who had been prevented from boarding the *Montevideo Maru* because they had technical skills useful to the Japanese, had been executed on the wharf at Kavieng, on the island of New Ireland, in 1944.[21] Thomas seemed interested in counting only white male survivors of internment. His calculations overlooked another group of Australians, ten nuns who had been interned in the Ramale Valley on the island of New Britain where they had worked as missionaries before the war.[22] Thomas had in fact spent the final weeks of his captivity in the Ramale Valley internment camp, which had been home to the nuns for much of the war.

Thomas's designation of 'us' ignored the nuns but it also, of course, completely negated the experiences of indigenous civilians who had endured the Japanese occupation of New Guinea. During his thirty years residence in the islands, Thomas had developed an extensive library which included long runs of academic anthropology journals, photographs of island life and research notes on indigenous societies.[23] In this he was unusual. Yet in ignoring the experiences of indigenous islanders as essentially unimportant, Thomas reflected a colonial attitude that prevailed among many members of the Australian community in New Guinea.

Like all of us, Thomas was a person of his time and place. The way he understood and interpreted his time as a captive of the Japanese was strongly influenced by his identity as a white man and member of the ruling elite. His memoir of internment barely disguises a sense that a natural racial order, in which whites were superior to islanders and Asians of any nationality, had been reversed by the victory of the Japanese. In an article written within months of his release, Gordon Thomas described the scene in Japanese-occupied Rabaul as 'topsy-turvy'. The internees were 'the one-time masters of Rabaul' now performing jobs previously reserved for indentured labourers.[24] The reversal began early. When the Europeans in New Guinea first surrendered to the Japanese, they were forced to carry the belongings of Asians who had also done so. 'The white man had become the servant of the East', Thomas commented. When rounded up into a hall, Thomas considered that hierarchies of colour had been reversed: 'Yellow ruled, white served'.[25]

Santo Tomas. Stanley. Ramale Valley. They are not names redolent with association in Australia, but for the men and women who spent the war interned by the Japanese they remain potent symbols of wartime detention. In comparison, the fate of 22 000 military POWs, members of the Second AIF defeated then captured by the Japanese, and the death during captivity of one-third of their number, is perhaps the defining feature of Australia's participation in the Pacific war.[26] It has attracted a wealth of memoir, reflection and academic study.[27] Yet imprisonment by the Japanese was a war experience shared by civilians, as the work of historians from the United States, the United Kingdom and the Netherlands on their own nationals has so clearly attested.[28] There was a group of Australians – men and women like Frank and Mary Merritt, Dorothy Jenner and Gordon Thomas – who also spent the Pacific war detained, imprisoned and cut off from contact with their families and friends.

In a historical period when the victims of warfare have become rather more central to public forms of commemoration and remembrance than the battlefield heroes and generals of an earlier era, and when stories of suffering, trauma and survival are an increasingly popular form of life writing, it is somewhat surprising that we still know so little about the experiences of Australian civilians interned by the Japanese. The lack of an instantly recognisable visual symbol has impeded memory, and fiction has perhaps distorted it, but there are other reasons too, which have much more to do with ambivalence. War histories are, by and large, military stories. Civilians, especially women and children, have long struggled to find a place within them. Civilians who were themselves directly and adversely affected by war have continued to remain peripheral to a national vision about war which continues to concentrate on military service and its effects on individuals and their families.

The relative invisibility of civilian internees in Australia cannot be explained, as it can elsewhere, by a lack of interest in or subconscious 'forgetting' of the Pacific war. Civilian internment has been considered peripheral to war histories in the United Kingdom and Europe because it occurred in the 'Far East'. For Europeans, the war to be won was that against fascism in Europe: events elsewhere were sideshows to the main event. This allowed little space for the war stories of people who had experienced an entirely different kind of war. The English had suffered through the Blitz, the Dutch had endured Nazi occupation. There was a perception at home, among Europeans, that those in the 'Far East' at least had better weather and no Nazis, whatever the extent of their actual privation.[29] One recent book by an American scholar suggests that in the United Kingdom and the United States there has been something akin to a historical 'amnesia' about the Pacific war, constituting as it did a humiliating defeat (at least initially), a challenge to white supremacy in the region and for the British, the final nail in the coffin of Empire.[30] Internees and POWs were an uncomfortable and unwelcome reminder of all that had gone wrong, and of what had been lost.

This is less true for Australia, where the phrase 'Far East' strikes a dull note. Even that arch-monarchist, Robert Menzies, was aware of this fact during his first prime ministership. In a speech broadcast in April 1939, Menzies reminded his listeners: 'What Great Britain calls the Far East is to us the near north'.[31] The experiences of the Pacific war would, in fact, come to dominate national memories of World War II in the years that followed. As a smaller nation, Australia had the luxury of deflecting the blame for military catastrophe on to a major power: the United Kingdom. Australians also have a knack of turning military defeat into celebrations of courage and spirit. Although World War I and Gallipoli in particular remain the pre-eminent and defining experience of war in Australia, World War II has the distinction of being the conflict in which the enemy attacked Australian territory, creating an unprecedented fear of invasion. The authenticity of the threat may now be in dispute, but this has done little to undermine the broader public belief in its veracity.[32] Prime Minister Paul Keating's political agenda in the 1990s, to foreground Australia as part of Asia and to point to weakness in the links with the United Kingdom as part of a republican agenda, renewed interest in the Pacific war as a key moment in both these relationships. The 'Australia remembers' campaign of 1995, which celebrated the fiftieth anniversary of the ending of the Pacific war, also concentrated public attention.[33] POWs were prominent in these commemorations but civilian internees were entirely overlooked by officialdom, although John Misto's play about women's internment, *Shoe-Horn Sonata*, won the Australia Remembers National Play Competition. Again, however noble the motivation, this was internment as entertainment and not as a form of official commemoration.

In Australia, it is not forgetfulness about the Pacific war but rather the ambiguous position of civilian internees in relation to common beliefs about participation in war, as well as the nature of sacrifice and entitlements to compensation for suffering, that begin to explain the limited public understanding of their experiences. By the mid-twentieth century in Australia, there were well-developed links between military service, sacrifice and the nation. The defence forces were expected to protect the nation and embody its values: their personal suffering was a sacrifice made out of duty to the nation. Public acknowledgement of this sacrifice was the essence of national commemoration. Entitlement to substantial repatriation benefits was its reward. Civilian internees had suffered in wartime, but they had not served the nation. Without service, there could be no commemoration, nor could there be entitlement. This was also a situation that prevailed in the United Kingdom, the United States and the Netherlands. The one exception to this rule was made for civilians interned in New Guinea, a group for whom the Australian government was prepared to accept a moral obligation, given that they were residents of Australian external territory at the time of their capture.

Moreover, internment camps confounded one of war talk's classic divisions: between the front, or battlefield, and the home front. Prison and internment camps were neither one nor the other. The battle was over, the camps' inmates were defeated or identified as 'enemies' of the occupying power. The camps were 'home' to their occupants, but without the sense of nurture or refuge that such a word usually signifies in wartime. In addition, these two zones of war – the front and home front – were usually aligned with particular gender roles. Battle was for men, the nurturing role of the home front was the proper arena for women (even though actual home front duties for many women included taking on jobs and roles previously deemed 'men-only').[34] The internment camp, an ambiguous zone, also posed dilemmas for masculinity and femininity. What did it mean for a woman to be detained by the enemy so far from her home? Was it emasculating for men to be defeated and controlled by those whom they had previously thought of as their racial inferiors? And who was to protect the women and children? Such tensions have always circled around the internment camps and their occupants, and have driven the interest of film-makers, novelists and playwrights. The very questions which have piqued the interest of creative producers have also meant that it has been difficult to incorporate internment camps into the traditional narratives of war and commemoration.

Returned internees were for the most part reticent, at least in public. By the 1990s those who had been children in the camps began to self-publish their memoirs but none have paralleled the commercial success of POW books.[35] The most well-known of these is probably Sheila Allen's *Diary of a Girl in Changi*, which has run to several printings.[36] Other civilian internees also kept a diary during internment, although this was always at the peril of discovery by their Japanese overseers, who had expressly forbidden it.[37] There were practical barriers too, because Japanese guards were not in the habit of distributing stationery supplies to internees, who had to make do with what was at hand. As a result, only a few diaries were kept and the number to have survived is even smaller. Dorothy Jenner, for instance, wrote her diary on toilet paper and, during inspections, hid it in the soles of her shoes. Jack Percival also kept a diary for most of his captivity. Percival was interned at Santo Tomas, and much of the diary was written on the back of laboratory test reports and student assignments that Percival found abandoned in the university's classrooms.[38]

Civilian internees were people who felt less bound to subscribe to the hyperbole of Anzac than POWs, and thereby have the capacity to tell us something different about the experience of captivity under the Japanese. They demonstrate the fragility of the concepts of 'mateship' and stoicism, integral components of the Anzac legend, as ways of understanding the behaviour of all Australians in wartime. Dorothy Jenner is perhaps the most flamboyant and idiosyncratic internee to flout that tradition, but others shared her sentiments and reservations about the effect of internment on individuals and the community. Internment also confronted contemporary ideas about what it meant to be a real man, a respectable woman and for both, what it meant to be white. The challenges were particularly acute for men like Gordon Thomas, long-term colonial residents who had placed considerable store in the prestige and superiority of the white race.

After their release from internment, civilian internees posed awkward questions for the state about just recompense and citizenship rights for those who could not claim service to the nation, but whose war experiences in enemy hands had been, in part, determined by their nationality. They also raised broader issues about the responsibilities of government towards its citizens who had chosen to live beyond the borders of the nation–state. The Merritt family's complaints about their repatriation costs from the Philippines had unwittingly exposed the ambiguous place that civilian internees occupied in understanding war, sacrifice and entitlement. They were not the only released internees to protest the privileged place of the citizen-soldier in the Australian repatriation and welfare system.

Australian civilian internees received a somewhat limited form of sympathy on their return and repatriation to Australia. This book seeks to explain why and to bear witness to the war experiences of civilian internees with both their own words and with mine. It seeks to recover lost stories, with an exploration of why they have been overlooked and with a historian's sensibility about the way they are told. It moves from looking at the initial confusion of invasion and defeat, to a consideration of the lived experience of captivity, particularly its psychological and physical strains, before examining the aftermath of war in terms of the legacy of internment and former internees' desire for recognition and compensation.

As citizens of a country fixated on the military experience of war, there have often been only limited places where the voices of civilians affected by war might be heard. We need to listen to these stories, if only to remind ourselves that the reach of war extends far beyond the immediate battlefield and that the costs of war do not belong to the military and their families alone. Sometimes internees' experiences of violence and privation make for distressing reading, at others their sense of grievance is bitter and overwhelming. There are moments too, when we are reminded that these were people for whom racial hierarchies were important. It has not always been easy to write about the bewilderment and pain that accompanied the erosion of privilege, for instance, when the privilege was in itself already problematic and other people suffered for it. Internees paid a terrible price for their presence in a foreign land, as one coloniser replaced another.

PART I

The Early 1940s

Events seemed so fantastic, that I pinched myself in order to see if I was having a bad dream or was really awake.

Malcolm Macfarlane, accountant, Thailand

Everyone knew we were for it.

Dorothy Jenner, Hong Kong, Christmas Day 1941

CASUALTIES OF WAR

In January 1942, when the Japanese invasion appeared imminent, New Guinea's most senior public servant, Government Secretary Harold Page, sought permission from Canberra to evacuate European civilians from the area. He was told to determine who were 'unnecessary civilians' but reminded that the withdrawal of any administrative officers was to be 'deprecated'. Essentially, Page's request had been refused. In the event, Rabaul fell to the Japanese within days.[1] Australian residents in the mandated territories felt a particular sense of betrayal and neglect by their government in relation to the defence of their home. They had expressed anxiety about an attack by the Japanese for some time, but only a small military garrison, known as 'Lark Force', had been stationed in Rabaul from 1941. The territories' residents were also unaware that, after Japan had declared war on the Allies in December 1941, the Australian government had decided for strategic reasons not to reinforce Rabaul and, as it were, to concede its loss in the event of an invasion. Despite the attempts of Lark Force to repel the Japanese when they did land in January 1942, it was easily overwhelmed by the sheer numbers of Japanese troops.[2] Later, Gordon Thomas recounted the disquiet among those who remained about the inadequate defence of Rabaul and the failure to evacuate civilians. One man told Thomas that civilians like himself had been left in New Guinea 'like bloody worms wriggling on a hook'.[3]

The rapidity of the Japanese advance thwarted the last-minute escape attempts of civilians in other parts of the region too. The day Dorothy Jenner was scheduled to fly out of Hong Kong to Manila, she walked out of the airport lounge and on to the tarmac to witness her plane being torn apart by a Japanese bomb. Although Jenner initially had no intention of staying in Hong Kong and ultimately had no choice, there were other longer-term residents determined to stay.[4] In the lead-up to war, despite the British advocating the evacuation of women and children in Hong Kong and imposing travel restrictions for the same group to Malaya, colonial governments had also issued reassurances about the strength of their own forces and the inferiority of the Japanese. These mixed messages lulled some members of colonial communities into false confidence, and a proportion even resented the effort to make them leave and took active measures to avoid doing so. Others, particularly Eurasians and those of Chinese heritage, foundered when their efforts to evacuate to the nearest friendly Allied nation, Australia, were rejected by an Australian government determined to maintain the integrity of the 'White Australia' policy.[5]

As the Japanese made their assault on British, American and Dutch territories in Asia and the Pacific, civilian Allied nationals found themselves in a tense and fraught situation. Evacuations, particularly of women and children, continued apace but there were simply not enough ships available to transport so many people at such short notice. People working in essential services, or as part of volunteer forces, were required to stay and assist in the territories' defence. To many of them, this participation in the defence of their homes led to a blurring of boundaries about what constituted 'service' during the invasion. The vulnerability of civilians was particularly acute in remote locations, far from the protection that sometimes numbers alone provided. Once they were trapped behind enemy lines, there was little the Australian government could do to help its civilian nationals. The unwillingness of the Japanese government to honour international protocols in relation to 'enemy aliens' in occupied territory meant information was sparse. Yet even in the confusion of invasion, concerns began to emerge that would become even more prominent as the years of war passed: that captivity would be a particularly perilous fate for women; that civilian internees held a worryingly ambiguous place in the protocols and practice of warfare; and that captivity under the Japanese was worse than mere imprisonment: it was a form of racial subordination.

Most white Australian women in New Guinea and its surrounding islands had left by the time the Japanese invaded in January 1942. On 14 December 1941, the administrator announced by radio that all women and children were to be compulsorily evacuated, except missionaries and nurses who might stay if they so wished.[6] Almost all of them needed no other word than this, and left as soon as they could, despite their misgivings about separation and anxiety about husbands and fathers. The condition on which the Australian government allowed the nuns to stay behind in Rabaul was that they undertook Red Cross work. The nuns immediately sewed red crosses on to their white habits.[7] Nurses, from the government hospital, Methodist mission and members of the Australian Army Nursing Service, would be very busy in the coming weeks and wished, liked the nuns, to remain loyal to those whom they served.[8]

The Anglican Bishop of New Guinea, Philip Strong, discouraged any missionaries – male or female – from leaving their posts. He suggested to his staff that they remain in the Territory 'under all circumstances and at all costs'.[9] For Europeans to evacuate when an invasion was imminent, Strong felt, would constitute a betrayal of trust. His diary describes the panicked flight of whites from the region as the war approached. By late January, Strong noted in his diary that the 'chief motto seems to be "Save yourself" or "Save the white man and never mind about the natives".'[10] Others too were critical of the preference shown to whites when it came to evacuation orders. No thought had been given to evacuating Chinese women and children who numbered in the thousands, and who were considered in danger owing to Japanese hostility towards the Chinese.[11] No one seems to have even remotely considered the fate of indigenous women on the islands.

The bishop's message about loyalty was heeded by priest James Benson, British-born but a long-term resident of Australia before his arrival in New Guinea as a missionary. He remained behind with two other Anglican missionaries, May Hayman and Mavis Parkinson, with whom he worked at Gona, on the northern coast of New Guinea. The younger of the two women was 24-year-old Mavis Parkinson, a teacher from Ipswich in Queensland, who had arrived at Gona only the previous year. May Hayman, a nurse in her early thirties originally from Adelaide, had been at the mission for six years. She had recently become engaged to Father Vivian Redlich, a fellow missionary who worked further inland at the Sangara Mission.[12] May Hayman had no desire to abandon her years of effort at the mission, and Mavis Parkinson was equally committed to her new calling. Theirs was to be a fateful decision.

Mavis Parkinson's parents were worried about her. As the war situation worsened, they contacted the Australian Board of Missions and sent a telegram to the bishop stating that they 'consider her return imperative'.[13] James Benson was also concerned. He was extremely anxious about the fate of his 'sisters' in the event of a Japanese invasion and began to lobby the bishop for an order to compel all the female missionaries back to Australia. As the Japanese moved closer to the mission settlement, Benson repeatedly begged the women to leave – he later remembered his feelings as a premonition of what was in store for them.[14] Parkinson and Hayman could not be shifted in their belief that it was their duty to stay, a message reinforced by Bishop Strong. All the men connected with the fate of the female missionaries are clear on this point: it reads as a defence as much as a justification.

The missionary women witnessed war at the front line. They were nearby when an American pilot parachuted too late from his burning plane. They carried the pilot's body into their small church and prayed for him. When the Japanese came ashore at Gona in July 1942, Benson and the two women fled into the jungle, leaving the hot dinner May Hayman had prepared in the oven. After several days of walking through the jungle, the party eventually found shelter near another mission compound. In the last letter she wrote to her family from this 'bush hideout', May Hayman sought to reassure them. 'We have not seen so much as a dead bird', she wrote in August 1942, 'but it has been very terrifying and nerve racking nevertheless'.[15] The delight she took in describing the precious possession of a spoon and plate, handmade beds and nights spent wrapped in mosquito netting was news received with some disquiet by her suburban Australian family. The last time Benson saw Mavis Parkinson and May Hayman, during an ambush by a Japanese patrol, they appeared to be running from the Japanese but called out and fell to the ground.[16] He continued to pray for them throughout the war, and to be tormented by the knowledge that they were in all likelihood dead. The tragedy had a particularly personal twist for Benson. He had initially come to New Guinea in the 1930s after a period of mourning for his own wife and three children, who had drowned near Goulburn in New South Wales when the family had attempted to cross a flooded river in their car. Benson had been the only member of his family to survive. Given this background, it is little wonder Benson had been so anxious. To his mind, the women's fate constituted a second fatal failure in his duty to protect the women closest to him. Benson's deceased wife came to him in dreams throughout the war, and he thought constantly about Hayman and Parkinson.

Figure 5: *Reverend James Benson, photographed in September 1945 after his liberation. Benson was taken captive by the Japanese after hiding in the bush with fellow missionaries Mavis Parkinson and May Hayman, who were executed.*

Another account suggests that Mavis Parkinson and May Hayman died together somewhat later. There is a witness statement, devastating in its simplicity, in the evidence collected as part of Sir William Webb's investigation into Japanese war crimes. An indigenous man told

Australian investigators what he knew about the murder of the missionaries. The sisters had spent the night in a garden. In the morning they were seen at a coffee house at Popondetta, inland from their mission station on the northern coast of New Guinea. They were surrounded by Japanese troops. The next detail is almost banal in its cruelty, considering what was to follow. The witness saw the soldiers tormenting the hungry sisters with biscuits – offering and then withdrawing the food. Soon tired of this game, the Japanese soldiers then walked the sisters about a kilometre to a plantation. Two of them started to dig a grave. Mavis Parkinson struggled to break free when one of the soldiers wrapped himself around her, but fell to the ground when he bayoneted her in the side. May Hayman had a towel around her eyes, but it is unclear from the witness statement whether she had seen her friend fall first, or only heard the sound in blindfolded darkness. Another soldier drove his bayonet into her throat. The women were buried in shallow graves that were near a track running into the plantation.[17] Bishop Strong sought to console May Hayman's family with the reassurance that 'in spite of what has happened', he was convinced that it was the right decision for her to remain behind in New Guinea 'and the only right one in God's sight'.[18] But his mind was uneasy. On a visit to Brisbane soon after their deaths, the bishop considered it would be too unsettling for him to visit Mavis Parkinson's family. Mavis Parkinson's father would not let the matter rest. He wrote 'hard and bitter' letters to Strong, insisting that he held the bishop responsible for his daughter's death. Finally, in April 1943, Bishop Strong went to Ipswich to visit the Parkinsons and had 'a very painful' interview with them that provided no salve for their grief. Later that year, Mavis Parkinson's sister interrupted a public meeting in Brisbane at which Strong was speaking, 'accusing [him] of killing her sister just as truly as if [he] had shot her'.[19]

The view that the murdered missionaries were women who *should* have been protected from the worst horrors of warfare dominates accounts of their fate. The story of another group of Australians in an equally remote location introduces the ways in which racial ideas influenced early perceptions of captivity. It also underscores the point that the initial period of invasion and the early days of capture could sometimes be the most vulnerable for enemy aliens. This incident concerns a group of men who were working in the mining industry in Siam (Thailand) in the early 1940s. The employees of tin-mining companies, by the very nature of their work, were located in relatively isolated parts of the region. Five Australians lived near Yala, which was inland on the thin finger of land that joins southern Siam with Malaya.[20] One of them, a mine superintendent, later recalled that the British had assured all the miners in the region that evacuation plans in the event of a war were in place, though residents were never provided with any details. When the Japanese arrived at a coastal town slightly further north, on 8 December 1941, the superintendent and his co-workers received no notification or instructions about how to proceed.[21] With a sense of impending crisis, the Australians sought each other out and spent the night together in a bungalow.[22]

It became evident from the moment of invasion that the local Siamese police were in sympathy with the Japanese cause. Within three days they had herded together the twenty-seven whites living in the area. The Australians later described the group as 'Europeans', implying that the Swiss, British and themselves shared a common identity, and that describing the fair-skinned as 'Europeans' was common, despite national differences. The entire group was housed in a small mine bungalow intended to accommodate two people. An officer who inspected the group told them about recent Japanese military victories, and added that 'all British persons will be exterminated'. On hearing this Norman Holt, a mild-mannered accountant from New South Wales, fainted.[23] Holt's father-in-law, a straight-talking Labor man who tirelessly lobbied the Australian government throughout the entire war and the years beyond to receive compensation for Holt's wife and son, would have been surprised. The father-in-law claimed throughout the war that Holt had in all probability been acting as a 'commando'.

The following evening the sleeping occupants of the bungalow were awoken by the blasts of hand grenades. Japanese guards then entered the chaos, dragged out some Indian prisoners who had recently joined the group and executed them. Another guard climbed underneath the raised bungalow and sprayed bullets up through the floor. When he had finished, other Japanese guards proceeded to shoot and bayonet those whom they thought were still alive. Believing their work finished, the guards left the bungalow and drove away in trucks. Those who had survived, by pretending to be dead, fled into the nearby jungle. One to do so was Norman Holt, who was later murdered while he slept by a party of armed Siamese in sympathy with the Japanese cause.[24]

Three other Australians had saved their own lives by climbing out of a window during the shooting. One of them, an accountant who worked for Thailand Tin Mines, Malcolm Macfarlane, stumbled down to a nearby swamp, and attempted to camouflage himself by slathering his body with mud. He climbed into a hollow tree and there spent the night, hoping that he would blend in with the trunk. 'My mind was partly on tigers', he later recalled, although the Japanese were probably prowling through his thoughts as well. Macfarlane was still in shock after witnessing the horror of massacre. 'The preceding events seemed so fantastic', Macfarlane wrote, 'that I pinched myself in order to see if I was having a bad dream or was really awake'.[25] Years later, when internees who had endured a long period of captivity were finally released, many of them described the return to freedom in similar terms, as if waking from a prolonged nightmare.

Two other Australians, including the manager at Straits Consolidated Ltd, Keith Craigie, seemed to have a clearer head. They agreed that those who were uninjured should hide in the jungle. However, at this point Craigie became separated from the group and was never seen alive again.[26] After the war, Craigie's widow received a letter from another survivor, a Swiss woman, explaining that Keith Craigie had in fact returned to the bungalow and helped to carry out her injured mother. 'I wish to express my admiration for your husband in returning to help us', she wrote. 'He was the only one who came back.'[27] Craigie's widow forwarded a copy of this letter on to the Australian government, suggesting that pride in her husband's decency in the face of terror might have been some salve for her grief. She was able to learn the full story about what happened at Yala from other survivors of the incident, who had wandered in the jungle for some time before being interned at civilian camps which had been established at Bangkok and at Changi.[28]

In the confusion of what later became known as the 'Yala incident', two Australian men – Norman Holt and Keith Craigie – had been murdered. They had been detained by the enemy but never actually entered an internment camp. The other survivors clearly felt that their friends had been killed, and they all had been singled out for this treatment by the invading Japanese and unsympathetic Siamese because they were 'Europeans'. This was not some kind of imagined persecution. The context of warfare had made them a declared enemy of the Japanese, but colonial tin-mining companies that extracted wealth from the Thai soil fostered enmities of much longer standing. There were parallels here with the experiences of the missionaries in New Guinea. Proximity and power might inspire loyalty, but they could breed ambivalence and resentment as well. By all accounts May Hayman's fiancé, Vivian Redlich, was an earnest and sincere missionary, but to this day it

28

is unclear if he was beheaded during the invasion by hostile villagers or the incoming Japanese.[29] Even if there had been a consciousness that the Europeans at Yala lived a privileged existence compared to their Thai subordinates, none could anticipate the horror of being locked in a bungalow and having bullets sprayed up through the floor and hand grenades thrown through the door. In this, they were victims of the Japanese army as much as they were the victims of the increasingly brutal nature of total warfare in the twentieth century, a feature of which was the blurring of boundaries between civilian and military targets and the 'cultivation of hatred' for the enemy.[30]

Hatred, particularly of a racial kind, created the conditions in which torture and persecution could thrive. The men at Yala had worked in the mining industry, and their knowledge about mineral resources and geography was at once attractive and threatening to the Japanese. Immediately before the war, some men in the industry had become involved in voluntary intelligence work and they too were vulnerable when mounting hostilities became declared warfare. One of them was Australian-born Geoffrey Scott-Settle, who was working in Bangkok as chief engineer and mineral buyer for a Russian company. Before the Japanese invasion, he had gathered intelligence for the British navy. Scott-Settle drew up plans of jungle tracks and landing beaches in Siam and forwarded them to Singapore. The Siamese police had been suspicious about his activities, and when Scott-Settle refused to co-operate with them, he was handed over to the Japanese military police, the Kempetai. This resulted in a four-month detention in a prison in southern Siam, where Scott-Settle's ribs and all his fingers were broken. He was confined to a cage and received more than 200 bayonet wounds. In an act of astonishing cruelty, a sword was inserted in his arm at the elbow and pushed beneath his skin until it emerged at his shoulder. The sword remained lodged in his arm for four days. Despite such torture, Scott-Settle's life was spared and ultimately he was transferred to Changi prison.[31]

Scott-Settle had been tortured for information, but other civilians actually participated in the fighting in an attempt to defend their territory from the invading Japanese. Australian civilian men living in British territories such as Borneo, Malaya, Singapore and Hong Kong had frequently joined volunteer defence corps in the years before the Japanese invasion. One woman who was evacuated to Sydney recalled that in October 1941 'practically every white man in Malaya was in camp training'.[32] In the mandated territories, eighty civilian men were

members of the New Guinea Volunteer Rifles and an unknown proportion of them joined the outnumbered AIF troops in the fight to
defend Rabaul.[33] Some women had also joined volunteer medical units
as nurses and aides so that they too could avoid evacuation orders and
stay behind to assist in the war effort.

At times of battle, the distinction between poorly trained and
equipped voluntary defence forces and members of the military was a
meaningless one. During the invasion of New Britain, an outnumbered
group of Australians that included soldiers and civilian volunteers had
planted a stick on the beach at Tol Plantation with a pair of white
underpants attached to it. This was at once an admission of defeat and
a potent symbol of humiliation. Despite this gesture of surrender the
men, military personnel and civilians alike, had their hands tied behind
their back and were individually and systematically bayoneted or shot.
Australian servicemen were massacred at Tol in this way. So too was
John Barrie, MBE, a civilian and manager of Rabaul's electricity company and an active member of the New Guinea Volunteer Rifles.[34]

The accounts of civilians who resisted the Japanese invasion and survived to tell the tale make it clear that members of the volunteer forces
considered themselves to have participated in front-line warfare. On
Boxing Day 1941, 51-year-old George Hooper sustained lasting injury
to his eyes when a bomb exploded in his face while he engaged in
a battle as a 'first gun & rifle shot' with the Selangor Local Defence
Corps. He later described his wartime role as being 'in action with the
Japanese', although he was never officially a member of any nation's
defence force.[35] In the mid-1950s, he still needed his young daughter to
escort him around the streets of Sydney and he did not receive repatriation benefits. Apart from exposing themselves to the danger of injury,
these civilians ran the extra risk of the Japanese assuming they were
in the military. After the Japanese victory, some civilian men who had
been part of the volunteer forces were placed in POW camps rather than
the internment centres established for civilians, which were sometimes
more benign than their military counterparts.[36]

In other locations, capture was not as dramatic but it was no less
shocking for those concerned. A man who considered himself 'An
Aussie Tramp in the Indies', Harry Slocombe, was surprised at the
rapidity of the Japanese advance when he heard the bombing of the
wharves and warehouses of the island of Celebes one Sunday night in
early February 1942. The following morning, at about 6 a.m., he saw a
column of Japanese soldiers march along the road. Soon afterwards, a

Japanese soldier arrived at his house on a bicycle, guided to the location by a 'native informer'. Slocombe, whose arm was bandaged following an injury he had received when handling a python, described the way fear gripped him:

> The Jap had an automatic in his hand. I slowly raised my eyes to his face & will never forget the expression I saw. I have had a lot of experiences with animals and have handled some very wicked big snakes 20 to 30 feet long [6 to 9 m], but I have never seen eyes to compare with what I saw that morning. The only way to describe them is to say that they were the eyes of the 'killer'.[37]

Fortunately for Slocombe, he was not long in the control of the 'killer', who was seriously affected by alcohol. It was a slow ride into town as Slocombe drove the car, with the 'killer' as a rear passenger who had his automatic rifle trained on Slocombe's back. Slocombe and the other Europeans in the area were eventually gathered together and placed under armed guard.

A similar process, in which people of Allied nationality were separated from the local population, occurred elsewhere. In Hong Kong and Singapore, for instance, Europeans were almost immediately required to register with the new Japanese authorities. In Hong Kong whites were initially corralled into the red-light area of the city and were 'interned like swine in Chinese Hotels and Brothels'.[38] They were subsequently marched, in full view of the local population, to Stanley prison, which would remain an internment camp for the rest of the war. It transpired that the brothels were luxurious compared to the sights that greeted the internees at Stanley, which Dorothy Jenner described as a 'scene of bloody slaughter'. Bodies were strewn throughout the prison, the stairs were smeared with blood and parts of the grounds were moist with decayed flesh and maggots.[39] Allied civilians were also marched under Japanese guard to the prison at Changi on the island of Singapore. In both Singapore and Hong Kong, the criminals were freed and the colonials imprisoned. It was a move designed to humiliate.[40] It took the men on Singapore over five hours to march along public boulevards to Changi prison. One Australian engineer was galled that women and children were subjected to the same treatment. After the war he claimed that his wife was 'subject to many indignities', including the fact that she, his son and many other women and children were marched nearly eighteen kilometres under Japanese guard to Changi.[41] For such men, internment involved the double humiliation of affronted racial pride and a stark reminder that their masculine duty to protect women and children had been compromised.

In his matchbox-sized diary, Ernest Henty, originally from Perth, described the procession to Changi as a 'hell of a hot walk' during which at least fifty men passed out from exhaustion. Henty was incensed that the governor, who had promised to walk with the men, drove by in a light truck and 'had the cheek to give us a cheery wave'. As the men marched in the gates, Henty thought to himself that there was little doubt that 'we are in for it at last'.[42] Henty's last comment registers a note of alarm and fear at the sudden reversal of fortune. It is a chord struck in other contemporary diaries. On Christmas Day 1941, 'day of our shame and surrender', Dorothy Jenner used the same language as her compatriot on Singapore: 'Everyone knew we were for it'.[43] The evocative phrase 'for it' suggests gnawing anxiety about the attitude of the victorious Japanese towards Allied civilians, given that they belonged to the racial group associated with colonial power. It was an anxiety that only increased when civilians discovered that they were to be segregated and interned.

The camps, once they had been established, varied in size, from major centres in the Netherlands East Indies which housed over 10 000 people to smaller, more remote camps with fewer than ten inmates. In Sumatra, for instance, it was generally the case that men were confined to prisons. Women and children tended to be herded into schools, churches and mission buildings.[44] On the islands of Singapore and Hong Kong respectively, Changi and Stanley became home to thousands of male and female European inmates. University campuses and mission schools were turned into mixed-sex internment camps in China, Bangkok and Manila. Although these camps were always overcrowded and the food was of limited or poor quality, they at least had the benefit of providing shelter. In other regions, particularly in the islands to the north of Australia, internees languished in fenced and guarded compounds that were barely more than campsites.

Australian nationals who had the misfortune to be interned were scattered throughout the region. Almost 380 Australian civilians were interned in Malaya and Singapore, most of them in Changi and, after transfer in 1944, Sime Road internment camps. The next most significant concentration occurred in occupied China, where 331 Australians spent the war interned in camps in Shanghai and north China. These camps ranged from condemned wooden huts built for British troops in the 1920s, to tobacco stores and boarding schools in the north. A further 139 were held in Hong Kong, most of them at Stanley prison but a few civilian men were detained at the island's POW camp. There was also a substantial number in the Australian mandated territories of New Guinea and Nauru and a few men on Ocean Island. In these islands so close to the north coast of Australia, over 300 people were captured, although most of them had perished within the first year of captivity when the *Montevideo Maru* sank. A further hundred or so were scattered throughout camps in the Netherlands East Indies, with the majority detained on Java and Sumatra. Approximately seventy-seven Australians were in the Philippines at Santo Tomas and Baguio camps, just over sixty in Japan itself and approximately forty Australian civilians were in Siam, most of them at Tha Phra Chandr, a university compound in Bangkok.[45]

The extent of internment and the location of the internees in most cases emerged only after the war was over and the internees had been liberated and repatriated to Australia. During the war, the Australian government had little information about the whereabouts or fate of Australians in enemy-occupied territory. Yet the Australian government realised, from at least early 1942, that conditions for Australians caught in Japanese-occupied territories would be difficult. They also sensed that internees were 'in for it'.

Commentators on the war, both behind the closed doors of government departments and in the public domain, were anxious about the treatment of people of Allied nationality in Japanese-occupied territories. They made specific comment on the potential for discrimination on the basis of not just nationality but also, more specifically, race. Escapees from Hong Kong provided information about conditions there during the invasion and early internment. In March 1942, Anthony Eden, the British foreign secretary and member of the War Cabinet, listed a catalogue of horrors that Europeans in Hong Kong had suffered.[46] In June 1942, an article in *Far Eastern Survey* stated that sometimes the Japanese deemed it expedient to exhibit 'special cruelty and contempt' towards one group, such as the British and Americans, in order to impress other prisoners, such as the Chinese and Indians.[47] Secret communications from the remaining Australian representatives in free China, the Australian legation at Chungking, also raised concern about the treatment of foreigners in specifically racial terms. In May 1942, they warned the government that in Hong Kong Chinese and Indians received more liberal food allowances and better accommodation than Europeans. The legation also passed on a rumour that the Dutch officers of a captured submarine had been treated to 'great hardships' in comparison to the 'excellent' treatment of the Javanese crew.[48] Even though it is clear that the Allies ultimately stopped commenting on Japanese abuses of their prisoners in order to prevent further retaliation, any relatives eager for news would have been able to access more than enough information to feed their anxiety.[49]

The British, in particular, were sensitive to treatment that to their minds seemed to demean them before the eyes of colonial and subject populations. One diplomatic official reported after his escape from Shanghai that political prisoners were housed in filthy and unsanitary conditions. He thought the intention was 'to demoralize them and to degrade them in the eyes of the Chinese'.[50] The primary aim of imprisonment, according to this observer, was humiliation. The proximity to local prisoners was another cause of concern. It was frequently mentioned as an intentional disregard of racial hierarchies. At Shanghai's Bridge House, which was a gaol controlled by the Kempetai, detainees were forced to live in cages infested with vermin.[51] These cages housed up to forty people of both sexes, most of whom were Chinese. One British report was appalled that white men were forced to share this confined space because many of the Chinese were criminals or 'suffering from disgusting contagious diseases'.[52] All of this information was published in British parliamentary papers, and copies of it passed on to the Australian government as evidence of the likely fate of Australians in Japanese-occupied territory.

Key officials were keenly aware that Japan was not a signatory to the 1929 Geneva Convention in relation to prisoners of war. Under the terms of that agreement, detaining powers were required to establish prisoner-of-war information bureaus and transmit the names of interned persons to the International Red Cross at Geneva.[53] There was also a loophole: the 1929 convention related to military *prisoners of war*. Internees had, in fact, no real protection by international law. This was made clear at the time by informed commentators. Writing in the *American Journal of International Law* in 1943, one American professor pointed out that: 'It is a striking fact that while there are elaborate provisions in treaties regulating the treatment of combatants who become prisoners of war, no comparable rules have been established as to civilians'.[54] In recognition of this, US authorities asked the Japanese to extend the provisions of the Geneva treaties regarding humane treatment to non-combatants. Other countries, honouring the spirit of the agreement, passed on the names of interned persons in conjunction with those of POWs to Geneva. The Japanese did neither. The Swiss were immediately prepared to act as a protecting power in all zones, but it soon became clear that in most cases the Japanese would not co-operate with international protocols.[55] After the Japanese invasion of China, the Japanese military evinced little concern for the international rules of law, did not educate officers about them, denigrated captives and accorded the treatment of enemy POWs and internees such little priority that it was a job given to marginal and minor bureaucrats. One Japanese scholar has concluded that Japan entered the war with 'virtually no policy for the treatment of prisoners, especially enemy civilian internees'. This indifference, lack of accountability and the sheer scale of internment, when combined with increasing pressure on Japan as the tide of war turned against them, created the conditions for mistreatment.[56] None of this was clear to the Allies in 1942, and there was some heart taken when, early that year, Swiss representatives were allowed access to British internees in Siam and a delegate of the International Red Cross was appointed to Shanghai.[57] The Red Cross also had information about the same time that interned civilians were receiving meat, fish, fresh fruit and vegetables, bread, butter, jam, tea, cream and sugar, with a bonus egg and coffee on Sundays.[58]

The optimism was short-lived and the rumours of tea with bread and jam were false. By April 1942 the British government was pessimistic about its efforts to obtain information and co-operation from the Japanese. Australia's High Commissioner in London, former Prime Minister Stanley Bruce, reported to his home government that the British were not confident that their objective to obtain camp reports, the personal particulars of prisoners and their humane treatment in Japanese-run camps could be met.[59] The Department of External Affairs told the prime minister's office that the attitude of the Japanese appeared to be that there was no obligation to permit visits either by the International Red Cross delegates or the Swiss, as representatives of the Protecting Power for British interests.[60] In November 1943, Stanley Bruce again conveyed British concern about Japanese behaviour in relation to the internees. Official protests about the situation had met with only 'evasive and cynical' replies.[61] This situation continued for the remainder of the war. In the face of such sparse information, the only alternative which remained open to the Australian government was an attempt to negotiate an exchange.

The first and only exchange of civilians between Australia and Japan took place early in the Pacific war. The British and Japanese governments negotiated the agreement, to which Australia was party. Nationals of British and Allied countries resident in the Japanese empire, or in parts of China and Siam controlled by Japan, were exchanged for Japanese nationals from the British empire. The exchange occurred in Portuguese East Africa (Mozambique), at Lourenço Marques (Maputo), in August and September 1942. Ships arrived at the Indian Ocean port city from England, India and Australia carrying Japanese nationals. Out of the total of 1800 Allied nationals who arrived at the port from Japanese territories, a mere thirty were Australian.[62] This included nine Australian officials and their dependants who had been members of the Australian legation in Tokyo.[63] The majority, known as 'non-officials', were missionaries returning from Korea and Manchuria. Several had been under house arrest, but only two of the repatriated Australians had been actually interned. The head of the Australian Presbyterian Mission in Korea, Dr Charles McLaren, was one. The other was an elderly businessman, Cyril Birnie, who had spent more than fifty years in Japan and a few final months in a Yokohama prison. The Australian government was disappointed about the failure to secure the exchange of any Australians from Siam. The British explained that preference was given to children and their mothers, invalids and their carers and the spouses (mainly wives) of officials. None of the Australians in Siam met these criteria.[64] No further exchanges occurred despite extensive negotiations in the remaining years of the war.[65]

Once back in Australia, and reunited with his wife and daughter who had left Korea in 1941, Dr McLaren submitted a report describing his eleven-week detention in a prison and subsequent internment. A long-term resident of Seoul and Chinju, a coastal town in the south of the country, Dr McLaren believed that he was marked as an opponent of the Japanese owing to his vocal opposition to compulsory conformity to Shinto practices. McLaren was at pains to ensure his guards were not falsely accused of mistreatment, but he did describe the physical discomforts endured in his cell. There was no furniture available for inmates, who slept on bare wooden boards. As the small cell was occupied by more and more people, body lice became a problem. McLaren noted that one day eighty lice were removed from his underpants, which was apparently a cell record. There were no facilities for washing. McLaren resorted to dipping a handkerchief in his tea, and scrubbing his skin and teeth with apple peel to imitate a feeling of cleanliness.[66]

McLaren's idiosyncratic report of his experience, which included exploration of his psyche, and that of his guards and cell-mates, was a disappointment to the Australian government, which had hoped to get some information about the conditions endured by internees from the reports of the individuals included in the exchange. Yet both McLaren and the only other man interned, Birnie, had relatively uncommon experiences and were not inmates of the large detention centres that had been established throughout the region in the previous six months. McLaren provided more information than officials probably wished: closely typed pages reminiscent of a missionary tract. Birnie, on the other hand, was reticent. He was unwilling to go into too many details about his experience, or to have his name connected with publicity about the ill-treatment of prisoners. Birnie retained substantial real estate and share portfolios in Japan and wanted them returned once hostilities had ended.

There was some consolation to be had from the exchange. Senior and experienced diplomatic staff had been returned from Japan, and at least twenty other Australians had been spared the ignominy of internment. There were also disappointments. The number who had been repatriated – thirty in all – was almost negligible. Not all who were contacted wanted to be repatriated. Before the Australian legation left Tokyo in 1942, the Charge d'Affaires approached Mother Mary Sheldon, the leader of the Sacre Coeur nuns in Japan, and urged her to consider the nuns' repatriation to Australia. Mother Sheldon refused, believing it was her duty and that of her Australian sisters to remain in Japan. Similar sentiments had motivated May Hayman and Mavis Parkinson, with a much less happy outcome. Mother Sheldon was not herself detained, but twelve of her Australian sisters were eventually interned for the duration of the war, to the distress of the order's mother superior and the nuns' Australian relatives.[67] Reluctance to repatriate was the exception rather than the rule: many internee diaries are permeated with the hope of repatriation, particularly in the early part of captivity. Furthermore, the reports prepared by the two men who had been imprisoned did not shed much light on the experiences of many other Australians caught in the region. The Australians considered that this exchange 'was overwhelmingly in favour of Japan'.[68]

The knowledge the Australian government did have about the fate of Australians was not encouraging. Within a month of their executions, the fates of Mavis Parkinson and May Hayman were known to the authorities. The main island of New Guinea was never completely surrendered to the Japanese, and word travelled through indigenous networks back to Australian representatives in Port Moresby. By October 1942 the families had received a letter of condolence from Bishop Strong, although his description of the women as being 'annihilated' must have been cold comfort indeed.[69] There was piecemeal information about the men in Yala, via the halting and tenuous diplomatic relationships the Japanese allowed in such a small number of cases.[70] The reports remained unconfirmed, however, and the families of the men concerned continued to live in hope. Hope, blended with fear and despair, was the common experience for the families of Australian civilians trapped in Japanese-occupied territories. There were almost 1500 other civilians about whom the Australian government had virtually no news. Most of them had been placed in internment camps, away from the eyes of the Red Cross or Swiss delegates. Their whereabouts and condition, as far as family and the government were concerned, remained unknown.

PART II

Captivity

The day of the British is over. I am ya boss.
Indian guard, Stanley Internment Camp

It's Xmas eve tomorrow, we are being deliberately starved, our systems are so short on proteins many of us can no longer hold our urine, our children are crying for food, the aged are dying from starvation.
Jack Percival, diary entry, 23 December 1944

RACE

In a state of shock and forcing herself to become accustomed to a new reality, in the immediate days after the surrender of Hong Kong Dorothy Jenner copied out the headlines of newspapers sympathetic to the Japanese victory and noted their insistence that British imperialism was broken and that it was the dawn of a new era.[1] Her papers include a handbill distributed by the Japanese, depicting a turbaned Indian riding an elephant, and a corpulent British man, wielding a whip, astride an Indian. The text which accompanied it was awkward:

> Elephant is employed by you and Englishman employs you/Elephant is given food by you and you are given whip by Englishman. Elephant obeys you and you are at the mercy of Englishman.[2]

Despite the imperfect language, the message was plain enough: you are oppressed by the English. The handbill is a prime example of the propaganda war launched by Japan, in which previously subject populations were assured that Japan's plans for a Greater East Asia Co-Prosperity Sphere would ensure 'Asia for the Asians'. Victorious Japanese forces encouraged local peoples to see their arrival as the end of an oppressive colonialism. There were complex military, strategic and political motives for the Japanese war offensive, not least of which was access to the rich resources of oil, rubber and tin in the territories that they occupied. The contemporaneous attempt to convince Asian peoples that Japanese occupation was liberation from Western dominance, however, added another level of anxiety for Allied civilians about what Japanese victory meant for them.

Gordon Thomas always firmly believed that the fight in the Pacific was less a contest between nations and more a war 'between the colours'.[3] This understanding of the conflict between Japan and the Allies as possessing a profoundly racial element, even if its origins were rather more political, economic and military, influenced the ways many internees understood the terms of their captivity.[4] Race, most particularly the cultivation of racial hatred for the enemy on both sides and the Japanese challenge to European colonialism and its associated doctrine of white supremacy, was an essential aspect of the Pacific war.[5] Men and women both evinced an early and heightened awareness that their previously privileged position as whites in colonial societies had come to a sudden and dramatic end. This was a profoundly unsettling experience on several counts. White prestige and its concomitant assumption of technical, military and intellectual superiority over subject populations had been undermined by defeat at the hands of an Asian opponent. Furthermore, Europeans were now at the mercy of an occupying power that had control over their movement and freedom. The irony of the reversal, in which the rulers became the ruled, was not lost on most observers, whatever their colour.

Before the war, Australian attitudes to the Japanese were in a slightly different register from those in relation to most other Asians, Pacific Islanders and Melanesians, given that the Japanese were not a colonised people and had emerged as an important naval power in the region as the twentieth century unfolded. Japanese culture and modernisation also had its many admirers among Western observers. The 1920s and 1930s had seen an increase in trade between Japan and Australia, and a willingness of some business and foreign policy commentators to question the wisdom of the White Australia policy, which had long caused offence to the Japanese.[6] Some historians have even suggested that continued immigration restrictions applied to the Japanese, particularly by the United States, and the American trade sanctions against them, actually left the Japanese little alternative but military aggression as a response to economic warfare.[7] Undoubtedly, however, increasing Japanese militarism in the 1930s, and Japan's declaration of war in 1941, challenged this softening, or at least reassessment in some circles, of the biological racism of the nineteenth century. The total underestimation of Japanese military power was also evidence of the continued racial arrogance of the West. The bedrock of racial attitudes to non-white peoples remained in place, and elements of it penetrated the surface at moments of crisis. *This is Japan*, the Cinesound newsreel shown at cinemas across Australia during the war years, depicted Japan's industrialisation and apparent 'civilisation' as a veneer. 'From these cities', the voice-over warned audiences, 'came the men who raped Chinese women in Nanking'.[8] While anti-fascist and anti-Nazi propaganda had focused on the behaviour of leaders, propaganda directed against the Japanese branded the entire Japanese people, and the ordinary soldier in particular, as possessing singularly evil traits.[9] It was little wonder that civilians trapped behind enemy lines were fearful.

The antipathy of the Japanese was clear enough, as the handbill collected by Dorothy Jenner attested, but subconscious fears soon surfaced that people indigenous to the region also did not hold members of their colonial and expatriate communities in affection. With the benefit of hindsight, it seemed to one tin-miner originally from Queensland who spent the war interned in Bangkok, that the Siamese had been 'against us' before the war.[10] Another remembered with some bitterness the scenes he witnessed in December 1941, when the Siamese national flag appeared in public crossed with the flag of the Rising Sun.[11] The sting of betrayal lingered in the memories of Malcolm Macfarlane about his trials at Yala during the same period. The miners had worked closely with the local Siamese for many years, but when the Japanese arrived most servants fled and others even seemed to delight in the sudden reversal of fortune. Siamese officials either commandeered the company's cars or disabled them, and a few helped themselves to alcohol available at the company's mess.[12] Macfarlane was unsure whether it was disloyalty or presumption that bothered him more. After his imprisonment, Macfarlane was clearly mortified to be detained with hardened criminals. His own clothing destroyed, he wore prison clothes, a blue cotton pair of short Chinese pants and matching shirt.[13] In this attire, the transition from master to subject was complete.

Disparagement of Europeans, and symbolic as well as literal distance from them, may well have been an act of self-preservation.[14] Indigenous peoples were sometimes loath to be associated with whites in case of reprisals from the Japanese. During her desperate trek through the jungles of New Guinea in her bid to outrun the Japanese, May Hayman felt that the people did not welcome them. 'We began to realize', she wrote to her family, 'that being white people the natives felt we might endanger their existence should the Japanese come and discover them befriending us'.[15] Although Hayman's party did receive shelter and food, ultimately they were betrayed to the Japanese by a less sympathetic local man. Yet many other Australians, particularly those in the armed forces, received invaluable and life-saving assistance in their fight against the Japanese in New Guinea. Sympathy with the Japanese cause was much clearer elsewhere, where overtly nationalist groups of Burmese, Filipinos and Indonesians openly collaborated with them.

Before the war, expatriates and colonials had worn their skin colour lightly, as a mark of distinction and with an expectation of deference. In these new conditions, whiteness was a liability and something to be concealed. After the Yala massacre, when at last Malcolm Macfarlane encountered some compassionate Siamese willing to shelter him, he covered his body in cloth to hide his white skin from the Japanese.[16] Australian nuns on New Britain remembered seeing one man attempting to escape the Japanese by riding a bicycle and 'blackening himself like a native'.[17] Others thought exaggerating difference might be their salvation. James Benson emphasised both his colour and civilian status by changing into his white cassock when surrendering to the Japanese after wandering dazed and alone in the jungle after an ambush. 'Even if they didn't understand the significance of the cassock,' he later wrote, 'it should at least be proof that I was no soldier'.[18]

In China, the marks of skin colour were supplemented by clothing that identified individuals as enemy aliens. The Japanese had occupied parts of North China since the 1930s. Once war against the Allies had been declared, all enemy nationals in the occupied parts of China were confined to their houses or, in Shanghai, to the British concession. Unlike the situation that prevailed elsewhere, civilians were not immediately interned. The Stranks family, Salvation Army missionaries from Australia, were detained in their own home in Peking for fifteen months between early December 1941 and March 1943.[19] They were also required to wear arm-bands in the street, with their nationality identified in Chinese characters. The British Residents' Association issued the red arm-bands on behalf of the Japanese authorities. For the purposes of this exercise Australians were classified as 'British' subjects and given a number. It did not invoke the same persecution as the Nazis' yellow Star of David, but it was racial distinction and for some, it smarted. Wearing an arm-band was experienced as an insult by John Burton, an accountant originally from Queensland who had worked in China for almost thirty years. As the Japanese began to circumscribe and monitor his activity, Burton approached the British Consulate General in Tientsin and had his credentials typed up. He had seen active service with the Queensland Imperial Bushmen in the Boer

War and had included on his testimonial that he was the 'Erstwhile Amateur Sprint Champion of Queensland 1897/1905'.[20] Burton had his managerial job title and length of service noted, and listed his past achievements. This was a man who perceived that age and seniority in his profession should release him from the humiliation of a common fate. But none of this spared him the indignity of wearing an arm-band or prevented him, ultimately, from spending the war in an internment camp. Perhaps age and weariness had corroded Burton's capacity to withstand the shocks of defeat. The teenage daughter of an Australian member of the Shanghai Municipal Police admitted that the arm-bands were intended to 'shame and isolate' the white community, but in her opinion they had the opposite effect: they became a badge of honour.[21]

Yet most internee memoirs barely disguise the sense of their authors that Japanese victory ushered in a new era in which familiar racial roles had been reversed. Resilience and defiance might be one response but discomfort and confusion were equally possible. Male internees were acutely conscious that the work the Japanese required them to perform was not in line with the labour usually performed by white men in the tropics. After his detention by a Japanese patrol, James Benson was ordered to piggyback a Japanese infantryman across a lagoon. 'I am not a coolie,' Benson insisted, 'I am a priest and a gentleman'.[22] Coolie work was not a white man's vocation. To Benson's mind, carrying human cargo was a job left for indigenous and Chinese workers, coolies, and not an appropriate job for a missionary. In a similar fashion, Gordon Thomas construed the work he and other Australian internees in New Guinea had to undertake unloading ships as 'real coolie work'. Thomas was happier later in his captivity when his group was required to help fit out tunnels with the assistance of Indian and Formosan prisoners. The presence of coloured assistants helped the white men re-establish their self-respect:

> It was not long before a portion of the dominant egoism, so generally displayed amongst the sovereign white race, was asserting itself. Having been coolies for so long it was remarkable how easily we donned the mantle of authority once again.[23]

Thomas's reflections on his internment by the Japanese are permeated by this sense that captivity was, for him, first and foremost an experience of racial subordination. Thomas was not alone in this view, given the social world in which he moved in the prewar era. His was a colonial community that had conventions and practices foreign even to mainland Australians, who were themselves not particularly noted for racial tolerance in the early 1940s. When the soldiers of Lark Force arrived in Rabaul in 1941, unschooled in the pretensions and more overt racism of the colonial *mastas*, there was disquiet among white residents about the erosion of respect. The newspaper Thomas edited, the *Rabaul Times*, published thinly veiled warnings to the visitors about their duties to maintain the prestige of the white race.[24] Although Australia held New Guinea under trust for the League of Nations only until the indigenous peoples were deemed fit for self-government, there was ambivalence among the white population in the territory itself about these ideals of independence for local people. The islands effectively functioned as Australian colonies with the concomitant inequities and injustices that colonialism brought to indigenous peoples. Social life and by-laws in the islands operated in strictly racial hierarchies, with whites at the top and indigenous people in a distinctly subordinate place.[25] One historian has considered that Australia had a 'mandate-managing reputation that was significantly better than its government deserved'.[26]

Thomas was a man aware of the racial dynamics of colonialism in New Guinea, having made an effort during his many years of residence in the islands to acquaint himself with anthropological studies of the indigenous peoples and to conduct research of his own. His prewar library, according to novelist Ion Idriess, 'was well known amongst the old island hands' and 'comprised a considerable amount of early day Papuan and New Guinea pioneering and history ("white" and native) that is now irreplaceable'. His collection of photographs and negatives, similarly, were well known as one of the best collections in the islands. Thomas had also gathered extensive information on 'native secret societies'. 'Such material could only be collected by a man who was resident in the Islands and was trusted by the natives to an extraordinary degree', Idriess thought.[27] Despite his intense interest in indigenous peoples and his apparently intimate relationship with various groups, Thomas never perceived them as equal partners. He always maintained that there was a 'native mind' that needed careful management and that whites were the true bearers of civilisation. For a man with these views, capture and detention by non-white overseers was an especially bitter pill to swallow. Thomas interpreted the rifle-whipping he received when surrendering to the Japanese in specifically racial terms as the Japanese soldier being presented with 'an outlet for his delight at having a white man at his mercy'.[28]

Given the longevity of cultural associations that linked non-white men with barbarity, internees were expecting physical cruelty. They were unprepared for antipathy and scorn. Subjection made them wince, but so too did the shock of being despised. Male internees, in particular, were amazed by the extent of hostility to whites among some Japanese they encountered. Gordon Thomas had 'felt about as popular as a blow-fly in a meat safe' when he first met with the Japanese invaders.[29] James Benson surrendered to a Japanese patrol, but initially struggled to get them to pay any attention to him. Benson, who had feared murder not disdain, was surprised when one of his captors quipped: 'I have no time for whites'.[30] Some internees continued to comment on this issue throughout their captivity. In March 1943, Harry Slocombe noted: 'The hatred these men have for the white race is unbelievable'.[31] World War I veteran Harold Murray, from country Victoria, had spent the 1930s in Malaya working as a mining engineer and he too was incredulous at the level of hostility to white men among the guards at Changi. He thought his Japanese overseers considered their European inmates to be 'white dogs'.[32] It was not just the Japanese who reminded the inmates of their reduced status. In Hong Kong, one Indian guard quipped to an internee, 'the day of the British is over. I am ya boss'.[33]

Being told by a black guard that 'I am ya boss' compounded the humiliation of incarceration. Sometimes internees coped with these challenges by invoking racial stereotypes and reworking them. There was comfort to be drawn from cliché, and some internees clung to the belief that, despite their current subordinate place, whites retained a monopoly on civilisation. For Gordon Thomas, the Japanese soldier's civilisation was merely a veneer, beneath which lay 'his original streak of savagery'.[34] The denigration of the Japanese as subhuman was another possible ploy, as frustration and powerlessness bred spite. Harry Slocombe recorded in his diary the camp scuttlebutt that the Japanese were descended from a Chinese prostitute having sex with an ape.[35] Government nurse Alice Bowman's memoir of her captivity in Rabaul and Japan remains replete with racial caricature, despite its publication forty years after the cessation of hostilities. The Japanese are described as short, bow-legged, simian, short-sighted, monosyllabic. Bowman claimed that 'their extraordinary physical smallness was a shock to us all'.[36] To her delight, one of the army nurses, Kay Parker, was six feet (1.8 m) tall and a source of fascination, she claimed, to the Japanese soldiers who were much shorter in stature. In this instance, typecasting the Japanese as short in stature and in awe of the height of a white woman reads as an attempt to contain the threat they posed to the author's sense of racial hierarchy, even if Kay Parker did indeed tower over her captors.

Other internees recorded their surprise that some Japanese military personnel they encountered upset the cartoon-like images of short and slight men that peopled their imagination. James Benson described the Kempetai who controlled the military prison in which he was housed as 'powerful men, almost as big-boned as an average Australian battalion'.[37] The Kempetai major in Rabaul was described by Gordon Thomas as possessing an almost Teutonic appearance, he was so tall, well-built, round-faced and immaculately dressed.[38] In both these descriptions strong physique does not appear as an innate attribute for the Japanese. Its origins and natural home are inevitably 'Teutonic' or even 'Australian'. Early in her internment, Rabaul nun Sister Berenice Twohill came into contact with tall air force men whom she considered especially nasty.[39] For her, physical strength equated with a heightened capacity for violence.

One of Charles McLaren's views, developed during his short time under Japanese guard in Korea, was that the 'Japanese mentality' found it hard to comprehend the unrelenting cheerfulness of British, American and Dutch internees.[40] There were others who mentally equipped themselves during internment by seeking solace in a belief in the superior fortitude of Western peoples. The former British Ambassador to Japan, Sir Robert Craigie, also considered that those interned in Yokohama prisons impressed their captors with their moral fibre and staying power.[41] When Gordon Thomas, who had been separated from most of Rabaul's civilian men, met them again about six months into captivity, he was struck by their changed appearance. There was one thing that remained unchanged though, which Thomas described as the most valued asset of the white man amongst coloured races – 'self respect, notwithstanding the indignities and humiliations each and everyone had to endure'.[42]

Camp leaders, on the other hand, were more acutely aware that pride often comes before a fall. In Changi, weekly newsletters reminded internees that whatever the previous order, they were prisoners now. 'Many of us still do not realise we are prisoners and not our own masters', British block commander Theo Stone insisted. Four months later, he again reminded his fellow internees that they had to realise that they were captives and therefore required to defer to their Sikh guards. They were standing not on solid ground but on remarkably thin ice.[43] Many who were interned in Changi actually preferred their Japanese guards to the Sikhs who replaced them in September 1942. At that time, the camp transferred from the control of the Japanese army to the Military Administration Department. One internee wryly commented that the Japanese had learnt, through the military debacle in Malaya, that 'we are not dangerous people'. The Sikhs, in contrast, were themselves controlled by the Japanese and were inclined to be 'punctilious and fussy'.[44] Harold Murray thought that some of the Sikh guards were particularly violent because this was their first chance to exercise control over whites. Murray interpreted this as an unfounded faith in Japanese rule and ingratitude for British efforts in Asia.[45] This was exactly the sort of attitude that camp leaders feared would lead to trouble. Deference to the guards was a problem for men in small camps as well as large. Harold Slocombe was amazed that the predominantly Dutch internees with whom he was interned continued to deceive themselves about the reality of their situation. 'It was a remarkable thing in this camp', Slocombe noted, 'that some civil servants could not realise that they were prisoners of war of the Nippon Empire and not the Toean Besars [Big Bosses] of pre-war days'.[46]

Camp leaders and acute observers of camp life were worried that disrespect would lead to retribution and, ultimately, violence. Certainly escape attempts were not tolerated. In early February 1942, for instance, only a month into his captivity Australian man Blakely Laycock attempted to escape from Santo Tomas. He and two other men were caught, tortured and executed by the Camp Commandant, Lieutenant Tomoyasu.[47] Retribution could also be swift for people suspected as acting as agents for the British. In Hong Kong Australian-born Chinese Herbert Wong only entered Stanley internment camp in January 1944. Wong, who was born in Melbourne but had lived in Hong Kong since his early twenties, was not initially interned: presumably his ancestry allowed him to blend with the local population. Yet Wong's sympathies remained firmly with the Allies, for whom he worked as a secret agent. Japanese discovery of these activities meant his admission to Stanley, where he was executed the following month.[48]

Violence and the summary execution of civilian internees, which did happen on occasion in the larger internment camps, were more common on remote islands where internees did not have the protection of numbers and witnesses. The fate of Australian civilians on two small islands in the central Pacific, Nauru and Ocean Island, illustrates this point well. The islands had been mined for phosphate since early in the century. Only seven whites remained behind voluntarily on Nauru; five were Australians and two were European missionaries. All of the Australians were beheaded, apparently in reprisal for Allied bombing of the island, in March 1943. The victims included the island's administrator since 1938, Lieutenant Colonel Chalmers, a World War I veteran from Tasmania. Another was Dr 'Bennie' Quin, a father of five who refused to abandon the hospital patients for whom he was responsible as the island's government medical officer. The widow of Frederic Harmer, an engineer also killed on Nauru, believed he stayed behind because he thought it was his duty to keep power and refrigeration running for the government officers and the British Phosphate Commission.[49]

On Ocean Island, a further two Australians were detained by the occupying Japanese, along with two British colleagues and two missionaries. The Japanese had arrived at Ocean Island about April 1942. Most of the Europeans and some of the Chinese population had already been evacuated. During the war, the Japanese dispersed a proportion of the indigenous Banabans and Gilbertese islanders, along with some Chinese, to other Pacific islands to work. Those who remained behind, an estimated 700, were believed to have been massacred in 1945. When the Allies came to reoccupy the island, very few had survived the occupation, and certainly no white men were recovered alive. Some had died from malnutrition and illness, and the fate of others was unclear.[50] Lindsay Cole, from Bairnsdale in Victoria, who worked for the British Phosphate Commission on Ocean Island, died there in 1943. His wife, who had escaped the island when pregnant with their first child, firmly believed that his body was discovered minus both hands. 'The horror of atrocities known to have occurred to one's husband', she later wrote, 'has permanently impaired my health'.[51]

Brutality certainly existed but it was not universal. James Benson was punched and kicked when originally detained by the Japanese on the Kokoda road, but was unharmed for the following three years of his captivity.[52] In contrast, Harry Slocombe's island camp was home to a particularly violent guard, 'The Bull'. Slocombe's diaries recall the frequent and often inexplicable beatings meted out to internees and the general depressions that followed such episodes.[53] Face slapping was as 'regular as the striking of the clock'. Slocombe felt ill listening to the 'heavy thud of these clubs on human flesh'.[54] His camp's inmates lived in fear of provoking attack from the guards, particularly the most violent. Violence also occurred elsewhere. Elizabeth Gibson, an Australian doctor interned in Borneo, reported that she was assaulted when it was perceived that she had not followed proper authority. A guard whom she described as 'brutal and callous', kicked her violently on both shins and hit her across the head, believing she acted without permission in relation to a medical matter.[55] In Manila's Santo Tomas, the violence was less general but extreme for those caught infringing camp rules. An Australian miner interned at Santo Tomas, Roy Stanford, told his brother not long after release that most internees had very little actual physical mistreatment from the Japanese and that 'their method was more subtle, just to slowly starve us to death'.[56] Dorothy Jenner made similar comment in relation to Stanley, and thought that the Japanese in control there were never especially cruel 'but there was a constant war of nerves'.[57]

Most internees were able to distinguish between the iniquity of the camp system more generally and the capacity for kindness from individual guards. Harry Slocombe, so disturbed by the violence in his camp, could also identify compassion when he saw it. In an early camp, he considered that the senior officer was an excellent camp commandant, who acted with justice and consideration towards his prisoners.[58] One of the few Australian men from Rabaul who did not perish aboard the *Montevideo Maru*, George McKechnie, recalled with gratitude the attention he had received from a Japanese doctor. The doctor had been called at the behest of his guard, who had broken protocol to do so.[59] One of McKechnie's fellow internees also recalled that one guard treated him 'always in a humane manner' and in fact informed on his fellow officers who had been involved in the massacre of some servicemen.[60] The internees at Stanley referred to one Japanese man, Watanabe, as a saint. An elderly man, Watanabe smuggled drugs into the camp for the inmates and towards the end of the war commandeered a truck with relief supplies and drove it into the grounds of Stanley. 'Among those devils', Dorothy Jenner wrote, 'we can find this thread of pure gold'.[61] Others saw aspects of Japanese culture that they actually admired. James Benson described the enthusiastic and respectful reunion of two Japanese friends as a 'gracious and dignified expression of friendship'.[62]

Benson was one of the few internees to meet Japanese who were not in the military during his period of detention. He met Seizo Okada, a war correspondent with the leading Japanese newspaper *Asahi Shimbun*, when Okada was on assignment on the island of New Britain.

After their meeting, Okada returned with books for Benson who was still detained in a military prison. Fellow journalist Gordon Thomas also met Okada and described him as 'a live-wire, energetic and full of beans'.[63] In conversations Benson and Okada shared, it soon became clear that Okada deplored the militarism that had pervaded Japanese life and policy. After the war, the two men kept a promise to correspond, and Okada told Benson that he had spoken so freely because 'I was so impatient to let you know that I was a human man of reasoning and free-thinking and conscience'.[64] Another Japanese Benson encountered, Ishii, also deplored militarism, convincing Benson that millions of intelligent people in Japan shared their views.[65]

Daily interaction also meant that internees saw the vulnerability of some of their guards, even if the possibility of violence or retribution was ever present. Harold Murray, who believed that the Sikhs were taking the opportunity to lord it over the whites, also admitted that many of them told him that, if they did not work for the Japanese, they and their families would starve.[66] The camp of missionaries near Rabaul played piano for their own entertainment, and the guards would gather round and call for encores. The compound was near the Japanese hospital and the internees would hear the screaming of shell-shocked Japanese soldiers. One nun felt that a lot of them were just like teenage boys 'dressed up as soldiers'.[67] Charles McLaren, confined to a Korean prison cell, was also at pains to acknowledge the consideration and human kindness shown to him by most of the guards. Nevertheless, he also reported the fate of American colleagues in the north of the country and the treatment meted out to fellow repatriates he met as he sailed as part of the civilian exchange to Lourenço Marques. 'There is another and blacker part of the picture', he wrote, 'and anyone who attempts to gloss over or explain away this grim and revolting story is partisan against the truth'.[68] McLaren described as 'broken' the senior businessmen from Kobe who had been interned and interrogated before their departure.

Opinion pieces and newspaper editorials on the subject of Japanese violence in internment and POW camps in the immediate aftermath of the camps' liberation focused on this behaviour as evidence of the 'inhumanity' and 'barbarity' of the Japanese. While it is easy enough to find former internees willing to explain away Japanese violence as barbarism, other internees sought to analyse and to understand the motivation behind the psychology of guards who were violent. Dorothy Jenner put it down to war itself. In the 1970s, she observed that Allied armies had killed, looted and perpetrated atrocities too:

Only we have white faces and pretend that this makes us automatically virtuous. It doesn't. I discovered many things in camp. One of them was that, just as there is good in all of us there is also evil in all of us. Good and evil cross national, racial and class boundaries.[69]

Harry Slocombe tried to move beyond racial stereotyping and analyse why the guard whom he referred to as 'The Bull' would wind himself up into a rage and beat the internees mercilessly. He consulted the camp doctor, who advised that the guard had some form of psychopathology. Slocombe thought that some of his captors had sadist tendencies and concluded that 'The Bull' was a 'hysterical maniac'.[70] This type of pseudo-Freudian analysis can also be found in the extraordinary reflections of Charles McLaren. McLaren argued that Freud had taught us that 'sadistic pleasure is a fact; and all of us, including the Japanese, are human'. He continued:

A confession is perhaps not out of order here. I still remember the zest with which as a child of five, I watched a chicken having its head cut off; its spurting neck and convulsed body. What a nasty affair! I also remember, as a boy of twelve, how I killed an unfortunate rabbit with my heel on its neck and felt some satisfaction in my power over it. What a revolting memory![71]

The attempt to understand sadistic tendencies in military guards, by examining his own predilection for violence, is a remarkably brave gesture, particularly in the climate of outright hostility to the Japanese that dominated in Australia in the early 1940s.

McLaren was an opinionated and forthright man, and one not afraid to express unconventional views. Long familiar with Asian culture, he was also a critic of the White Australia policy and Australia's 'racial prejudices and fears', which he felt damaged the country's reputation among Asian peoples. Alice Bowman also thought that the White Australia policy was a very sore point with her captors, but developed an interpretation quite at odds with McLaren's. She considered Japanese resentment a 'contradiction of standards', given Japan's own lengthy period of isolation from foreign influence. Bowman sought to justify the White Australia policy as being a logical product of its time, a desire to maintain standards, wages and jobs for whites by restricting the entry of coloured labour.[72]

For others, the experience of internment confirmed their belief in the need for Australia to maintain its policy of restricted immigration. Harold Murray commented on the Eurasian or indigenous wives of interned men whom he observed during his years in Changi. These women had taken on the burden of their husband's nationality when the Japanese arrived. One of them, 'Nan' Hooper, was Siamese and seventeen years younger than her husband, George. They had a son, Harold, who had been born on the island of Penang. During the Japanese invasion, Nan helped to nurse wounded Australian soldiers in Singapore's Cathay building. She and her son were later interned in Changi.[73] Despite the sacrifices made by women like 'Nan' Hooper, the hearts of men like Harold Murray remained hard. He reported with dismay that in the women's section there were:

> Women of all shades of colour from white, very few having that colour, to jet black, and the children in large numbers of lighter shades, there are very few real white children in camp; about a dozen in all.

The sight of coloured wives and mixed race children, Murray commented, was enough to make him a confirmed White Australian.[74]

One of the children Murray might have seen was Sheila Allen, who had never really known her Malayan mother, but identified strongly as a 'British' subject because her Australian father had assumed responsibility for her education and well-being. She showed not a moment's hesitation in registering for internment. Her unusual diary entry for 28 February 1942 – 'At last! Interned and what trouble we had to get ourselves here' – registers a note of relief that she will remain aligned with the British.[75] Unlike other Allied nationals, who had been compelled to enter internment camps, Eurasians could choose to remain outside. A desire to remain identified with the colonials, so forcefully expressed by a voluntary internment, did not shelter Eurasians from ongoing prejudice once within the camp walls. For her troubles, Sheila Allen was referred to by some fellow inmates in Changi as 'That slit-eyed Chink!'[76] Jean Gittins, another Eurasian woman who had volunteered for internment in the hope she might be exchanged to Australia, where her children had been evacuated, wrote explicitly about the racism in Stanley camp on Hong Kong. Some of the British in camp felt that, were it not for the many Eurasians in the camp, there would be sufficient food for them. Relatives and friends were allowed to send in weekly parcels and Eurasians in particular benefited from this. The 'pure' British were the least likely to receive such parcels, and resented those internees who did.[77] European families further objected to the concentration of Eurasian families in one block of the camp. The governing council agreed that this was 'highly

Figure 6: *Daughters of Mary Immaculate, indigenous sisters who risked their lives to smuggle food into Ramale Valley internment camp for interned missionary priests and nuns.*

undesirable' and dispersed the Eurasians throughout other blocks in the camp.[78]

Civilian internees everywhere, from the hills and valleys of New Britain to the residents of urban Santo Tomas, relied on help from outside sources. This could be in the form of overt assistance, as was the case with the relatives of Eurasians in Hong Kong, covert gifts or the willingness of those 'outside' to conduct black-market trade. One man in his early forties from New South Wales, Stanley Pinkerton, had worked in the Philippines Cold Stores before the war. Early in his internment at Santo Tomas, he managed to get meat delivered to the camp from the stores. An American war correspondent who was interned with him later wrote a letter of thanks to the Australian prime minister, describing Pinkerton's efforts as a 'bangup job'.[79] In North Borneo, Elizabeth Gibson was so grateful for the help she received from one Chinese family in Kuching that she made a point of mentioning their efforts during her interrogation by Australian intelligence officers after she was released. 'Had they been discovered by the Japs it would have been certain death', Gibson insisted.[80] It might be considered an advantage that civilian internees, many of whom had lived in the region for years and had extensive local connections, enjoyed over POWs. As recent arrivals with almost no connection to the surrounding communities, POWs were very differently placed.

For those like Gibson, interned close to places where they had lived for some time, networks and contacts with local people were vital to survival. When Charles McLaren was in jail, his Korean servant was permitted to deliver food to the cell. McLaren claimed that he was 'filled with an abiding gratitude' for her loyalty and the efforts of other Korean friends during his incarceration.[81] Similarly, the nuns in New Britain received help from the 'native sisters', indigenous women affiliated with their order of nuns. The sisters would leave sweet potatoes and taro for the internees to collect. The indigenous sisters helped the internees survive under threat of death and torture, a loyalty not forgotten in the postwar years. The nuns always remembered the kindness of their indigenous friends when speaking publicly about their captivity.

Upon release, some internees tried to provide immediate assistance to the people who had been so essential to their survival. Theo Stone wrote to the Australian Red Cross specifically to win special consideration for local people who had helped the internees. He appended a list of those who had provided help to internees at considerable risk to their personal safety. Stone was grateful for what he saw as 'Asiatic devotion to our side'.[82] Those internees interviewed by war correspondents after their liberation also stressed the help they had received: 'All returned internees spoke highly of the Chinese, who were most harshly treated but continually risked their lives to smuggle food and money to the internees', one report on Singapore proclaimed.[83] Some were also at pains to highlight the even greater suffering endured by ethnic Chinese, Indians and Filipinos at the hands of the Japanese. Patients returning from Hong Kong internment camps aboard the Royal Navy hospital ship *Oxfordshire* wanted journalists to tell their readers about 'wholesale massacre of Chinese civilians, inhuman torture of loyal Indian soldiers and incredible sufferings from disease and hunger'.[84] The internees' appreciation of the assistance they received from outside the camps and their acknowledgement that suffering was often more acute among the non-interned local populations are aspects of internment history that are lost if interest is too strongly focused on the dynamic between captor and captive alone.

Dorothy Jenner even admitted to imagining that, when the British in Hong Kong were defeated by the Japanese, the march to Stanley prison would be watched by former servants only too eager to spit upon their former masters. Instead, she witnessed countless acts of tireless fidelity.[85] A few internees recounted their efforts to disabuse the locals of the perception that the Japanese were good for them. James Benson's memoir recounts a conversation he had with a young indigenous man from the Aitape district of New Guinea. 'Japan good fella', he told Benson. The Japanese gave the indigenous people 'plenty fella beer, plenty whisky, plenty saki . . . He no make im Kanak boy work tu mas'. This was in explicit contrast to the 'White man . . . I no bloody good. He make Kanaka boy work all day'.[86] Benson felt duty-bound to contradict him, telling him that the ready availability of alcohol would kill them all. Benson's conversation with the young man occurred early in the war, when the extent of the Japanese military's own empire-building ambitions and the ultimate incompatibility of such ambitions with self-determination for indigenous peoples were not quite apparent to some of the subject populations.

For Benson, it was not just misplaced loyalty that irritated, it was the inversion of hierarchies of race that had come to seem natural in the colonial environment. In the Philippines, the journalist Jack Percival noted somewhat more perceptively in July 1944:

> the taste of what Japanese-sponsored 'independence' actually means and memories of the prosperous times before the Japanese invaded the islands will outweigh the primary feeling of tremendous hurt at being deserted and abandoned to their fate by the United States.
>
> However, one thing is sure – when the forces of reoccupation beat the Japanese to their knees they will still have to contend with a Filipino insurrecto element. The period of martial law in certain parts of the Philippines will, therefore, be somewhat lengthy.[87]

Percival also recognised that the indigenous people 'outside' the camp walls suffered privation just as much, if not more, than internees themselves. He was incredulous that internee patrols in Santo Tomas would hand over Filipinos they found jumping the camp walls and pilfering from internees. In February 1944 he wrote:

> They doubtless reason: 'If my family and myself are starving, the whites inside who have plenty won't miss a little'.
>
> I am in favour of giving them a licking and chucking them back over the wall, but it must be bad propaganda on the 'Outside' if it becomes known that the internees are handing Filipinos over to the Japanese.[88]

Percival knew that, despite the internees' detention behind camp walls by the Japanese, the boundaries between 'inside' and 'outside' remained porous and that internees were dependent on the trade and good will of the local people for their survival. He also recognised that, despite the internees' own suffering and – by the end – near starvation, conditions were just as grim outside the camp walls. This was a situation that also prevailed in other territories occupied by the Japanese. In 1945, one Australian official reported that as the last Allied nationals were escorted from Yangchow internment camp 'the Chinese populace were already surging in through the gates to loot the Mission compound that they occupied'.[89]

As former members of a powerful minority in British, American and Dutch colonies, where whiteness had most often signalled privilege and position, internees experienced captivity as both a reversal of racial hierarchies and reinforcement of racial distinction. Many recognised that their very survival was dependent on maintaining good relationships with indigenous peoples, and expressed a deep and abiding sense of gratitude for the help they received from them. The more perceptive internees realised that the initial Japanese victory, even if the Allies did win the war, had lowered their prestige for ever more. Some coped with the humiliation of captivity by resorting to stereotypes about the 'savagery' of the other peoples in contrast to their own civilisation. In some sense this was a predictable response, given the centuries of racial thinking which had constructed non-white peoples as inferior, and which was one of the central justifications of colonial rule in the societies in which internees lived. It also reflected a psychological need to retain some sense of superiority in a situation of subjection. Yet for some, life in captivity exposed war and colonialism as important contexts for the behaviour of Japanese captors and guards drawn from previously subject populations. It became clear that not all Japanese were barbarians and not all whites were civilised in the face of hardship and deprivation.

3

COMMUNITY AND CONFLICT

In February 2004, at the dedication ceremony of the Australian ex-POW memorial, the governor-general, retired Major-General Michael Jeffrey, declared that in captivity, Australians had demonstrated a 'triumph of the enduring bonds of mateship'.[1] His comments reflected a broader cultural tendency, one also present in POW memoirs and literature, to tailor the rather ambiguous experiences of defeat and capture in order to suit the cloth of the Anzac legend. The concept of mateship has been essential to this process. The diaries and memoirs of civilian internment reveal a different captivity. It is not mateship that is the striking feature of these commentaries on camp life, although there were often instances of unity and common purpose among the internees. The overwhelming impression of these 'communities under stress', as one American internee labelled them, is of competition over access to scarce resources and frequent interpersonal conflict.[2] The exception tended to be groups of priests, nuns and nurses, who had lived communally before their captivity and were better placed to deal with its challenges. Most internment camps brought together previously disparate social groups, unaccustomed to communal living in close quarters. The divisions and disagreements within camp communities, and the selfish behaviour of some of their members, undermine any easy correlation we might be tempted to make between adversity and unity.

It is easy to assume that the effect on internees of classification as an 'enemy alien' by the occupying Japanese and instructions to proceed to a civilian internment centre undermined the social distinctions of prewar colonial societies. Whatever their previous social position, all were captives now. As Jack Percival put it, 'the righteous have been herded together with untried murderers, crooks, professional gamblers, swindlers and knaves of all ilks'.[3] Early in his captivity Gordon Thomas considered that internment had both a humbling and levelling effect. Not only was the prestige of Europeans undermined in the eyes of indigenous people, distinctions of rank within the white community were blurred. Social, business and political position had been 'torn off each one of us like a garment and thrown on to the fire of humiliation, fed by the fuel of indignities. We were socially naked', Thomas recalled. Government officials were now on the same level as their lowest-paid clerks, business executives lined up with office boys and all of them, in the eyes of their new Japanese guards, 'were less than the lowest coolie from Chinatown'.[4] Audrey Begley, whose family of Salvation Army missionaries was interned at Yangchow civilian assembly centre in China from March 1943, also thought that the levelling effect began early. She was one of a large group of Europeans living in Shanghai who were gathered together and ordered aboard a succession of coastal steamers and freight barges on a journey north to their allotted internment camp. The lack of sanitary facilities on the boat peeled away privilege and distinction. The only toileting was a can, surrounded by a circle of others to form a barrier of privacy. Class distinction paled overnight, Begley remembered, as the internees were subject to the democracy of basic bodily functions.[5] Historians of the internment experience have often extended these impressions to the entire period of captivity by writing about the 'enforced egalitarianism of total poverty' and arguing that 'class and social status were ultimately useless tools for internment'.[6]

These descriptions of internment as erasing distinction described the early period of captivity, when the initial trappings of rank and position had been nullified by defeat, a new regime was installed and internees realised their common fate. It was also soon apparent that the Japanese administration would not provide infrastructure sufficient to deal with the numbers of people who crowded into most camps; neither did they provide adequate or nutritionally balanced food. Most camps had to be self-sufficient; internees could not rely on the irregular delivery of rations. This of necessity required co-operation. Inmates of the larger, mixed-sex camps in the Philippines, China, Hong Kong and Singapore realised early on that some form of organisation would be necessary for communal life on such a scale. Internees set their minds to solving the problem of infrastructure in relation to sanitation and cooking, in particular. The internal chain of command ran from the dormitory, block or wing level up to camp executive committees. Each level had its elected delegates and chairpersons, and Australians were active participants. Stanley, a camp comprised of many different 'blocks' of former prison cells and guardhouses, had representatives known as 'blockheads'. The outspoken Dorothy Jenner soon found herself elected to the job, which in some respects was like being handed a poisoned chalice. She confided to her diary after her election: 'committee a hellish one – I am automatically everybody's enemy'.[7] Another Australian woman on the governing committee, health committee and disciplinary board in a Chinese internment camp also acted as assistant camp accountant and was group captain of sixty-four women, a task she later described as 'very nerve-wrecking [sic]'.[8]

Yet the positions were coveted as providing a modicum of power in an essentially subjected situation. Even the children noticed: 'Didn't know there are so many women interested in running and organising of our camp', Sheila Allen remarked.[9] Australians were certainly elected to represent the interests of other internees, but none took on leadership roles within the camps. A journalist interned in China, Jean Armstrong, worked on the general committee of her Shanghai camp for sixteen months. Jack Percival represented the interests of about 500 men from Santo Tomas on the British advisory committee. A Salvation Army officer originally from Colac, Keith Begley, was elected to represent the interests of his group at Yangchow. Those with senior bureaucratic, judicial and church positions in prewar life tended to take pre-eminence on camp committees.[10] In this way, despite the necessity to make do, distinctions between different types of internees began to emerge early in internment and they tended to replicate the hierarchies of prewar colonial societies.

Although they were represented on management committees, Australians in camps remained aware that they were members of a national minority. Most of the camps were dominated by the numerical majority, and this varied according to region. Philippines internment camps were dominated by Americans; those in Hong Kong, Singapore, China and Borneo by the British; and Netherlands East Indies camps, home to the vast majority of all civilian internees, by the Dutch. This prompted the Australians in Stanley internment camp to form an 'Australian society' as a way of protecting the interests of their fellow nationals, although this group too was prone to infighting. Dorothy Jenner considered that in Stanley there were '92 *Australians* who think they are G[od] Almighty, or who are living down the stigma of colonial birth'.[11] The Japanese considered Australians as 'British' subjects, which technically they were, given that legislation creating Australian nationality did not become law until 1948. In the rare instances that the Japanese provided information to the Red Cross or the Swiss on the composition of internment camps, they tended not to distinguish between Australians and other British subjects.

Although aligned both legally and culturally with the British, the Australians in camp did not always feel embraced by them, as Jenner's comment about the 'stigma of colonial birth' suggests. Sheila Allen found comfort in the British attitude, perhaps because she had never actually been to Australia. She thought Changi had a British air of formality that helped to keep the community together. The more worldly mining veteran, Harold Murray, was irritated by the British he encountered in Changi. He thought it 'was the characteristic of people of Great Britain to be always minding other people's business and wondering why people of other races do not like them'. Dorothy Jenner also found fault with the attitude of her fellow British subjects. She claimed that the British made a point of treating the Australians as different, and making them feel inferior.[12] At Santo Tomas, Jack Percival clashed with the British Advisory Committee, whom he referred to as the 'Pukka Sahibs, Far East, Incorporated'. The committee was given the task of drawing up lists of individuals to nominate for exchange, if one were to eventuate, but Percival felt a place on the list was influenced more by 'old school tie' than genuine need. His criticisms of the process led to 'talk in certain quarters about that uncouth chap from Australia'. Percival considered that, in camp, the men's urinals had replaced the club as the real site of power and scene of negotiation. His resentment lay in the lack of process and transparency – he also complained elsewhere in his diary about 'secrecy, star chamber and closed door methods when dealing with the affairs of internees seeing that everybody's neck was in it' – but his telling comments about the urinals also indicated that female members of the camp were excluded from much of the decision-making as well.[13] This was the case in Santo Tomas and other large mixed-sex camps such as Stanley, where only one woman out of a possible 900 ever appeared on its most powerful main committee.[14]

It was the attitude of British internees to Australians that called forth relatively rare yet overt discussions in diaries and memoirs about the meaning and significance of Australian nationality. As Dorothy Jenner put it, the condescension of the British made her a 'raging patriot'.[15]

An integral part of British disdain of Australia and Australians had always been related to its origins as a penal colony, although the irony of the British and Australians now sharing an experience of incarceration seems to have passed without notice. Only one internee seems to have made reference to the parallels between his own experience as a prisoner and Australia's convict heritage. One morning in April 1943, about forty men from Harry Slocombe's internment camp were forced to drag a broken-down street roller along the road. The use of man-power put Slocombe in mind of 'the early days of Australia pictures'. The only difference, he noted, was that the overseer in camp used a rattan instead of the whip more familiar to the convict system.[16] Although Slocombe distinguished between the rattan and the whip, when newspaper cartoonists came to represent 'Japanese sadists' in control of Australian prisoners when the war was over, they did not and, in a possibly symbolic gesture, placed the lash in the hands of the guard. The awkward parallel potentially suggested is between the 'stain' of the convict heritage and the experience of Australians in war.

There were other aspects of camp life and of the physical environment that called forth reminders of Australia, sometimes through the power of contrast. The persistent rainfall during monsoon season at Slocombe's Makassar camp led him to quip in his diary that 'if any state in Australia is having a bit of a drought at present I would be pleased to supply a couple of inches a day'.[17] Other experiences suggested more direct parallels. Harold Murray was appalled at the cavalier attitude of the Japanese to the removal of trees on the island of Singapore. He compared his Japanese overlords to farmers and councillors in rural Victoria, who would not rest until they had cut down rows of trees for the sake of mere convenience. The avenues of Singapore, planted for shade and beauty, were denuded as the internees consumed more and more wood for cooking and firing. 'The whole landscape is becoming like a Mallee scene except the desolation is not so bad here as in the Mallee', he reflected in August 1944.[18] One of the nuns on another island, New Britain, was put in mind of the awe which greeted the completion of an Australian icon as the men of her camp started digging from opposite ends of a hill to eventually achieve a continuous maze of interconnecting tunnels. When the first two connected 'it was almost like the Sydney Harbour Bridge again when the cranes went across and it fitted exactly'.[19] Moments of despair and of joy called forth reminders of home, but for others it was the sheer size of the Australian continent which came to stand for the hope that one day captivity would end. In

Hong Kong, Dorothy Jenner thought often about 'that great big wide country down there' when she visited a private rock to pray. Australia 'represented space and freedom, in a way which it is difficult to explain to anyone who has never been deprived of [it]', she later reflected.[20]

Although national differences persisted among the internees, camp executive committees established rules for communal living that sought to erase them as far as practicable. Those that survive from Yangchow Civil Assembly Centre reflect the emphasis on creating harmony and order. Rule One described the camp as 'the best home for those who live in it' that would function best if people respected one another and obeyed the rules.[21] Rule Three specified that there were to be no complaints about food or living conditions, a policy it must have been almost impossible to enforce. The committees also organised squads to perform the labour necessary to feed the community, ensure their well-being and keep conditions as sanitary as was possible. In Stanley there were squads for cutting wood, gardening, trenching, rations, sanitation and the kitchen. Similar squads operated in other large camps. Committees devised work rosters and rules about the number of hours of labour each internee performed but these had to be modified as sickness and hunger claimed their victims. In Santo Tomas, Roy Stanford worked in the carpenter's shop which, by the end of the war, had produced 3000 beds. By the end of his captivity, only eleven men out of thirty assigned to the shop were actually well enough to work.[22] Although some were legitimately excused from work by internee doctors on the grounds of illness, there were constant disputes over the hours of work and the contribution of camp members to the functioning of the camps. In Stanley in September 1942, the vegetable cutters and woodcutters went on strike when their extra rations were cut owing to camp shortages. 'Their slogan "a matter of principle" met with no sympathy', according to Dorothy Jenner, who soon filled their places with more willing workers.[23] Harold Murray's diary records his frustration at the carping of some camp members about the allocation and distribution of work in Changi, men who he claimed were known as 'the moaners'. He considered that most of the 'moaners' were Englishmen 'who thought they were carrying the world on their backs'. He was quick to note that such individuals were in the minority overall but that they made their presence felt and posed awkward problems for camp committees.[24]

The division of labour in mixed-sex camps was largely on gender lines but not always so. The children stayed with the women, in both mixed-sex camps and the women-only camps in the Netherlands East

Indies. In the women-only camps, it was a traumatic parting for all concerned when boys were forced to transfer to men-only camps when they reached the age of ten or eleven. In the mixed-sex camps, men usually dug the trenches while women were more likely to undertake garden work. Mary Stanford worked in the camp vegetable garden, one of the privileges of which was the right to pick quantities of an edible weed. She would then take the bucket of weed back to her husband at the carpenter's shop, and they would remove the thorns and stems. It was like a 'good spinach', her husband recalled.[25] 'Wood fatigues' at Changi were men's jobs: cutting down rubber trees and hauling them back to the gaol by handcart.[26] At Santo Tomas, one Australian man washed the laundry for the children's and isolation hospital every day for three years.[27]

There were distinct benefits for women who found themselves interned alongside men. The occupational backgrounds of some men in camp – the doctors, chemists, engineers, agricultural experts, for instance – were essential to the establishment of a camp infrastructure to deal with issues of sanitation, health and welfare. While the women-only camps, which were concentrated in the Netherlands East Indies, contained a handful of doctors, scientists and educators, professionals formed a much smaller proportion of the overall population and, as a consequence, these female internees endured a much more difficult captivity. This is not to detract from the ingenuity, application and persistence of some women in the camps. Some of the early studies of women's internment, conducted in the 1970s, tended to err on the side of celebration, excited by the strength and fortitude of mostly middle-class women in difficult circumstances who demonstrated the lie of myths about feminine vulnerability and hopelessness. To quote one: 'Ironically, it can now be seen that what was illuminated by the women's imprisonment was its exact reverse – Women's Liberation'.[28] But the structural reality that in the early 1940s women were much less likely to be educated, practising professionals in fields essential to the maintenance of a secure environment, such as related to engineering and sanitation, placed them at a distinct disadvantage if they were suddenly left to their own devices.[29] This was compounded by the concentration of women-only camps on the islands of Java and Sumatra, where conditions were extremely harsh, internees were severely malnourished and tropical diseases claimed thousands of victims.

Those designing their own work rosters and working in camp gardens, kitchens, carpentry shops and on sanitary duties at least had the comparative luxury of working to maintain themselves and other inmates. This was an important boost to internees' psychological well-being.[30] Although some historians state that civilian internees did not undertake forced labour for the Japanese in mines and on railways, some Australian internees claim that they were indeed forced to work for them.[31] A teacher from Adelaide who had been employed by the Malayan Education Department, Claude Coats, was one civilian who had the misfortune to be transported from Changi to work on the railway. There were others in his position, despite the fact that in Australia the Burma–Thai and railway is remembered as an experience of military POWs. A 40-year-old man from Perth who was working for an Australian gold-mining company in Malaya at the time of the Japanese invasion, Robert Marriott, was another civilian who worked on the railway. He had joined the Federated Malay States Volunteer Force, and actively fought against the Japanese during the battle for Malaya, then Singapore. After spending most of 1942 in Changi, Marriott spent the rest of the war in POW camps along the railway. Despite his official designation as a civilian internee, Marriott identified as a POW: 'I am not a civilian internee but a prisoner of war captured at the surrender of Singapore', he insisted in the early 1950s.[32] A civil engineering graduate of the University of Melbourne, George Robertson, was also officially a civilian internee but died of beriberi and malaria while working alongside POWs on the railway in 1945. Before the war, he had worked for the Johore government in the Drainage and Irrigation Department.[33] In the segregated camps on Java and Sumatra, women were often compelled to undertake heavy labour for their Japanese overseers, under threat of severe discipline and punishment.[34]

Camp committees were powerless to prevent the Japanese from forcing civilians to depart for distant labour projects, nor could they protest against heavy labour assignments in the face of severe retribution. In less-trying camps than those in the East Indies, they did try to ensure the smooth functioning of the camp and facilitate everyday living by sheer effort of organisation. The Begleys remembered that 'life in camp was organised to reflect the ordered society from which internees had come'.[35] In Yangchow there were school lessons, adult education classes, scouts, guides, brownies and cubs. Education classes were run for adults too, both in China and other large camps, in order to stave off boredom. Others with skills that might be useful for their fellow internees once the war was over ran specialist classes. Harry Slocombe

Figure 7: *Ian Begley, top row, third from left, photographed on 1 August 1945 at Yangchow internment camp in northern China. Begley, the son of Salvation Army missionaries, was interned along with his parents and siblings.*

ran English classes for his largely Dutch camp mates.[36] William Tingle, former bantam-weight champion of the Orient, and sports director of the Shanghai municipal council before his internment, put his athletic and organisational skills to use in his camp. He acted as sports director of the interned youth in his Chinese internment camp.[37] Religious communities also paid special care to older and younger members. Sisters Berenice and Flavia were two of the younger members of their religious community, and relatively recent arrivals in Rabaul. Their older sisters, long-resident in the region, attempted to make sure their younger colleagues did not waste their years in camp. One hut in the camp was set aside for study. Berenice and Flavia, who were great friends, referred to the hut as 'the university'.[38] They went down there each day for some quiet time to study the native language of the area. In almost every camp with children, an enormous effort was poured into attempting to ensure some level of continuity in the children's education. Bernice Archer's extensive study of internment in the Asia–Pacific region concluded that women dominated these teaching staffs and 'must be considered a major force behind the normalization, order and discipline in the camps'.[39]

Care of the young and, at the other end of the life cycle, respect for the dead were unifying features of most camps. Dorothy Jenner, not a devout Christian by any other measure, thought that attending church services at Stanley camp was important because it showed the Japanese that the internees were united. For the same reason, everyone always attended funeral services, whether they knew the deceased or not.[40] Although she was only a teenager, Sheila Allen also recognised the basic cohesion of the group in the willingness of many of them to look after the most vulnerable. Allen appreciated the sacrifice, hard work and co-operation of every woman in camp. 'There are mothers who worry about us', she wrote. After praising all levels of the camp, from doctors, teachers, the entertainment committee down to the sweepers, drain workers and kitchen squad, Allen noted that the children were a responsibility taken seriously by the adult internees.[41]

One camp that appears to have functioned relatively harmoniously throughout the war was formed on the island of New Britain. The internment camp formed at Vunapope, near Rabaul, was home to hundreds of missionaries, male and female. In all, seventeen nationalities were represented in the camp. They maintained religious observances in camp, an important thread binding them to the time before the war. Community prayers and spiritual readings confirmed and strengthened faith. Prayer was 'the essential freedom, transcending all locks and bars, all walls and frontiers'.[42] Most internees were members of the Community of the Sacred Heart, which was predominantly a German mission, although the leader of the camp was a Polish bishop. The Japanese administration in New Guinea had interned German nationals, despite the fact that Germany was also an Axis power. Other Allied nationalities in the camp did not resent their incarceration with German missionaries, whom they considered 'every bit as anti-Nazi as the British Bretheren'.[43] Australian nuns of the order of Our Lady of the Sacred Heart, who ranged in age from their mid-twenties to quite elderly women in their seventies, were among the camp's residents.

The religious community, some of whom were accustomed to creating missions in relatively remote areas, set to work building the infrastructure of their camp. The missionaries from around the Rabaul area initially lived in fenced-off huts behind the Catholic convent at Vunapope. They pooled the resources of several self-supporting missions – livestock, garden equipment, cooking facilities – to produce a functional camp community. The nuns even moved their piano, pushing it nearly five kilometres to their new compound.[44] Ultimately, the

Figure 8: *Australian nuns' sleeping quarters at Ramale Valley internment camp, New Britain. Internees had been confined to the bottom of a ravine by the Japanese, and had built the accommodation themselves.*

extent of Allied bombing raids forced the camp's male members to tunnel into the hills near the campsite – shelter that the Japanese commandeered when the compound was eventually destroyed by bombing in May 1944. At that time, the Japanese military in control of the camp sent the internees to live at the bottom of a ravine in Ramale. The gorge was so deep and the forest so thick that at first the internees couldn't even see the sky, Sister Berenice remembered.[45] She spent many days shifting washing lines so that damp clothes might dry in rare glimmers of sunlight. James Benson described it as a 'wild, fantastic place; a sheer-sided gorge torn out of the soft volcanic rock of the Bittagalip Hills'. A stream ran along the floor of the ravine. Eventually, the site's occupation by hundreds of people began to kill the undergrowth and more light began to penetrate the valley. The male internees built bush shelters and more tunnels, where they all lived for eighteen months. Each religious community had its own shelter built on a terrace of the ravine near a tunnel.[46] The Japanese built a wooden platform around the top of the gorge to keep an eye on the activities of its inhabitants. Some members of the Kempetai would stand on the edge of the cliff and urinate into the gorge below.[47] This was a closely watched and guarded group, but their survival was largely the result of their own initiative and efforts.

The relatively harmonious functioning of the camp is recalled in the memoirs of James Benson, who had spent the months before his arrival there in a crowded cell in a military police camp run by the Kempetai. Benson thought the camp was the 'City of Peace'. When Benson arrived in July 1943, semi-starved and in poor health, the religious community immediately rallied to assist him. This was the time before bombing raids had destroyed much of their carefully built infrastructure. Dropping his filthy pants and singlet into a bucket, Benson washed and changed into fresh clothes and dried himself with a towel. He slept in a bed with a pillow and sheets. He spent most of the night stroking and patting the sheets to confirm for himself that they were still there. As if finally meeting with a much-anticipated lover, Benson was 'too happy to sleep'. He was overcome with the sensual satisfaction of smooth fabric and familiar voices. 'I fear that the kind and gracious company made me feel very foolish and emotional – I had not spoken two consecutive sentences to a white man for well over a year'.[48] For Benson, a long period of physical and sensory deprivation had come to an end. Even though still a captive, for the first time in years this was an experience shared with his own kind.

Benson's impressions of the camp as a functional community are borne out by Gordon Thomas, who arrived there only towards the end of the war. Thomas was both impressed and astonished at the harmony that seemed to prevail among this 'polyglot assembly'.[49] The contrast with his own small group of internees – four men in total including James Ellis, George McKechnie and Alfred Creswick – was stark. The repetition of camp life, the boredom, the irritation with fellow internees in too-close quarters: these are the qualities that come across in most other camp diaries. The size of the camp appeared to be irrelevant to the consistency of this complaint: it was made by people living in small, closely guarded groups, as well as those who spent their war in internment camps that had thousands of inmates. Harry Slocombe constantly referred in his diary to the nervous strain of his fellow internees and their propensity for petty arguments.[50] Gordon Thomas described a similar process at work amongst his group. One man's action or remark was 'furtively and venomously dissected and analysed' by the others in his group. The frustrations of powerlessness caused them to turn on one another. 'Our outlook was becoming distorted, our minds warped', Thomas remembered.[51] On Christmas Day 1944, Jack Percival witnessed one internee stab another in the neck when he was asked to attend a roll call, a sign of nerves and frustration if ever there was one.[52] In Stanley, Dorothy Jenner witnessed 'fisticuffs' between one married couple, and on the same day, another situation where one internee referred to another as an 'old bitch', 'and the fun began – one thing led to another, glasses were clawed off noses, wind pipes clutched & noses bloodied'.[53] The strain of uncertainty also caused men in Changi to become irritable 'and the mole hills looked like mountains and a number were beginning to lose heart', Harold Murray wrote in 1944. He confessed to attending church services just to get away from his area of the camp. It got on his nerves to see the same faces morning, noon and night.[54] The female inmates of Changi, housed in their own section, also showed signs of tension. Even Sheila Allen, temperamentally disposed to see the best rather than the worst in a situation, noted in December 1943 that it didn't seem to take much to start a quarrel. Similarly, committee meetings at the women's section always contained 'a lot of arguments and back-stabbings'.[55]

Captivity was inevitably stressful and it was difficult to avoid unwanted company. Most camps comprised social groups that, in ordinary times, infrequently mixed together. 'The camp was a complex of cultural and social diversity', the missionary Begleys recalled, and consequently 'tensions often led to arguments'.[56] Australian nurses captured in Rabaul and transported to Japan were prone to argue and irritate one another, but they also demonstrated that ties that preceded captivity were the least likely to fray. According to Alice Bowman the relative smallness of their camp and the length of captivity 'gave vent to constant paltry disagreement'. Bowman and seven others had worked at the government hospital; the other nurses in her camp were affiliated with either the army or the Methodist mission. Group identity remained strong throughout captivity. 'We were from three classified organisations of our profession and tended to remain within our own secure circle,' she recalled, 'probably this was the greatest cause of dissent. However, we were always staunch and unified in real crisis'.[57] This blend of pre-captivity loyalties and new group identity is reflected in a book owned by Joyce Olroyd-Harris, a government nurse, which she retained throughout captivity. The book was inscribed as a gift from 'Chris', the nickname for Methodist missionary nurse Jean Christopher. It contains poems written by the one member of the group who was not a nurse, planter and hotel proprietor Kay Bignall. Inside the back cover there is also a handmade Christmas card, addressed to Joyce and signed 'The Methos'. The women clearly cared for one another enough to make gifts and share poems but the distinctiveness of the groups remained.[58]

Conflicts also arose because people were living in overcrowded conditions with inadequate food and limited resources. In Changi, some internees stole from other inmates' luggage and filched rations from the kitchen. The leader of one block described stealing food as the 'crowning cad's performance' and the 'meanest form of pilfering'. In Hong Kong, there was 'the most awful thieving and racketeering among ladies' who worked in the kitchen. In Santo Tomas, by November 1944 competition for food was so intense that a baby's bottle of milk was stolen at midnight when the child's mother left her room for a moment.[59]

Internees unsurprisingly found it necessary to establish quasi-legal tribunals to ensure discipline in the camps. At Changi and Stanley, for instance, disciplinary boards were established within six months of internment. Internees came before the boards to settle personal disputes over the theft of property and assault and to mediate conflict over the behaviour of the camp's children. Childless inmates were often driven to distraction by the waywardness and noise of other people's children. One woman who was on the disciplinary board in Yangchow camp later recalled that this job was 'very strenuous as there were many delinquents' in her camp.[60]

The main crime of those who appeared before these tribunals appears to have been selfishness in an environment where everyone suffered deprivation. Some internees were placed before a board by various committees, who suspected their workers of attempting to defraud camp canteens and other distribution centres for their own benefit and that of their friends. Others broke camp rules. In Hong Kong, one woman was brought before the board for requesting a double-decker wooden bed, which she proceeded to use for firewood.[61] The boards meted out a range of punishments, from reprimands to depriving guilty members of block cooking and bakery facilities, cigarette issues and canteen purchases for a period of time to hard labour for theft.[62] By 1944, Jack Percival considered that within the walls of Santo Tomas, itself an internment camp, were three other gaols: one each for male and female internees that were run by internee committees and a 'Japanese gaol' for those 'under investigation by the Japanese'. Those in the internee gaols included 'alcoholics, those convicted for petty larceny and two internees who stole rice "Because we were hungry"'. With his typical acerbic wit, Percival also noted that the internee gaols did not house those who most deserved the community's punishment and vilification: 'the racketeers who are now selling sugar, bully beef and powdered milk' at a vastly inflated profit to other internees.[63]

Racketeers earned the vilification of most members of the camp community; so did those who collaborated with the Japanese. In April 1944, Percival complained that 'there are so many white Japanese, ranging from cooperators to just plain stool pigeons'. 'White Japanese' was also a term used by Harold Murray, who claimed that in Changi there were Englishmen 'hand in glove with the Nips' who provided more trouble for the other internees than their Malay and Sikh guards. The collaboration in these cases appeared to be matters of expedience, as it was in Harry Slocombe's camp, when some men accepted money and favours from the Japanese in exchange for reporting on the activities of their fellow prisoners.[64]

In the camps, racketeering among internees, the abuse of privilege and other displays of selfishness were a constant source of irritation to Percival and others like him. In China, in the early days after liberation, enmities that were barely concealed within the camps burst through to the surface. The injuries of class and race clearly continued to be felt within the camp walls. One correspondent to a Shanghai newspaper, upon his release, immediately put pen to paper and suggested discrimination against mixed-race people was endemic amongst the British elite. 'The good old selfish spirit of "Look out for yourself, Jack, I'm in the lifeboat" was demonstrated in all the camps', he wrote. 'And it was not the under-privileged who was the worst offender, it was the man who should have set a better example, the "big shot"'.[65] Dorothy Jenner thought so too:

> When people become anonymous they become hateful. Judges & dustmen look the same in the cookhouse & are just as light-fingered. Society – or its segments – with nothing to lose or gain don't possess the dignity of denizens of the jungle. Rogues have more stature than snivelling, grabbing members of this community – taipans [bosses] caught with their pants down – Externally there is little difference these days between the millionaire and the park dosser. I'll take the simple dosser, he's kinder.[66]

In contrast, Gordon Thomas considered that internment reversed the social order. He described those who had previously been the 'have-nots' of society as 'prison plutocrats'. According to Thomas, men used to living by their wits had an advantage in camp over those used to living by their cheque-books. 'It was guts that counted in those days, not gold.' Jack Percival also considered that the racketeering of canteen goods in Santo Tomas was financed by businessmen who in prewar days wore 'the cloak of respectability and are pillars of the church'.[67]

The racketeering and corruption appear to have been so intense in Santo Tomas camp that it created, according to Percival, two classes of internees: the 'haves' and the 'have-nots'. The 'haves' were those with continuing access to resources, whether through conduits to assets in the 'outside' world or as a result of criminal activity within the camp (which involved hoarding canteen supplies and selling them at inflated prices to other inmates) or via collaboration with the Japanese. This minority of camp inmates could afford to pay other internees to perform their share of community labour. Consequently, the health of the 'haves' was maintained at the expense of the 'have-nots', who were required to work more on substantially less food. 'So', Percival railed in May 1944:

> there is the portion of worn out Have-Nots who have been on the borderline of starvation for $2\frac{1}{2}$ years, who have little resistance left to stand up to the worst phase of internment, which is rapidly approaching, and, furthermore, have no food reserves to tide them over.[68]

Earlier in captivity, in September 1942, Dorothy Jenner had also considered that there were distinct classes of inmates in Stanley, and she thought her job as a block representative was clear: 'I am looking after the have-nots'.[69]

Percival's comments make clear that while an extreme situation might have prevailed in Santo Tomas, internees with continuing access to resources and contacts with the outside world also had an advantage inside the camp walls. Although escapes from Japanese internment camps were extremely rare, and usually resulted in swift recapture and execution, the camp boundaries remained permeable in terms of traffic into the camp for black-market goods and trading. Outside help was necessary for survival because most internees entered camp with very few possessions and because of the paucity of rations supplied by the Japanese. Depending on the circumstances of their capture, most internees entered captivity with little more than a suitcase of possessions, if that. Those already displaced from their homes were at a distinct disadvantage. Sheila Allen, her Australian father, John Allen, and his Siamese wife, Vichim, entered Changi with very few personal possessions. They had already fled down the Malay peninsula from Ipoh and lost their remaining belongings when their accommodation in Singapore had been bombed. The survivors of the ships bombed as they attempted to leave Singapore were also at a disadvantage in their Sumatran camps. They arrived with literally nothing but what remained of the clothes on their back, while the local Dutch internees at least had time to pack a suitcase. A thriving black market developed when the assistance of local people was not permitted, or closely policed. In such circumstances, a few remaining possessions assumed enormous value. At Tjideng women's camp in Java, internees swapped clothing for fruit through a hole in the fence.[70]

There was also some permeability of the camp's boundaries in terms of access by the Red Cross and the Swiss consul, although this occurred in only a very few camps. Australians in China, Hong Kong and Bangkok, along with those in Japan itself, enjoyed two advantages not available to 'enemy nationals' resident in other parts of Japanese-occupied territory. The Japanese in these regions allowed the Swiss consul to maintain contact, albeit irregular, with people of Allied nationalities and provided them with small cash payments to purchase goods from the camp canteens.[71]

Leonard Stranks, interned at Weishin in China, recalled that he received four payments of 'comfort fund money' during his internment. Stranks, his wife and two daughters received the money but the Japanese set the exchange rate so low that all the family could afford to buy with their money was one kilogram of peanuts. After three or four payments, the camp's executive committee advised the internees to refuse the money.[72] Assistance from the Red Cross was piecemeal and according to the whim of the Japanese in control. The vast majority of internees never saw a Red Cross parcel; a few received one or two throughout their captivity that they rationed like water in the desert. The Philippines internees, for example, received one parcel from the Red Cross in December 1943 and those who did not carefully store and ration this food almost starved, according to Roy Stanford.

Red Cross access to camps also sometimes allowed family members separated by war to learn of each other's whereabouts. This was a particularly useful resource for the Begley family. Australians by birth, Keith and Edith Begley married in China and had spent most of their life there, engaged in missionary work. By the early 1940s, they had three children who remained at Tientsin Grammar School in northern China while Keith and Edith undertook work for the Salvation Army in Hong Kong. Interned in Stanley after the fall of Hong Kong, the Begleys had no knowledge of the fate of their children. The Red Cross representative who visited their camp was able to discover that another Australian Salvation Army family, the Stranks, had taken in their children when the Japanese had closed the school. The Red Cross was also able to convince the Japanese authorities to reunite the family in Shanghai. In February 1943 the Begley parents were released from Stanley internment camp to resume the care of their children in China, whom they had not seen for two and a half years.[73]

The experience also gave Keith Begley precious knowledge about what would be needed if he were ever interned again (which he was within months). Before his next internment, Begley gathered together the requisites of a cobbler – 'shoe-lasts, twine, bees wax to treat the twine, curved needles, pieces of leather, rubber heels tacks'. He kept his fellow internees at his next internment camp, Yangchow, well shod. Footwear was essential in the cold Chinese winters, especially when internees were forced to dig trenches in the snow and stand in them while the Japanese conducted roll call each day. Begley also repaired cricket balls and soft balls for the children.[74] The Begley family memoir presents such actions as pure altruism, which they may well have been. But Dorothy Jenner, who shared the early part of the Begleys' internment at Stanley, considered them 'real racketeers'.[75] Whatever their motivation, the Begleys were survivors.

Some families learned about their loved ones through very rare radio broadcasts from the camp. Oswald Goulter, an Australian-born missionary for the United Christian Missionary Society in China, sent a message over short-wave radio on 13 March 1944. Like many other missionaries, Goulter had decided to stay at his post when given the chance to evacuate.[76] The East Asian Residents Association forwarded the text of the message to his sister in Colac. It read:

> Dear folks and everybody in Australia. Life goes on quietly here. I am still teaching at the University. Have robust health and sleep 10 hours every night. My own little garden grows lettuce, tomatoes and onions. Have had no letters for an age. Note carefully. Write me.[77]

News that the family received from the Australian legation in Chungking suggested that much of the message was in code. Oswald was in 'only fair' health, and received food parcels from some supporters outside the camp.[78]

Limited diplomatic contact with Japan also meant that internees there sometimes received word from their families. Sir Mark Sheldon, brother of the leader of Australian Sacre Coeur nuns in Japan, was able to use his connections and money to send a few cablegrams to his sister during the war. This would have been beyond the means of most Australians: one sent during 1944 cost Sir Mark over £8 (about a month's wages). Mother Maude Lennon's brother, Mr Herbert Lennon, had to be content with reassurance from the Prime Minister's Department that 'everything possible was being done to assist Australian nuns in Japan' in response to this heartfelt, handwritten plea:

> [The nuns were taken] from their lovely Tokio convent at short notice & sent into the interior of Japan to a concentration camp. My dear aged & only nun sister, Mother M. Lennon, who is nearly 70 is ill in the Hospital . . . Surely these dear ladies . . . should be returned to Australia . . . otherwise these dear people especially aged will pass out from the trials of bombing etc which will no doubt be in evidence in Japan.

Despite Mr Lennon's faith in the power of his government, by 1944 virtually all information from the Japanese in relation to internees had ceased. It was not until November 1945 that Herbert Lennon received official confirmation from the government that his sister was safe and had survived her internment.[79]

Families received at most one or two communications from Australians interned in the region, while internees themselves in rare instances received Red Cross postcards but in most cases heard nothing. This did not mean that the camp community was impervious to the outside world. Covert relations with indigenous peoples continued in almost every case, and legitimate interaction with Red Cross and the Swiss in a limited number of others. Although it is easy to imagine that internment reduced all inmates to the same level, in fact an internal prison hierarchy developed that rewarded those with plain cunning and for whom rank and privilege from prewar colonial societies continued to provide access to positions of authority within the camp walls. Positions of real authority within mixed-sex internee communities were the preserve of men. Internment was a problem of community; it also posed unique tests and temptations for individual men and women.

4

COLLABORATION

In October 1942 a British diplomatic official returning to England after an exchange with Japan reported that there had almost certainly been cases of 'gratuitous collaboration with the Japanese, but only the future can show how serious or far-reaching their effect will be'.[1] The effect on the Allied war effort was small indeed, but participation in such activities besmirched the reputations of those involved for a long while thereafter. One of the cases to which the diplomat referred was that of a small group of men and women, based in Shanghai, who formed themselves into an organisation that urged Australia to break its alliance with the United Kingdom and to forge its own path in Asia, at peace with Japan. Political conviction, expedience and social injury blended in ways that are difficult to untangle, and prompted the members of this group to earn the opprobrium of their fellow expatriates by conducting radio broadcasts and writing newspaper columns critical of the Australian government. The Japanese were particularly interested in encouraging Allied nationals to broadcast on their behalf, and also placed pressure on other Australians in internment camps elsewhere, such as Hong Kong, to work for them. In Stanley, Dorothy Jenner came under pressure to do so, as did Douglas Murdoch, a cousin of the better-known Sir Keith. Almost all of the Australians who became involved in this form of collaboration spent at least part of the war in an internment camp. If reluctance to endure internment had motivated the actions of most of them, it was a strategy that ultimately backfired.

A respected figure in his community, the officer in charge of the Salvation Army in Shanghai, Brigadier George Walker, was identified early in the war by the Japanese as someone with whom they would like to work. Walker was a missionary in the prime of his career. He had left Australia in the 1920s with his new bride, Jessie, also a Salvation Army officer, and had spent the next twenty years working as a missionary in India and China. The Walkers had four children, two of whom, teenagers Joan and Wilbur, still lived with them in Shanghai. In November 1942, just short of his fiftieth birthday, Walker was arrested, imprisoned at Haiphong Road and tortured. The Japanese wanted Walker to broadcast messages addressed to other Allied nationals, urging them to reconsider their position on the war. If they wanted a willing collaborator, the Japanese had picked the wrong man. Walker's family was harassed as a result of his steadfast refusal to co-operate with his captors. Unlike most families in Shanghai, who were interned together in mixed-sex camps, the Walkers endured the war apart, uncertain of one another's fate.[2]

George Walker had the misfortune to endure a long period of torture, but in other cases the Japanese attempted to lure Allied nationals to broadcast for them with promises of release from internment. The Japanese commandant of Stanley, Lieutenant Commander Takasaki, invited Dorothy Jenner to put her journalistic skills to use for the Japanese. In July 1942, Jenner attended Takasaki's quarters for a hot chocolate and was offered the opportunity to leave the camp and work in Shanghai for the Japanese newsagency, Domai. The Japanese wanted her to urge Australian troops to lay down their arms and join the Co-Prosperity Sphere. Jenner was surprised to find that she enjoyed meeting Takasaki, whom she considered 'a Cambridge man with elegant manners' and great personal charm. She also found it easy to refuse by telling him she had no money and no friends in Shanghai. When asked again the following day, Jenner sidestepped the issue by saying she had no desire to go back to the front line, but Takasaki assured her Shanghai was peaceful, which Jenner considered to be a lie.[3] Jenner's refusals were further testament to her acuity. They were a model of expedience as euphemistic denials that avoided provoking confrontation on direct, political grounds.

The ease of her refusal, and its acceptance by Takasaki without consequence, gave Jenner licence to be scathing about other internees who had been tempted by his offer. Douglas Murdoch, who before the war had worked as an engineer for Cable & Wireless Ltd in Hong Kong, tried to justify his decision to accept the Japanese offer for release from Stanley in exchange for relocation to Shanghai. As a member of the famous Murdoch clan, whose children were being cared for in Perth by the chancellor of the University of Western Australia, Professor Walter Murdoch, Douglas Murdoch appeared to be searching in vain for opportunities to earn a similar level of distinction. Murdoch told his fellow internees his release would allow him to further Australia's interests in its trade relations with Japan and to assist the aid work of the International Red Cross on behalf of the internees. With her usual bluntness, Jenner noted in her diary that the story was 'all bulls—'. She thought that Murdoch was actually attempting to further his own ambitions and angling for a future trade commissionership. The senior British man in the camp expressed his opinion to Jenner that Murdoch was a 'vain fool' and told Murdoch and his wife, Joyce, who was thinking of accompanying him, to reconsider.[4] The peer pressure was to no avail, and Murdoch was released from internment and relocated to Shanghai, courtesy of the Japanese. The Murdochs were provided with apartments at the Cathay Hotel in Shanghai. Ultimately, though, they entered Yangchow internment camp, but somewhat later than other Allied nationals.

After the war, Murdoch told his own version of the story. He claimed that the Japanese had transferred him to Shanghai for 'interrogation'. Murdoch argued that the Japanese thought he had connections with the Australian diplomatic corps, given that he had completed national service before the war.[5] This seems unlikely, given that there is evidence that the Japanese were in fact trying to tempt the politically expedient to broadcast for them.[6] Murdoch's link between national service and diplomacy also appears to have been drawing a long bow. Murdoch stated that his 'interrogation' lasted for six months before his transfer to Yangchow internment camp. The later opinion of Australian diplomatic officials in China was that Murdoch had flirted with the idea of collaboration but had eventually decided against it.[7] It is incontrovertible that Murdoch spent most of his war in internment, and that its after-effects continued to plague him for many years. The trade commissionership never eventuated and Murdoch was dogged by poor health and ailing fortunes. In 1947 Cable & Wireless retired him as being 'permanently unfit for future service'. His marriage to Joyce had ended in divorce. In December 1952 Murdoch suffered a 'nervous collapse' and his doctor considered that he was suffering from 'acute anxiety state [and] general nervous and physical exhaustion'. The doctor concluded that 'his future is definitely clouded'.[8]

Perhaps contemplating collaboration with the Japanese had played on Murdoch's conscience. He was not the only Australian at this time who may have done so and several others took more significant steps towards open support for the Japanese position. In Shanghai a group of Australians had formed a 'Break Away from Britain League', which eventually and more commonly became known as the 'Independent Australia League'. The Australian security services were briefly concerned that the movement had links with the 'Australia First' movement on mainland Australia, but this fear proved baseless.[9] The Independent Australia League's founder, Alan Willoughby Raymond, was a man who had publicly advocated in an article in the *Bulletin* as early as May 1940 that Australia should improve its trading links with Asia. In July 1942, after Australia and Japan were at war but before the internment of Allied nationals in Shanghai, Raymond published another article entitled 'Australians play with fire' in the *Shanghai Evening Post*. The cover of the edition sported a full-colour illustration of a Japanese soldier in the foreground, bayonet to the ready, emerging from the silhouettes of other Asian peoples in the backgrounds with the words 'Guardians of East Asia's Co-prosperity Sphere' emblazoned on the cover. In the article, Raymond attempted to convince readers that Australia's defence and trade ties with the United Kingdom worked only to the advantage of the United Kingdom. Describing Australia as a 'British lacky [sic]', the article deemed it necessary for Australia to forge an independent path. 'Geographically and economically,' Raymond argued, 'we are a natural complement of Asia'. Australia should therefore join Japan's East Asia Co-prosperity Sphere.[10] Throughout the war he continued to publish columns in the *Shanghai Evening Post* under the heading 'An Aussie's Point of View', critical of the Australian government's unwillingness to pursue foreign policy independent of the United Kingdom or the United States.[11]

Interviewed after the war by the Australian Security Service, Raymond claimed that, after the fall of Singapore, he was convinced that Australia should adopt an independent foreign policy. He had left Australia in 1940 because he did not agree with Australia's support of the European war, 'which I regarded as unwarranted and as a selfish action on the part of Britain'. He also couldn't find a job. 'Myself and a group of friends decided', he recounted, 'that if we could get Australia to declare independence she could not only take care of her own dire situation in a more realistic manner, but could also prepare for a better future'.[12] The first meeting of the Independent Australia League was held in Shanghai in March 1942, with about a dozen people in attendance.[13]

The Japanese were keen to accommodate Allied nationals prepared to criticise their own governments' policies. Accordingly, facilities were created for the Independent Australia League to begin broadcasting its message over a German radio station in Shanghai. Further south, Australian security services were able to hear the contents of the radio broadcasts out of Shanghai, and the director general rather dramatically labelled Alan Raymond the 'Australian Lord Haw Haw'. The broadcasts continued for the remainder of the war.[14] A British woman interned in Shanghai later claimed that between broadcasts, Raymond and his friends in the League would meet at the Astor Hotel and at the Broadway Mansions in Shanghai.[15] Raymond maintained that he had 'successfully resisted innumerable attempts to convert my efforts to Japanese propaganda' and that he was 'at no time employed by the Japanese in any way'.[16] Yet he was one of the few Australians in Shanghai to avoid internment, and he was also able to have his mother returned to Shanghai from internment at Stanley in Hong Kong.

Another member of the League was John Holland, an Australian in his early thirties who was the black sheep of a respectable West Australian family. After a falling out with his father, Holland had left Perth and pursued work on the east coast. His career in car sales appeared to falter during the Depression, when a conviction for cheque forgery earned Holland a spell in Emu Plains Prison. In 1937, Holland left Australia and tried his hand at journalism as well as continuing sporadic work in the 'motor car business'. An intelligence officer later described him as an 'opportunist' who was used to 'living by his wits' in prewar Singapore and Shanghai.[17] He had this in common with Alan Raymond, who had been back and forth between Australia, Shanghai and Hong Kong before the war. In mid-1942, John Holland had written to his father, a well-known Perth doctor, in an attempt to explain how he was faring in Shanghai during the war. Holland told his father that he belonged to an 'Australian Political Party' that was 'endeavouring to promote a separate peace with Japan'. Accordingly, he was now broadcasting in Shanghai each evening. 'Naturally this is a very serious statement for me to make,' Holland conceded, 'but I am prepared to stand by the results of it, as we people in the Far East have better conception of what the score is than you folks at home'. Six months later, Holland offered his services to the Japanese, and in November

1942 they flew him to Tokyo to continue broadcasting his anti-Allied message. 'I do hope you will not condemn me', Holland asked his father, expressing the hope that they would talk more fully at war's end. 'After all, we are entitled to our own politics', he concluded.[18]

Alan Raymond was also assisted in his work by Wynette Cecilia McDonald, a woman in her early thirties, who was the daughter of a University of Melbourne botanist, Ewan McDonald. Wynette McDonald had arrived in Shanghai in 1940 with her lover, a Swedish man named Lindquist, who had previously run a hairdressing shop in Melbourne.[19] Short of funds, McDonald had immediately called upon Vivian Bowden, the Australian trade commissioner, in his capacity as president of the Australian and New Zealand Society of Shanghai. Bowden assisted Wynette McDonald in her search for accommodation, paid some of her hotel bills and eventually helped her find a position at fellow Australian Ruby Taylor's Peter Pan School. Bowden admitted that the teaching job was poorly paid. McDonald had already begun to attract the attention of authorities because she socialised with German and Japanese men. The manager of the YWCA Hostel in which she was staying contacted Bowden and told him that Wynette McDonald was a young woman with strong views about the war and who seemed 'very bitter against England'.[20] Although she paid her a pittance, Ruby Taylor thought McDonald was clever and a good teacher. In conversation, however, McDonald was overtly critical of the White Australia policy and this made Ruby Taylor suspicious. One Monday morning when McDonald failed to show up for work, Ruby Taylor went through her desk and found documents belonging to the Royal Navy. She immediately contacted Bowden, who advised instant dismissal. It transpired that Lindquist had been working at the naval office and found the crumpled letter in a wastebasket. Bowden thought the retrieved telegram was 'a deliberate – if clumsy – attempt at spying'.[21]

It appears at this point that Wynette McDonald began working for Alan Raymond, and became more heavily involved in the Independent Australia League. In a move that was not politically astute with the expatriate population, given their feelings, as part of the Japanese celebration of the fall of Singapore Wynette McDonald and Lindquist drove along the Bund in Shanghai in an open car with a Japanese naval officer. Soon after, McDonald commenced her broadcasts on 'Japan and the Japanese' on Shanghai's radio station and also promoted the idea of Australia reaching a separate peace with Japan. Clearly, however, McDonald's antics were not taken too seriously, at least at first, by other expatriates. One later remembered that the broadcasts 'at first amused the British colony so much they made a point of tuning in to her sessions'. In an early talk, McDonald had asserted that Australia's prime minister (Curtin) was an 'evil and corrupting influence' and 'that this son of a policeman had actually murdered the late Prime Minister', Joe Lyons, by giving him poison.[22]

Unlike Raymond, McDonald did spend some time in a Shanghai internment camp during the war. Interned at Lungwha, she was not popular with the other internees. Ruby Taylor, her former employer, claimed that Wynette McDonald was a known fraterniser and a constant visitor to the quarters of the Japanese officers. On New Year's Night 1944, McDonald escaped from the internment camp. In a newspaper interview given when she returned to Australia, Wynette McDonald claimed to have dyed her skin with iodine and walnut oil to appear Chinese, thereby allowing her to slip past the guards. Yet she claimed to have been recaptured and spent the remainder of the war in solitary confinement.[23] Interviews conducted by the Australian Security Service with McDonald's fellow internees provided a different account of McDonald's departure from the camp. The internees claimed that McDonald's 'escape' was a ruse, organised by the Japanese camp commandant, with whom McDonald had associated before her internment. In support of these claims, the internees argued that usually escape attempts were followed by a suspension of privileges for all internees. Instead, in McDonald's case, the commandant announced that she had been recaptured and was undergoing solitary confinement. McDonald was never seen in camp again. According to a British woman, whom the Australian Security Service believed to be a credible witness, it later became clear that McDonald lived out the war in a furnished apartment 'where she received and entertained her Japanese friends'.[24]

After the war, both Alan Raymond and Wynette McDonald admitted to members of the Australian Security Service that they had been members of the Independent Australia League and had conducted radio broadcasts in Shanghai. Raymond was unrepentant about either his actions or his political beliefs but he was canny enough to insist that he was never in Japanese pay and 'always prayed that the Allies would win the war and that Australia would be safe'.[25] Wynette McDonald's political position was never as clearly articulated as Raymond's and after the war she attempted to argue that her involvement in the radio broadcasts had actually been an attempt to *assist* the Allied war effort. 'I at no period had intended to co-operate with them', she told an Australian investigator, 'but had walked in fear of the bridge house [prison]'. McDonald argued that her radio session, 'Japan and the Japanese', contained extracts from a book that she thought might have information useful to the Allies, such as Japanese population statistics and details about military bases. McDonald thought that the Japanese eventually saw through her plan, and then gave her more overtly political material to read out. At that juncture, McDonald assaulted Alan Raymond and was dismissed from the radio station. 'Whilst I was working at this station at no period did I do it with the intention of helping the Japanese', McDonald repeated, 'but for purely patriotic reasons the money I received was enough for hire of my typewriter, transportation and cigarettes'.[26] Her relationship with Raymond had not inspired any loyalty; McDonald revealed almost immediately that she would be prepared to give evidence against him.[27] Perhaps Raymond was not a man who inspired confidence. His own elderly mother agreed to give evidence against him if she could gain a berth on a repatriation ship back to Australia.

In their efforts to mount a case for treason against Alan Raymond and Wynette McDonald, the Australian Security Service gathered letters that diplomatic representatives had written during the war about their activities and interviewed former internees and associates of the pair. Although this evidence was collected in an effort to prove that Raymond and McDonald collaborated with the Japanese, it also reveals that both Raymond and McDonald were largely shunned by the British community in Shanghai. Their embrace of the opportunity to broadcast for the Japanese may have been an expedient choice – perhaps one more politically motivated in Raymond's case than McDonald's – in a situation where internment was the only alternative but it is also possible that it stemmed from, or was at least fuelled by, social injury. The incidental criticisms made of Raymond and McDonald by members of their community also reveal that while Raymond was distrusted for his business dealings, McDonald drew opprobrium for her morality and sexuality. Both were ostracised because they appeared Eurasian.

Australian diplomatic staff and security agents mentioned in their investigations that Raymond and McDonald appeared 'Eurasian', assuming that this alone might explain their behaviour and be sufficient reason to doubt their claims to be Australian subjects. During the war, employees of Australia's Department of External Affairs remained at their posts at the Australian legation in Chungking; while

Shanghai was occupied by the Japanese and most foreign residents were interned, Chungking, inland in western China, remained 'free'. Legation staff conveyed as much information as possible back to their superiors in Canberra on the activities of suspected Australian collaborators. Patrick Shaw, who had been included in the exchange of diplomatic staff from Japan and was stationed in Chungking by 1943, told the Australian government that Alan Raymond, 'by appearance looks partly Eurasian' and claimed that Wynette McDonald 'is Eurasian'. McDonald's Eurasian appearance probably explains the security service's assertion that she 'claims Australian birth but is generally disbelieved'.[28] A woman with whom McDonald was interned claimed that 'one of the contributing factors to McDonald's hatred of Britain and the British Empire is her mother, who is of mixed French parentage', as if it were a causal relationship.[29] Wynette McDonald's mother, Winifred Le Blanc, was in fact born in Footscray, in Melbourne, in 1891 to a father who appears to have been French Canadian but it is unclear whether there was anything 'mixed' about his forebears. The security files contain no photographs of Wynette McDonald, so it is not even possible to speculate about whether her appearance encouraged people in their beliefs about her origins. There was no other evidence offered for the claims that Raymond was Eurasian, apart from photographs on top of his newspaper columns that show him as a fair-skinned man with dark hair and a pencil-thin moustache. Raymond had been born in Melbourne to English parents, and grew up in Sydney.[30]

Raymond's Eurasian appearance was one strike against him as far as the British community in Shanghai was concerned; his 'unsavoury reputation' was another. Raymond had initially travelled to China during the Depression, when still a young man in his twenties, and had attempted to make a career for himself in sales and trade. He did not meet with much success and endured the ignominy of being 'posted' in the Shangahi Club for unpaid debts. Raymond had also been involved in horseracing, primarily as 'a trainer of other people's ponies', but according to reports also socialised with the less-principled members of the Shanghai racing fraternity, and allegedly engaged in malpractice.[31] Given such dealings, Raymond was apparently a man of no standing whatever in the business community of Shanghai. The disapproval of the company he kept extended to 'low Chinese women', Japanese and Germans. Raymond was, one report concluded, 'an object of loathing among reputable Britishers in Shanghai'.[32] Bowden concluded his report on Alan Raymond with the following damning indictment:

While it is perhaps a natural democratic tendency to accept men at face value, in the case of Raymond it is a form of misrepresentation that might enable him to make arrangements with business houses or others in Australia which in evidence of his past career, would be more likely to bring theirs or Australia's name into discredit rather than achieve any good for them.[33]

These criticisms of Alan Raymond, and his unwelcome presence in the white business community of Shanghai, circled around his occupational and trade credentials, but the ostracism endured by Wynette McDonald arose more from moral judgements about her sexual behaviour. McDonald had arrived in Shanghai with a man, Lindquist, to whom she was not married. Lindquist claimed to have left Melbourne because Australians suspected everybody who had any trace of a foreign accent, adding that he feared that the government would intern him as an enemy alien.[34] Perhaps his German-sounding accent was not welcome in Shanghai, either. The suspicions that McDonald's lover aroused were not quelled by her reports that German internees in the Netherlands East Indies, through which she had travelled on her way to China, were not well treated there.[35] Bowden considered Lindquist 'a derelict', and another long-term British resident of Shanghai stated that in the eyes of the Anglo-Saxon community, Lindquist was a 'common confidence trickster'.[36]

McDonald's association with Lindquist did not endear her to the British residents of Shanghai, which may explain why they later claimed that from the day of her arrival McDonald more frequently associated with Germans and Japanese. Consequently, 'British and Americans were reluctant to accept her as one of their own'.[37] The sequence of McDonald's choices is ambiguous in the reports: did she associate with Germans and Japanese because the British ostracised her, or was the social shunning a consequence of her associations? Whatever the chronology of events may have been, McDonald's open criticism of the White Australia policy, along with her willingness to socialise with Axis nationals, meant that she was not accepted within the British community. Her alleged fraternisation with Japanese officers and guards during the internment period and thereafter, with the implication that she had offered them sexual favours, made the destruction of McDonald's reputation complete. In 1940, Trade Commissioner Bowden had criticised McDonald's activities yet retained a modicum of respect for her, noting his opinion that, despite her apparent unwillingness to accept advice, she was 'not without intelligence and with a good deal of spirit'.[38] By the end of the war, an Australian Legation staff member openly referred in an official report to the 'wide and innocent eyed Miss McDonald' as a 'harlot' who 'acknowledges nearly a hundred lovers but says that no. 67 the Jap guard when she was in jug was the only one she really loved'.[39] By the time Wynette McDonald was on her repatriation ship back to Australia, the construction of her as a deviant, sexually licentious woman reached its fullest expression in the report of a security officer that claimed that 'she is described as morally unsound and, in another quarter, to have Lesbian tendencies'.[40]

Social isolation before the outbreak of war also seems to have contributed to the suspicion that another Australian woman, Doris de Villa, collaborated with the Japanese in the Philippines. Doris de Villa was not interned by the Japanese and this was immediate cause for speculation among the expatriate population in Manila, most of whom spent the war behind the gates of Santo Tomas. Although Doris de Villa later claimed that 'the people in the camp were much better off than we were outside', her freedom throughout the war years made the de Villas the subject of conjecture and innuendo.[41] Rumour among other internees had it that Doris de Villa, her husband, Edward, and their son had lived in spacious apartments after the Japanese occupied Manila and interned other Allied nationals. There were further claims, all unsubstantiated, that Edward de Villa had collected car keys of other white residents in the city and handed them to the Japanese and had offered his services as a geologist to them.[42] After the war, even the Australian security services thought the suspicions 'may be treated with a degree of reserve, in view of possible personal animosities engendered by other repatriates from internment camps in Manila'.[43] Although these allegations were never proven, two facts remained. First, Edward de Villa had disappeared after being interviewed by the Japanese in late 1944, and his wife never saw him again. Doris de Villa returned to Australia as a widow, accompanied by her son. Second, Doris de Villa was never interned by the Japanese. Was her freedom a matter of collaboration, as other internees claimed, or mere expedience?

Doris Stubbs was born in Llanelly, in north-eastern Victoria, on Christmas Day 1896. When she was almost thirty, she had married Edward Manso de Villa, a geologist of English and French heritage who, it might be assumed, was rather more worldly than Doris. Dr Edward de Villa had been raised in Belgium and France, taken degrees at King's College, London, then travelled the world furthering his career as a geologist. He had already married once, in Vancouver, and was sep-arated from his Canadian wife and son. De Villa had worked in the Straits Settlement, Federated Malay States, China, the Netherlands East Indies and, by the 1920s, in Australia. Doris Stubbs had known de Villa only three months when she married him in 1926, and they almost immediately departed for Java. The couple lived in various parts of South-East Asia and China before settling in the Philippines in the mid-1930s. Before leaving, both Doris and Edward de Villa had applied for Australian passports but they had been refused because the British Home Office advised that Edward de Villa could not be regarded as a British subject. As Edward de Villa's wife, Doris's application was also refused, given the standard practice at the time of wives assuming their husbands' nationality upon marriage.

When the Japanese arrived in Manila, Edward de Villa claimed French nationality to avoid internment by the Japanese.[44] It appears that Doris de Villa agreed with her husband's strategy to avoid intern-ment, because she later claimed that she had not been interned owing to her neutral status. This revelation caused an intake of breath among security service officers in Sydney, who described it as 'extraordinary' given that Doris de Villa maintained that she had 'lost' her French passport and claimed repatriation to Australia as a British subject.[45] Doris de Villa always contended that life outside the internment camp was just as difficult as life inside it. She sold her jewellery and clothes in order to survive, food was in short supply, and ultimately her hus-band had been arrested by the Japanese. Doris de Villa believed that her husband had been murdered by the Japanese because she 'was told that another man who was taken with him had his head cut off'. Doris de Villa's sexual integrity was never called into question in either the rumours that accompanied her back to Australia or in subsequent inves-tigations into her activities. Nevertheless, the security officer who inter-viewed de Villa could not help himself asking, after she referred to the arrest and disappearance of her husband, whether she had been 'inter-fered with after they took your husband'. 'No' was all Doris de Villa said in reply.[46]

It is clear that Doris de Villa did not regret her decision to avoid internment. The animosity directed towards her from other internees was largely the result of beliefs about her husband's activities. The main crime Doris de Villa appears to have committed was to enjoy freedom while other members of her community endured captivity. She did not experience her whiteness as reason enough to throw in her lot with that of other expatriates in the city, despite a common view of the war as having a profoundly racial aspect. The injury of this was compounded when Doris de Villa and her son moved into Santo Tomas once it was liberated, to seek shelter from potential attacks by guerillas and to join the queue for repatriation. It also transpired that the de Villas had been socially isolated members of their expatriate community before the Japanese occupation. According to enquiries by the Australian security services, Edward de Villa 'drank to excess' and the couple 'did not mix freely with the other European residents' in Manila. Edward de Villa's travels about the world as a geologist appear to have ground to a halt in the Philippines, where he remained for a decade, the longest stop on his previously demanding itinerary. It appears that 'owing to his mode of living and excessive drinking' de Villa was unable to complete jobs for which he had been engaged and the family became 'financially embarrassed'.[47] Although Doris de Villa claimed in an interview after the war that her husband had earned 'big money', it seems that the days of financial security may well have been over before the Japanese arrived. If Edward de Villa had viewed the arrival of the Japanese in expedient terms, as a chance to revive his flagging fortunes, it had not worked. By the end of the war his reputation, and that of his wife, were in tatters. And the hardship continued. In 1946, Doris de Villa asked the Australian government if 'something more can be done for me than being put on the dole' and that she and her son 'have been living upon the charity of my sister since returning to Australia but all good things must come to an end'.[48]

The common element among those Australians who appear to have collaborated with the Japanese, or at least enjoyed a relationship with the Japanese that allowed them to avoid internment, was a sense of being outsiders in expatriate communities notoriously sensitive about policing the boundaries of class and race in their relatively small social worlds. Perhaps they were individuals with nothing much to lose or, in the case of Douglas Murdoch, a man whose ambitions and one suspects, pressure to live up to the expectations of the family name, might have temporarily skewed perceptions about the correct and acceptable way to fulfil them. It should be remembered, though, that the number of Australians involved in broadcasting for the Japanese and other forms of collaboration was extremely small. Most Allied nationals captured by the Japanese entered internment camps and attempted to adapt to the pressures of communal living and to deal with its physical, mental and emotional challenges.

The homecoming of Australians suspected of collaboration with the Japanese was closely monitored by the security services. Doris de Villa was watched by intelligence officers from the moment she arrived on Australian shores. Security service officers mingled with the crowd of returning internees on the train she took from Townsville to Sydney and reported on the family with whom she stayed overnight in Brisbane. Mail that Doris de Villa received at her sister's house was intercepted. At one point, the Red Cross even agreed to a security service officer posing as one of their aid workers as a way of extracting further information from her.[49] Nothing Doris de Villa did or said during this period suggested that she had collaborated with the Japanese.

Although many civilian internees felt let down and disappointed by the services and assistance that their government provided to them after their liberation, there were a few who must have been eternally grateful. Alan Raymond, Wynette McDonald and John Holland had the diligence of officers in the Attorney-General's Department and in the Crown Solicitor's office to thank for their escape from prosecution. Despite the best efforts of the Australian Security Service, the Australian government's senior legal officers decided there was insufficient evidence available to mount a prima facie case of treason against them. Only one, John Holland, went on to make the mistake of leaving safe territory.

The Australian Security Service firmly believed that Alan Raymond and Wynette McDonald were collaborators, and always referred to them as such in correspondence. As early as October 1945, the Commonwealth Attorney-General's Department had decided there was insufficient evidence with which to charge either Raymond or McDonald with treason. After carefully examining the texts of Raymond's speeches and his newspaper articles, the Attorney-General's Department agreed that they were of an overtly political character but, critically, there was 'no suggestion in any of the commentaries that Australia should join Japan'. There could only be a prima facie case of treason established against Raymond 'if it could be proved that he intended to assist Japan'.[50] Still not satisfied, however, the security service sent one of their own, Captain Blackett, to Japan and China in November 1945 to see if he could gather further evidence against them and to interview Holland, Raymond and McDonald.

Blackett went first to Tokyo, where he interviewed Holland, who was in Sugamo prison. Holland had been arrested by the US army on 20 September 1945 at Sapporo, on the north island of Japan, while he was sitting in a barber's chair in the Grand Hotel.[51] After speaking with Holland, Blackett formed the opinion that there *was* a prima facie case of treason against him. Blackett then went to Shanghai and met with senior figures in the British and American intelligence community, who conveyed their belief that there was insufficient evidence to charge Raymond and McDonald with treason.[52] Further interviews with McDonald, Raymond and other people who knew them in Shanghai were all to no avail. The Attorney-General's Department remained convinced there was no point in charging either Raymond or McDonald with treason.[53] Counsel advising the Commonwealth Government, Richard Windeyer, KC, and Rex Chambers, were of the opinion that there was 'little doubt that [Raymond] was guilty of treason, but there was not, however, sufficient evidence to support an indictment'.[54] Although Raymond never stood trial for his wartime activities, a letter written from the Commonwealth Investigation Service to the Department of Immigration in 1948, when Raymond applied for an Australian passport, clearly states the service's feelings on the matter. 'Although insufficient evidence can be obtained with which to charge Raymond with treason', the letter claimed:

> there is no doubt that he did collaborate with the Japanese and his activities in that direction caused considerable feeling amongst loyal people who were in Shanghai during the war . . . This man showed himself to be a traitor during the war.[55]

The situation was slightly different for John Holland, who had already been arrested by the Americans. By October 1945, his family were aware of his fate. In the Senate, Senator Dorothy Tangney from Western Australia urged that next of kin be notified of the whereabouts of the 'suspected war criminals'. 'I have in mind, particularly, the members of a family who would much prefer that their son were dead than that he should be found guilty of the crime of which he is suspected.'[56] The family was not named in Parliament but, after another six months with no word, Senator Tangney had written privately to the Minister for the Army on behalf of the Hollands. Tangney pointed out that John Holland's father, Dr J. J. Holland, was 'a well-known and high [sic] respected citizen of Perth'. Despite Dr Holland's profile, the enquiries about John Holland had in fact been initiated by his sisters, who claimed on behalf of the family that 'the shock and worry was getting them all down'. [57] One sister tried to convince the Australian Security Service that 'she was sure he was broadcasting under compulsion'.[58]

Dr Holland, who appears to have always had a fractious relationship with his son, remained tight-lipped. His son's claim, almost four years previously, that 'we all are entitled to our views' had seemed misguided then, and even more so now.

The Attorney-General's Department and the Crown Solicitor had been prevaricating on a decision about whether or not to prosecute John Holland since at least November 1945. Finally, in May 1946, the legal experts advised that there was still insufficient evidence against Holland to charge him with treason, and that he should therefore be released to Sydney. After his return, Holland did not remain for long in Australia, perhaps conscious that the government was willing, if unable, to charge him with treason. By September 1946, he had left Fremantle after finding work as a member of a ship's crew. Holland eventually made his way to England aboard a tanker and was arrested by Scotland Yard detectives on board ship in February 1947.[59] Like other British subjects accused of broadcasting for the enemy, Holland was prosecuted under Defence Regulation 2A, which contained a maximum penalty of life imprisonment. British prosecutors thought that charging him with treason, which carried the death penalty, would not be suitable for broadcasters like Holland, 'renegades who were not thought to be deserving of death'.[60]

On 25 March 1947, John Joseph Holland was convicted at Central Criminal Court, London, of engaging in subversive wartime acts in China and Japan. 'I should think it was vanity on your part which caused you to think that a person like yourself could have some influence on the policy of Australia', the Lord Chief Justice chided Holland. Nevertheless, in sentencing, the Lord Chief Justice stated that he was persuaded by defence counsel's argument that Holland 'fell out' with the Japanese, refused to continue broadcasting for them, and subsequently endured over two years in a Japanese prison. 'What you did in lending yourself to the Japanese came back on you like a boomerang and landed you in this torture hell in Japanese prisons for $2^{1}/_{2}$ years.' The early postwar reputation of the Japanese as particularly brutal captors served Holland well in his moment of need. 'It would be idle affection of my part', the Lord Chief Justice confessed, 'if I did not remember that a British subject who was imprisoned by the Japanese was subject to what can only be called terrible torture during that time'.[61] Yet the transcripts of the case contain surprisingly little reference to the treatment Holland received, save for inappropriate clothing in the cold Japanese winter. Ultimately, the Chief Justice considered that despite

Holland's foolishness he had suffered enough. Consequently he took what he described as a 'wholly exceptional course' and bound Holland over in the sum of £10 to be of good behaviour for the next five years.

When finding Holland guilty but giving him a suspended sentence, the Chief Justice explicitly mentioned the Australian government's unwillingness or legal incapacity, he was not sure which, to prosecute Holland. 'They took no proceedings against you and they allowed you to leave Australia', he noted with some incredulity.[62] It was not merely Holland's spell in a Japanese prison but also his own country's reluctance to prosecute him that allowed John Holland to walk from the Old Bailey a free man in the northern spring of 1947.

5

SEX AND HEALTH

Dorothy Jenner was no prude. Her memoir recounts with considerable relish the series of lovers she enjoyed during her time in the United States, England and Europe throughout the 1920s and 1930s. Yet when she was interned at Stanley, Jenner made the decision to remain celibate. 'Even though this was very much against my real nature,' she later recalled, 'I made a pact with myself that I would never get into a position where I could be discovered by a Japanese guard in an embarrassing position'. For Jenner, the decision was a matter of both personal and national honour. 'I wouldn't give a Jap soldier the pleasure of being able to snigger at me, and through me, my country.'[1]

In retrospect, Jenner's decision to become a 'nun', as she put it, may well have appeared a patriotic act. The diaries she wrote during captivity, however, reflect a far greater concern with the camp guards' proclivity for policing sexual activity among the inmates than with any intention to uphold national honour. Being caught 'in the act', according to Jenner's calculations, would make a woman far more vulnerable to sexual attack from a Sikh or Japanese guard, a fate she feared throughout her time in Stanley. Jenner's diaries record incidents in which 'fornicators' were caught by Sikh guards and forced to report to the Japanese commandant.[2] Although choosing to remain celibate herself, there is an element of voyeurism in Jenner's listing of all the places that couples chose for their trysts: broom closets, freshly dug but still empty graves and the flat roofs of internee billets. The Japanese could observe all of these places through field-glasses from their headquarters, she noted. The Japanese might have been watching, but Jenner herself was making notes and quite possibly longing for that period in her own life when sex seemed less fraught with danger.

In the postwar period, the greatest cultural interest in internment's sexual aspect rested with the interaction between Asian guards and their white captives. There was no real surprise in this, given the long fascination in Western cultures with the detention of Europeans by cultural 'others', and the anxieties about transgression, boundaries and colonialism that they expressed. This genre of story has long been known as the 'captivity narrative'.[3] The sexual threat of the captor was certainly an issue for internees, as Dorothy Jenner's thoughts and fears so readily attest, but internee diaries were much more focused on relationships within the internee community than between internees and their guards. Internee diarists were interested in sex but they were also curious about gender, and how men and women responded differently to the challenges of internment. The body – its desires, physical and mental health – was of constant concern to internees throughout their captivity.

If civilians were conscious of their racial identity, they were equally aware that captivity posed particular dilemmas for women. The desperation to evacuate white women from Allied colonies and territories did not merely stem from the belief that war was ultimately men's work and that women did not belong in the battle zone. It was driven just as much, if not more, by assumptions about the non-white man as the sexual predator of white women. The belief that sexual excess was a feature of racial inferiority and the less-commonly stated subtext that sexual interaction between a white woman and a non-white man issued a challenge to white masculinity, was widespread in colonial communities. In the Australian territory of Papua, for instance, this confluence of ideas received expression in the White Women's Protection Ordinance of 1926, which prescribed the death penalty for the rape or *attempted* rape of a *European* women or girl.[4] Such an ordinance expressed fear about white women's vulnerability, but it also contained a warning to women who might express desire across the racial divide.

Wartime propaganda emphasised the potential for sexual violence that inhered in the Japanese soldier and implied that white women would be particularly vulnerable. One often-reproduced cartoon depicted a King Kong-like Japanese soldier holding aloft the naked body of a white woman.[5] This was at once a literal representation of the threat the Japanese were imagined to pose to white women, and a symbolic representation of the vulnerability of the nation to the penetration and domination by the Japanese enemy. Furthermore, Japanese military victory and occupation had compromised European men's ability to protect 'their' women.

Sex was a threatening topic, and not one which Australian men wanted to discuss with their new Japanese overseers. 'Sex, so far as the Japs were concerned, was an open subject to be discussed by any-one at any time', Gordon Thomas recalled. 'It was as much a part of the Nip life as horse-racing is in Australia.' After the occupation of Rabaul, he explicitly resented Japanese soldiers and sailors asking him about the attractions of 'Australian marys'. 'Mary' was common par-lance in the island territories for an indigenous woman. 'The mere word "mary" immediately riled us when used in connection with Australian women, and we would turn our heads away in disgust.'[6] Thomas con-sidered it further insult to have Australian women even talked about by the Japanese, and in refusing to discuss them also attempted to continue shielding them from the prying eyes of the Japanese.

Fears about the potential for sexual violence in the Japanese army were not entirely without foundation. As newsreels and cartoons revealed, the Rape of Nanking and the abuse of Chinese women during the Japanese occupation were relatively well known. Dorothy Jenner's diary entry on Boxing Day 1941, the day after the British surrender of Hong Kong, immediately registered her fear. The women at her hotel had gathered together in one room. 'An unspoken thought – held on tongues – Were we to be the victims of their mauling? W[oul]d we be man handled – raped?' A few lines later, Jenner face-tiously dismisses her initial encounter with the occupying Japanese as 'leaving us ruffled but unraped – Like the old maid we were rather annoyed at being overlooked'.[7] Despite this apparent glibness, Jenner's diaries and notes from captivity repeatedly and almost com-pulsively return to the topic of rape and sexual interaction between guards and female internees. Unusually, Jenner also mentions the names of women she believed to have been raped during both the occupa-tion and later internment. In other accounts there is a tacit assumption that anonymity should prevail. Jenner's papers also contain an exten-sive and graphic description of the sexual violence perpetrated against Chinese and British nurses at Happy Valley Relief Hospital during the invasion of Hong Kong.[8] Other Australian women who encountered the Japanese during the invasion have also admitted fears for their sex-ual safety but none has ever admitted publicly that she was a victim of rape.

Australian nuns in Rabaul, accustomed to their single-sex community, were also terrified. After the Japanese victory, the nuns were confined to their convent. The two-storey building overlooked the harbour
and had wide verandahs to take advantage of the views and sea breeze.
At night, the guards would continually patrol the wooden verandahs,
their footfall echoing throughout the convent. Like the more worldly
women in Hong Kong, in the early days of captivity the nuns slept in
one room together and refused to undress.[9] The nurses from the government hospital had also been moved to the convent and were wary of
the guards. They claim to have not been actually harmed, but were also
frightened when at night the guards would enter their rooms and touch
their bodies. One of them, Queenslander Alice Bowman, thought perhaps the soldiers were under orders *not* to molest the women, because
they would retreat quickly when the women protested.[10] Dorothy
Jenner also reported that Japanese officers at Stanley would attempt
to prevent guards from sexually harassing the female internees. She
described her fear of drunken guards conducting 'sweetheart hunts' as
being so intense that each time it occurred she would hide in the toilet.
'The [officers] always protected us', she concluded, 'unless you were one
of the ones *they* wanted'.[11]

Bowman's memoir and newspaper interviews with the women at
war's end were full of bravado but they read, ultimately, as a thin veneer
for fear. To describe experiences as 'hair-raising', as Bowman does, is
a ploy of comic deflection that serves to neutralise the fear that once
existed. It cannot have been comforting for the women to be constantly
asked by soldiers if they were virgins. At night, the nurses in Rabaul
slept with a phial of morphine beside their beds, with plans to swallow it
if a sexual attack occurred. In the early days after the fall of Hong Kong,
Dorothy Jenner had asked local British policemen to shoot her if she
were about to be raped.[12] For these women, rape by a Japanese soldier
was a fate worse than death. In denying molestation these women protect their own reputations as much as they do the actions of the guards,
but other research has also suggested that sexual violence against white
women was relatively rare. It was Chinese, Korean and other indigenous women in Japanese-occupied territory who bore the brunt of sexual aggression.[13] And, as Jenner's compulsive return to the topic in her
diaries and notes from captivity suggests, for some white women the
intense fear of rape, if not its actual occurrence, constituted a traumatic
experience that they revisited throughout internment.

The Japanese were not the only non-white men that interned women came into contact with during their captivity. Many of the guards were indeed Japanese military personnel, but there were also Sikhs, Koreans, Formosans, Indonesians and Chinese who oversaw and disciplined the inmates. Undoubtedly, some white women chose to become sexually involved with their overseers, although this remains a topic shrouded in secrecy and silence. In the Netherlands, for example, there is a small population of people born in the 1940s of mixed Indies Dutch–Japanese parentage. Other camp inmates have commented on this phenomenon but the voices of those directly concerned have rarely been heard. This may well be because fellow internees denigrated them. Australian army nurses interned on Sumatra referred to the women who chose to 'fraternise' as 'Jap girlfriends' and 'the satin sheet brigade'.[14] In Hong Kong, Dorothy Jenner wrote in equally disparaging terms about the 'young society harlots' who seduced their Chinese superintendents in order to improve their accommodation in camp. She also complained in August 1942 that each night some of the female internees played '"whoopee" with Jap authorities', a practice which she considered 'a thorough disgrace'.[15] Sheila Allen noted that after the internees evacuated Changi and moved to Sime Road, some of the huts were known as 'Brothel Houses', in reference to the sexual contact that occurred there between interned women and their guards.[16]

Yet captivity and deprivation could blur the fine line between choice and compulsion. Although only a teenager at the time, one of Sheila Allen's diary entries alluded to the dilemma: 'Would we sell ourselves? – I don't know – maybe there are cases but who are we to judge morally – can we honestly say that but "For the Grace of God" there go I?'[17] It has been well documented elsewhere that some women who did become sexually involved with their overseers used it as a means of gaining much-needed food and medicine, for their children, relatives and friends. Some middle-aged women volunteered themselves to save their virginal teenage daughters from a similar fate.[18] Although some internees like Dorothy Jenner derided such behaviour, those who benefited from it were eternally grateful. There were also other, less fortunate women, who had been robbed of any choice.

In the Indies, at least 200 Dutch women were abducted from their camps and subjected to daily, multiple rapes.[19] Other female inmates called them 'rabbits' and threw stones at them when they returned to camp, unaware that the women had been forcibly removed by the

Japanese authorities.[20] No Australian women are reported to have been involved in the compulsory recruitment of white women into military sexual slavery for the Japanese military. A group of Australian army nurses interned on Sumatra have admitted the pressure placed on them to work as 'comfort women' but have always vehemently denied that they acceded to such demands or were ever forced into submitting to them.[21] It remains a controversial point with activists on behalf of the former 'comfort women' that although the Dutch later tried a Japanese accused on the grounds of 'having forced Dutch women to practice prostitution', no member of the Japanese military was ever tried for similar war crimes in the cases of tens of thousands of Asian women subjected to a similar fate.[22] Despite these tensions, one of the Dutch survivors, Jan Ruff O'Herne, who later migrated to Australia, has become a well-known advocate for women to 'break the silence' surrounding rape in war and the systematic exploitation of women licensed by the Japanese military's system of sexual slavery.[23]

Some Australian internees witnessed the system at first hand. In Rabaul, for instance, internees laboured on the wharves unloading Japanese ships. One group witnessed the arrival of hundreds of Korean 'comfort women', many of whom were 'little more than children'. They wore brightly coloured kimonos, elaborately dressed hair and wooden shoes. The internees unloaded their luggage and carried it to the lines of waiting trucks. One Irish priest wondered 'what his Holiness would say if he knew I was portering for prostitutes'.[24] Despite the 'portering for prostitutes' comment, Korean workmen resident in Rabaul told the Australian internees that the women had arrived under false pretences. The women had believed they were coming south to work in factories and coffee plantations. It would not be until the 1990s that similarly affected women spoke publicly about their abuse and forced participation in what they preferred to call 'military sexual slavery'. Many thousands of Korean, Filipina and other women indigenous to the region were subjected to a similar fate.[25]

Although female internees reported their fear of rape, particularly early in their captivity, the diaries and papers of male internees are remarkably silent on the topic of sexual violence. They do not even admit fear. Male-to-male sexual violence, or even consensual sex, between guards and prisoners, or among prisoners themselves, is a barely explored aspect of captivity under the Japanese.

Despite writers' willingness to detail the peccadilloes of their fellow internees, in most accounts there is a virtual silence about same-sex relationships in captivity. Jenner mentions the names of known homo-sexual men in her camp, whom she referred to as 'pansy chaps', as matters of fact rather than as the revelation of a shameful secret but does not dwell further on either male homosexuality or lesbianism. Given the prevalence of such associations in other prison populations, their complete absence would be unlikely in internment camps, particularly those that enforced segregation of the sexes. In the end, internee reticence on such matters may well leave us little option but to respect the silences and ambiguities that often accompany intense friendships, both within and outside captivity.

Some internees claimed in bitter moments that they were too hungry to care about sex. In Changi, for instance, Harold Murray had certainly noticed that the women were scantily clad in the hot and humid climate but claimed that the semi-starvation diet made food of greater interest to men than sex. 'We had other things to worry about', he noted: 'Dress and all that went with it was not in the running, food had the whole field.'[26] Murray viewed the 'sun tops' – a modest form of bikini top but still unusually risqué for respectable women in the 1940s – of the women in Changi from across the way. His own wife was at home in Australia but married couples in Changi were eventually permitted a few visits to each other at 'relatives' meetings', although they were never allowed privacy or to cohabit. In contrast, married couples in Stanley were allowed to live together. Jenner was typically tongue-in-cheek about this, referring to one block of the camp as 'Adultery Annex', and revealing that people who had previously been 'sub rosa practitioners' were now living openly together.[27] For happily married couples, the creation of mixed-sex camps was most likely a relief because it meant that they did not face the daunting prospect of separation during war. This was certainly true for Jack and Joyce Percival at Santo Tomas. It posed other dilemmas for women used to living in segregated communities. The twelve Australian Sacre Coeur nuns based in Tokyo, for instance, were initially removed from their convent and placed in a mixed-sex camp in a Tokyo surburb. One nun, Sister Mary Hastings, noted her surprise when they were transferred to accommodation which was also home to interned priests and male missionaries. The men immediately set to work helping the nuns establish their sleeping quarters. 'I have had many queer experiences in my life', one of her sisters commented, 'but I never expected to get my bed made by a Jesuit'.[28]

The Percivals and other couples mixed freely in the much larger Santo Tomas, and often ate meals together in the 'shanties' that were eventually constructed between the campus buildings. But at night husbands and wives went their separate ways to the respective male and female quarters of the camp. This was until February 1944, when the Japanese allowed married couples to live together again for a brief time. Jack Percival described the scene of preparations 'for the restoration of conjugal rights due to the benevolence of the Imperial Japanese army'. The camp amplification system played the 'Wedding March' as internees carried bedding down to the shanties. 'Not a great deal of work has been done in camp today', Percival reported the following night. 'Departmental heads were late for duty, and a number of the garbage gang seem very bleary-eyed.'[29] The arrangement lasted less than a month. In Manila, the Japanese more typically discouraged sexual relations between camp inmates, even married couples, in the certainty that abstinence was the best contraceptive of them all. As far as they were concerned, there were already enough mouths to feed.

Percival's own 'conjugal rights' with his wife had been restored during the brief respite from sexual segregation, but any joy, relief or satisfaction he might have found in their reunion did not make its way into his diary. The critical eye Percival was willing to cast over his fellow internees, never extended – at least in written from – to his own feelings about his wife or their marriage during the years of internment. This is a topic upon which he was resolutely silent. The absence of comment is in fact unsurprising given Percival's stoicism and his tendency to write his diary as a *de facto* newspaper column. Although Dorothy Jenner was a journalist too, and also composed her diary entries with a reporter's eye, her detailing of sexual practices has a level of intimacy missing from Percival's notes. This may well have been an extension of Jenner's frankness about sexual matters and intense interest in sexuality, which form a strong presence in both the internment diaries and her published memoir.

Percival was most inclined to document the effects of internment on others rather than his own relationship with his wife. He likened the camp to a 'parochial community' in which 'tongues wagged', but they were more likely to do so about illegitimate births and adultery than married couples seeking a rare moment's privacy and intimacy. Percival was himself critical of the 'lounge lizards' and 'cuckoos in the nest' who preyed upon the wives of men interned elsewhere in POW camps.[30] Dorothy Jenner, who had been scathing about interned women who fraternised with Japanese officers, was less concerned about relationships with a similar purpose within the internee population. One of her friends was a Hong Kong-based Australian prostitute, who in camp continued working in exchange for food, which she shared with Jenner.[31] Despite Jenner's broadmindedness, at least in relation to some practices, Percival's comments also make clear that some internees placed pressure on others to conform to standards of morality that held marriage as sacrosanct and disapproved of sexual activity outside its bounds. This might have been repressive for some internees but in other cases it had its virtues. Percival, for instance, noted in his diary that 'girls in the children's playground are extremely buxom and great vigilance against sex abuses in this mixed camp is maintained by parents and officials. There has been no sex crime yet'.[32] Percival's further speculation that a diet high in rice had led to advanced breast development in young teenage girls strikes an odd note in his mostly detached reflections, but his acknowledgement of the potential for pedophilia within the camp is a rare admission that internees were aware of its possible occurrence and took steps to police it. The children, although vulnerable, sometimes took matters into their own hands. In one camp in China, the teenage boys sought revenge on a known pederast by luring him to a lonely dark place and painting his penis with gentian violet, an antiseptic distinguished by its lurid purple dye. This was a clever act of public outing and shaming in a community that lived in dormitories and took communal showers.[33]

The vigilance about respectability among some camp members, and uncertainty about how long the war might last, might go some way towards explaining marriages celebrated in camp that in retrospect might have seemed a bit hasty. In December 1942 Lionel Buttfield and Phyllis Lynch, who was not yet twenty-one, married in Santo Tomas in the presence of fellow Australians as witnesses. Their daughter Pamela was born the following year, and a son, Frank, within weeks of the camp's liberation.[34] The Buttfields were two of seventy babies born in Santo Tomas, although over thirty had been conceived before internment. Jack Percival's son, Jack Jr, fell into the latter category.[35] The Buttfields' marriage did not survive the transition to freedom and by the early 1950s both Lionel and Phyllis had remarried; Phyllis retained custody of their daughter, Pamela, and their son, Frank, lived with his father.[36]

Others met partners with whom they formed lifelong relationships. Nelma Davies, the daughter of Australian Salvation Army missionaries in China, recalled that the day she married her British husband Edwin in their internment camp, she had lost so much weight that she was able to wear a child's first communion dress as her wedding frock. Mrs Davies still possesses the toastracks composed of steel heel-clips and the storage containers made from flattened food tins that fellow inmates presented to the couple as wedding presents.[37] As committed Christians, but also young people in love, the Davies considered that the only way their relationship could be consummated in captivity was by having it blessed by the Church.

The enthusiasm for weddings displayed in the gifts handmade for the Davies and the willingness of women to risk conceiving a baby in such conditions have been interpreted by other historians of internment as life-affirming actions in an environment where uncertainty often prevailed. Marriage and childbearing in camp 'defied Japanese attempts to destroy the virility of Western colonial communities', Bernice Archer has suggested, 'and were a public proclamation of the community's endurance, continuity and future'.[38] The semi-starvation conditions, especially towards the end of internment, also affected women's menstrual cycles. The absence of regularity is often a conduit to unplanned conceptions, in internment as much as anywhere else.

While marriage and conception were life-affirming choices for some, not all internees were overjoyed at the boost to their numbers that babies, planned or otherwise, provided. There were people contemptuous of women who conceived during internment, and about the proportion of rations allocated to children by executive committees. Dorothy Jenner, childless throughout her life, resented the extra rations given to children in an effort to boost their calcium supplies. Jean Gittins, who chose to be interned in Stanley for her own safety, was a mother herself and especially critical of women who conceived during internment. At Stanley, pregnant women were given double rations. Gittins thought this practice was outrageous, claiming that these women usually 'drew them only for their husband or lover as the case may be'.[39]

Despite Dorothy Jenner's and Jean Gittins's circumspection, many mothers in captivity made enormous physical sacrifices in an effort to ensure that their children would survive. Gittins's own children had been safely evacuated to Australia and she did not face the daily challenge of providing enough food for them. In time-honoured traditions common in many impoverished families, internee mothers sacrificed their own requirement for food in order to provide for their children. Edith Begley's children were teenagers in their Chinese internment camp, but adolescence is a hungry time and she often went without so that her children could have more.[40] One of the most extraordinary

Figure 9: *Frank and Molly Jefferson, and their daughter Julie, greeted by a relative after their repatriation from Santo Tomas internment camp.*

acts of concern blended with anxiety was performed by Molly Jefferson, interned with her husband Frank and daughter Julie in Santo Tomas. 'With every available money Frank & I could get hold of we bought up milk & were able to give Julie 1 cup a day for a long while', she wrote in one of her first letters to family in Australia after they were released. Mrs Jefferson also had her own blood injected into her daughter, in the belief that this would pass on essential vitamins and minerals which Julie missed out on in their internment camp. She did so 'until it was taking too much out of me, so in these ways we were able to keep Julie fairly well, all she had was Measles & they seemed to do her good'.[41]

Owing to the paucity of medicines and the prevalence of diseases like beriberi, dysentery and malaria, particularly in the tropical zones, some mothers were forced to watch helplessly as their children died. One woman originally from Sydney, Noeline Ossendryver, gave her daughter life and watched her die in an internment camp. 'At her birth, as at her death, there was no doctor there to help us', she later recalled. Noeline, whose husband was a veterinary surgeon in the Dutch army, had arrived in camp with her eldest child, a son, and gave birth to her

Figure 10: *Noeline (L) and Roma (R) Ossendryver photographed after returning to Australia from internment in Java. Roma's son Arnold (L) was born in camp. Noeline's daughter Elaine was also born in camp, but did not survive her internment.*

daughter, Elaine, in October 1942. In the early weeks of pregnancy during the Japanese invasion of Batavia, Noeline had the company of her sister-in-law and fellow Australian Roma Ossendryver, a former model also from Sydney, throughout her captivity. In November 1944, the families moved to the overcrowded Struiswyk Gaol in Batavia and lived in a stone cell that had moss growing across the floor, where they 'could see our children fading before our eyes'. Elaine died in the early hours of a June morning in 1945, after her mother and aunt had conducted an all-night vigil with the sparing use of a two-inch candle.[42] Roma had also been pregnant early in her captivity but she was fortunate that her son, Arnold, born in a Bandung camp, survived his internment.[43]

Elaine Ossendryver could not be helped but there were children who pulled through. Audrey Stanford, interned in Santo Tomas with her parents, developed a serious kidney infection. She was given the last sacrament but her illness coincided with the only delivery of comfort kits from the Red Cross that the Japanese allowed throughout the entire war. With the assistance of drugs she survived but the recovery took months. Writing to Audrey's aunt in Sydney at the end of the war, her father remembered that 'It was a very worrying time for us, and pulled Mary down a lot'.[44] In camps where death from treatable illness was not uncommon, it was an enormous relief for mothers when their children made a recovery. When Gwen Kirwan's four-year-old son William returned to the women's section after his long spell in Changi's hospital, her eyes were 'shining with a can-it-be-true-he's-back expression', according to Sheila Allen.[45] But she continued to worry about his health and was still anxious in the 1950s about the after-effects of internment on William's development and future prospects. When applying for a small grant from the Australian government, Gwen Kirwan included a photograph of her son taken upon liberation to show just how small he was for his age. She also included another, taken just before the Japanese occupation of Malaya, which showed William to be a chubby, sandy-haired three-year-old. She noted on the back: 'A glance at this healthy child shows that [before internment] this healthy child had nothing but perfect health'.[46]

Jack Percival's diary demonstrates that it was not only mothers who feared for their children in captivity. Fathers, when they were nearby, watched with increasing anxiety as the children failed to thrive and showed the effects of malnourishment. In 1944 Percival noted in his diary that the camp's children were 'developing bellies such as we used to see in famine photos from China' and observed that the playing fields were deserted because very few of the children had any energy to spare. In the one exception to his general practice of reporting others' feelings, rather than his own, Percival remained acutely conscious throughout his captivity that his son had never known true freedom. 'Our child has never seen a tablecloth, doesn't know what candy is, has never seen a street or a house', Percival lamented. 'Next month will be my son's [second] birthday as a prisoner of war', he remarked with sadness in April 1944, 'into which state he was born – poor little blighter'.[47] Percival did his best to find spots of beauty and interest for his son within the gloom of the internment camp. In July 1944 Percival was able to give his son some indication of what a lighted Christmas tree looked like when a swarm of fireflies descended upon a huge acacia tree. It was an evening of low cloud, and the insects glowed 'like gems displayed on black velvet'. Percival continued:

Figure 11: *Joyce Percival and her son, Jack Jr, born in Santo Tomas internment camp.* '*Our child has never seen a tablecloth, doesn't know what candy is, has never seen a street or a house*', *Jack Percival senior lamented in May 1944.*

They were so thick that they seemed to crust the umbrella-shaped foliage, creating a glittering wealth of beauty such has shaded the head of no maharaja at the Durbar of Dehli nor no East Indies sultan. It was a sight of singular beauty amid the sordidness of the Japanese concentration camp. The show ended for the kid when I caught six of the largest,

108

put them in a match-box and released them in his screened crib. The glow they diffused lit up the interior of the cot like the candles on a birthday cake in a darkened room.[48]

This is one of the most moving passages in Percival's diary, and the richness of its imagery and the determination to show the child a form of beauty is testament to the depth of Percival's anguish about the privations his son endured in Santo Tomas.

Parents worried about the health and education of their children but internment was also particularly hard on the elderly and infirm. Harry Slocombe, in his fifties, noted in his diary that 'most of us men at middle age are finding the going pretty hard on the food we are getting, the young men are doing fine'.[49] In camps where food was, initially at least, less of an issue, the change in diet and circumstance was thought by some to have the opposite effect. Gordon Thomas observed that the elderly men in his community previously prone to liver and ulcer problems actually improved in health. Cut off from their daily supply of alcohol, forced to undertake physical work, some men who had previously been overweight alcoholics seemed to take a turn for the better.[50] Early in internment, one man in Changi made a request that a photographer from outside the camp be allowed in to photograph him, so that his wife, who had always complained about his weight, could see him now.[51] The outcome was not always so bright. In Yangchow internment camp in northern China, one alcoholic suffered such severe withdrawal symptoms that he 'became mentally unbalanced and finally was buried in the small cemetery at the rear of the camp hospital'.[52] But being relatively fit and strong had benefits other than immediate good health. It also meant people in such positions might work a bit harder to get extra rations for themselves and their families. In Santo Tomas, Australian mining engineer Roy Stanford worked as carpenter, which gave him additional rations.

Internees everywhere, whatever their age, were obsessed with rations and the food supply. As the years dragged on, hunger and captivity were common bedfellows. Internment diaries often contain list upon list, column after column, of ration issues, calorie equivalents, calculations of expenditure and the shifting prices of canteen goods (ever upwards) that reflect the energy internees devoted to securing their daily rice. Two months into internment in Changi, the camp executive committee noted that 'next to release, the most important topic is probably food'.[53] This would not change throughout captivity and worsened each year.

Food supplies were insufficient for camp populations, and they were also of very poor quality. By 1944 Harold Murray was commenting in his diary that he had come 'to loath the look of that watery soup' that not even a pig in Australia would deign to eat.[54] In February the same year the meat allowance at Santo Tomas had been entirely discontinued and replaced with what Jack Percival described as 'baskets of stinking fish, seemingly containing loot from all the gold-fish bowls in the far east'. 'All have been thrown onto the starvation diet,' he continued, 'which would cause a riot if served in any penitentiary in Australia, Britain or the USA'.[55]

The final year of internment was the most difficult for internees everywhere. On the island of New Britain, the nuns living at the bottom of the ravine in the Ramale Valley ate boiled pigweed as the staple of their diet. Far away in Tokyo, their Sacre Coeur sisters felt the food shortages as much as every other member of Japanese society as the war worsened. 'We were often reduced to lying on the bed for want of strength to stand up', Sister Mary Hastings recalled.[56] By the end of their captivity, internees at Santo Tomas, always poorly fed, were surviving on less than 3000 kilojoules per day. (Around 7500 kJ would be the daily requirement of an inactive adult.) The average weight loss was about 22 kilograms per adult. 'We were a walking bunch of skeletons when the Americans came in', Stanford told his brother, 'and not all could walk'.[57]

Jack Percival, whose own weight plummeted to under 42 kilograms compared to his prewar weight of 68 kilograms, documented the physical deterioration of his fellow internees at Santo Tomas very carefully. In February 1944 he noticed that 'food panics' had set in and that people were surrounding the rope barriers outside the food stalls like hungry wolves. It was a situation set to worsen. Later the same year Percival observed that previously strong men had not the strength to climb stairs, that most women's legs looked like match sticks and that the babies cried almost constantly with hunger. 'The skin on the faces of men and women is stretched, sallow and taut like on skulls of a head hunters' collection', he wrote. Young men, once the stalwarts of work crews, began fainting in the food lines. In September 1944 Percival predicted that it was now a race between the incoming troops and the grim reaper, 'with starvation and disease his chief aides'.[58] Molly Jefferson would have agreed. She believed that her family had been released from Santo Tomas just in time to save her husband's life: 'we were afraid for him', she confessed to his aunts after liberation. 'He was skin & bone, legs and face all bloated, many men of his age died, or are still quite ill in hospital', she confided.[59]

The paucity of food was paralleled by inadequate medical supplies. Health and the treatment of illness were constant concerns. Australians interned closest to the homeland of the enemy, Japan, fared better, in general, than those in Japanese-occupied territories further south. Internment was relatively benign in China, where fewer than 4 per cent of Australians interned died, most of whom were aged and ill before their internment. The death rate among Australian civilians at Changi was 7 per cent.[60] Nevertheless, poor food, inadequate medical care and the stress of captivity had exacerbated existing illnesses. The most physically trying conditions were endured in regions geographically closest to Australia: the islands of the mandated territory and those of the Indonesian archipelago. On Java, the island where the Ossendryvers had been interned, and Sumatra, conditions were extremely harsh and death rates high; over 70 per cent of all Allied civilian deaths in captivity occurred on these two islands alone. At least 15 per cent of Australians interned on the Indonesian islands died. Father and son, David and John Evans, were two of the casualties. Both men had worked in the mining industry, David Evans as an engineer and his son John as a dredgemaster. Both succumbed to dysentery and beriberi in their Sumatran internment camp in 1944.[61]

The Evanses endured illness that could not be treated without proper medication but in other situations internee doctors and nurses worked small wonders with the limited materials they had at hand. Elizabeth Gibson made calcium from eggshells and iron tonic from rusty nails and lime juice.[62] The ability to cobble together medicines and treat infections and wounds with inadequate resources meant that doctors and nurses were much-valued members of camp communities. The esteem with which his fellow internees regarded Dr Keith Graham, a missionary doctor in his early thirties originally from Ballarat, was confirmed after the war when one of them wrote to the Australian government. In early 1946, an American who had worked as Dr Graham's assistant in their Shanghai internment camp, wished to express to the Australian Minister for External Affairs his 'grateful appreciation for the fine work done by your fellow country-man'. He wrote:

> I do not think any man could have worked so hard, could have treated internees so fairly, could have faced realties so honestly as did Keith Graham. At times he was not well himself but he never let that interfere

with his work. He met well-nigh insurmountable obstacles with courage and ingenuity and never once did his sense of humour fail him. Australia should be well proud of a man of this caliber; it is certainly true that the unselfish services of men of this type will go far toward cementing the peace for which the world today is crying.[63]

When the internees were liberated, the press particularly highlighted the role that female doctors and nurses had played in ensuring the survival of camp members. Dr Jeanette Robinson and Sister Helen Latta, Australian women who had been interned in Changi and Sime Road in Singapore, were later described as providing 'superb care' for their fellow inmates.[64] While the glowing testimonial to Keith Graham supports the adulation of doctors and nurses in later press reports, there is also evidence to suggest that medical practitioners could also fall prey to less admirable qualities of selfishness and greed. In Santo Tomas, Jack Percival noted the case of two missionary doctors, one male and one female, who refused to assist others in the camp unless they received private quarters for their families. 'As a result of their demand 19 women and babies were emptied out of a room to make way for them', Percival noted with some disgust.[65] It was grist to his mill that internment brought out self-interest in some and altruism in others.

Despite the sobering note struck by Percival's anecdote, veneration of doctors is also a common feature of stories and narratives about life in POW camps. There is little doubting the dedication and ingenuity of interned doctors, and the appreciation of many patients who benefited from their care. There is also a subtext here, though, which recognises that, despite their captivity by the Japanese, doctors and nurses were able to perform the work within the camp for which they had been trained. There was a continuity of professional identity that allowed dignity to continue in the face of defeat. It was one of the few areas of internment where men and women were accorded equal eminence.

Doctors may well have survived internment with their professional identities intact but for many others, men in particular, one of the major challenges posed by internment was the maintenance of pride and dignity in a situation of defeat and confinement by an enemy once considered immeasurably inferior to them. The overturning of the established order, and the detention of women and children for whom men were responsible and who they ought to protect from the worst horrors of warfare prompted, in the words of one historian, a 'crisis of masculinity'.[66] Gordon Thomas rolled together these ideas about masculinity, the duty to protect and horror at the failure to do so in his description of the Japanese invasion. According to Thomas, during the invasion Rabaul was 'truly ravished':

> Tens of thousands of Nip soldiers were spoiling and moiling the town; entering our houses, ransacking our wardrobes, destroying our little household gods, our books and papers; gloating over the photos of our women-folk with their little slotty-sexy eyes, mentally raping them.[67]

In the extended sexual metaphor Thomas employs to describe the invasion, he construes the territories as a possession rightfully owned by white men like himself and unjustly despoiled by the Japanese.

Defeat was emasculating, but confinement was itself a feminised state, with its connotations of passivity and powerlessness.[68] Camp newsletters made overt comment on the 'domestication' of men, who in camp, cooked, washed, cleaned and sewed.[69] One cartoon published in the Santo Tomas 'Internews' depicted a man dressed in an apron, throwing his hands in the air shouting 'this is punishment enough'. In the background is a woman saying 'get busy you @#* loafer'.[70] The intention of the stories and the cartoons that often accompanied them was to amuse and make light of the situation but, like much humour, there was an undercurrent of contradiction and discomfort upon which it drew. It suggested that some male internees experienced the subjection of their situation as emasculating. This was also evident when Harry Slocombe wanted to collect the stories of his fellow internees for his diary, with the promise that when he was free the world would know what captivity was really like. Apart from the fear of spies and recriminations if the diaries were discovered, real enough in Slocombe's camp, he also encountered resistance from the men because they felt 'too humiliated' to recall their experiences.[71]

Dorothy Jenner sensed the frustration of the men with whom she was interned and linked it to socially dominant constructions and experiences of masculinity and femininity. Women, she thought, were used to taking the back seat, to being under the directions of others. Although she herself had experienced a more active and adventurous life than most women of her class and generation, Jenner recognised that other women spent much of their time dependent on the decisions of men. '[W]hereas women can simply sit and wait, men can't', she observed in her memoir. 'They have to be doing. I saw this very clearly in camp. The women could cope with that situation far better than the men.'[72]

Jack Percival admitted as much immediately after his release, when he told his employer that:

> the worst feature of the whole damned show was sitting, waiting thinking 'Henderson [his superior] will think you let him down'. However, I am now making double efforts to put up a show for you.[73]

A study of American internees at Baguio internment camp in the Philippines also concluded that 'incarceration deprived more of the men than the women of their customary occupations', thereby adding a level of stress and difficulty.[74] Mothers, for instance, remained responsible for the care of their children, with an even greater level of interaction and responsibility than the prewar period, when white children were routinely cared for by amahs and indigenous nannies.

In Shirley Hazzard's novel *The Great Fire*, part of which is set in immediate postwar Hong Kong, Australian war crimes investigator Peter Exley describes to his old friend, and main character in the novel, Aldred Leith, the way internment at Stanley affected men and women differently. The women, particularly mothers, recalled their fears and anxieties, the contingencies of camp life and the strategies they used to entertain themselves and keep their chins up. The men, according to Exley, 'invented illusions of order, coherence, authority . . . It was the sense of form, I suppose; of remaining answerable to what had been one's standards'.[75] This is, of course, a novelist's interpretation of the meaning of internment and the ways in which men attempted to retain their masculine identity, yet it is finely wrought. Bernice Archer also considers that the administrative structures that internees developed to manage camp life, the various departments, newspapers, tribunals, organised forms of leisure and so on were a 'dynamic, virile approach to internment' that helped men to 'reinvent, or perhaps reaffirm, themselves as the virile, undiminished pre-internment colonialists'.[76]

Archer views such strategies as ways of overcoming some of the physically emasculating effects of internment. Nakedness and public exposure were two realities of captivity that shamed individual men. Early in his internment, Gordon Thomas described the way in which Japanese guards would only allow internees to visit the latrines at allotted times and in groups, 'publicly performing the function which even the most immodest of men reserve as a purely private affair'.[77] James Benson, who was forced to share a prison cell in Rabaul with Japanese military criminals, felt that the 'elemental needs of the situation' caused men to lose all reticence and outward modesty. 'In a few weeks we became as unselfconscious as a lot of animals.'[78] For a committed Christian, conscious of the difference between man and beast, this was a humiliating fate. Nakedness and filth shamed Benson, making him feel as low as an animal, but it bothered him more than it did others.

The situation in Benson's crowded cell was an extreme version of a fate common to many internees who lived in close quarters in a tropical environment. Such conditions loosened some men's bodily inhibitions. In Changi, Harold Murray observed that men who had been reluctant to walk around naked in their own bedrooms now 'roamed the camp grounds very close to Adam before the Fall'.[79] Camp leaders were initially concerned that decorum be maintained and that bodies be covered up. In Changi, one block commandant complained about men's inadequate dress, objecting to men wearing 'scanties', or loincloths, in the food lines. 'We are in prison', he warned his fellow internees, 'but we are still decent people'.[80] Middle-class masculinity, in this mid-century period, was innately linked to the maintenance of public decorum and respectability even in the most dire circumstances.

For James Benson, the physical degradation of captivity was profoundly confronting to his former sense of self. While he was in prison, Benson could not bathe and his body was covered in lice. The deterioration of his body was immensely distressing and Benson's appearance began to disgust him. 'The spectacle must have been pretty horrible', he later remembered, describing in some detail his protruding ribs, legs swollen from beriberi and the boils that covered almost his entire body. 'My hunger distressed me less than my bodily filth', he insisted.[81] Benson also experienced the weakening of his body as an erosion of his manliness and took steps to assert some control in a desperate situation. He later admitted to growing a beard as a token of sorrow for his missing missionary colleagues. This was a tradition of the villagers whom he and the women wished to serve; it was also a potent symbol of masculinity. Gordon Thomas, who had not worn a beard before the war, also grew one in captivity because he thought the Japanese had some respect for the elderly, and it made him look older.[82] It also made him appear more immediately like a mature man who might command respect. One wonders, though, whether it had the desired effect. The Japanese referred to him as 'Yagi San' (Mr Goat), owing to the greyness of his beard.[83]

These attempts to re-masculinise appearance, and the 'invented illusions of order, coherence, authority', certainly convey a sense of the ways in which men attempted to compensate for the emotional

challenges of internment. They also tell us only part of the story of
male responses to captivity. Some men certainly experienced aspects of
their internment as emasculating, but then were fortunate enough to
find strategies and resources that helped them to re-establish or reaffirm
a masculine identity. Others did not. According to Dorothy Jenner, 'it
was always men who suffered from the worst depressions'. 'I'm not being
sexist', she assured her readers of a memoir written in the 1970s. 'It's a
fact. We never had a woman commit suicide. It was always men.'[84]

Sheila Allen's father, John Allen, a mining engineer from Melbourne, was unable to bear the trial of internment. The actual cause
of his death is unclear but his mental deterioration, withdrawal into his
own world, and refusal to eat could be interpreted as a suicide of sorts.
John Allen was interned in the men's section of Changi and at relatives' meetings he was allowed briefly to see his daughter. The reunions
were a source of joy and anticipation for Sheila Allen but she sensed the
increasing depression in her father. He was dwelling more on the past
and expressed feelings of guilt at not having spent more time with his
daughter. Living up to his financial if not his emotional responsibilities,
John Allen sent Sheila to live with nuns at a convent school for most of
the year before internment. It was a distancing that bothered him less at
the time than it did during internment, when Sheila resided only metres
from him, yet in conditions of absolute abjection. John Allen seemed
to run together ideas of neglect of duty in the past with a failure in his
duty to protect in the present. In July 1943 Sheila described her father
as 'not at all well – I am worried about him'. Two years later, his deterioration was advanced. He had begun stealing from other internees,
earning him social disgrace and bashings from his fellow inmates. Sheila
noticed that 'he rambles a lot about the past – not making much sense
really. He seems such a child in his manner and I am worried about his
mental state'. John Allen began to withdraw further into his depression and by May 1945 appeared at a relatives' meeting wrapped in
a small towel, thin, unshaven and with his hair uncombed. Within
a few weeks, three months' short of Changi's liberation, he was dead.[85]

John Allen's mental deterioration is reported to us through the journal entries of his daughter Sheila, who also reported the suicide of a
doctor in the camp. 'I wonder how many more will go the same way?'
she reflected. 'Sometimes it isn't easy to be cheerful – especially when
the "bug" hits you and you feel as if your inside is coming out in bits
and pieces.' Despite Dorothy Jenner's observation that the women were
less prone to depression than men, Allen in this instance provides a

description of something very akin to despair. On another occasion she described one of the residents of the women's section, Mrs Flowers , singing nursery rhymes in a high-pitched voice, throwing hammers at the children and asking fellow inmates if they thought she was mad.[86] Yet it remains the case that such expressions of mental disturbance are more common in the papers of men. For some, like Charles McLaren who had joined the exchange of civilians with Japan in mid-1942, the depression was clinical and of long standing. A doctor himself, McLaren was frank about his lifelong struggle with mental illness. McLaren's greatest fear was not the actions of Japanese guards, but the unpredictability of his mental state. To his enormous relief, however, McLaren left his cell 'with a mind entirely untroubled'.[87] It was only later, when he was under house arrest at the home of another Australian missionary couple, that his depression returned.

Gordon Thomas was more reticent about his own medical history when he came to write his memoir of internment. Although providing pen portraits of the disposition and idiosyncrasies of the three other men with whom he was interned at Rabaul's freezer works, like Percival, Thomas did not disclose much about his own feelings and mental health. It is astonishing, for instance, that nowhere in his memoir of internment by the Japanese does Thomas mention that during World War I, while still a civilian, he had been captured and interned by the Germans in New Guinea. After his release, Thomas subsequently enlisted in the First AIF, but was discharged medically unfit owing to his nervous debility. During his medical interview, Thomas claimed that he 'first began to be troubled by nervousness when interned in German New Guinea 1914'. On examination, Thomas also claimed to suffer epileptic fits, although his doctor had not witnessed one and Thomas himself had answered 'no' when asked about a history of seizures on his enlistment form. Thomas also stated that he had experienced insomnia and nerves in the four years since his release from internment by the Germans. According to the doctor, Thomas had 'never done physical work', a distinct disadvantage for a soldier. Ultimately, Thomas was considered to be 'completely run down' upon his return to Australia. After seeing action in France, he had completed his service on orderly duties in England. Thomas was diagnosed with 'effort syndrome', an anxiety disorder epitomised by heart palpitations, laboured breathing and exhaustion after slight exertion.[88]

This medical history would suggest that internment and manual labour while interned by the Japanese must have posed profound difficulties for Thomas. Previously plagued by a form of chronic fatigue and anxiety, Thomas's memoir instead presents us with a man who endured captivity and its trials with an almost stoic resignation. It might be possible to argue that Thomas had made a recovery in the more than twenty years that had elapsed since World War I. A letter from his doctor, written after liberation, would suggest that he had not. 'The cardiac conditions' that Thomas suffered from, were

> directly referable to the fatigue of forced duties, to the anxiety for personal safety from years of frequent bombing, the anxiety about the fate of his wife and friends, and property assets, the inadequacy of kind and quality of diet and the rigors of exposure – all this in a man of indoor cultural pursuits rather than one of manual outdoor work.[89]

The uncertainty of their fate and the frustrations of confinement troubled other men who were prepared to admit as much, at least to themselves. Harry Slocombe thought that 'nervousness' was more pronounced among the older camp members, among whose number he counted himself. In February 1943, one of Slocombe's room-mates who was normally 'very level headed' had hysterics for almost two hours. The previous month, Slocombe noted that it had been eleven months since he had been interned. 'I have just had another look at the calendar to make sure that it was not eleven years', he noted in his diary.[90]

Harold Murray also found difficulty with the open-ended nature of his captivity. 'The future life in an internment camp was not the best', Murray claimed, 'and there was no appearance of ever getting out of it alive'. All of the internees, according to Murray, wore a 'mask' and during the day it was firmly in place and 'one faced the world as best one could'. At night, 'when one was alone with himself the mask fell from his soul and he knew he felt the worse', and sleep did not come easily. 'In the silence of the night,' he confessed, 'one did "drop his bundle" there was no mistake about that. I am writing for myself and I think that goes for the rest of those that were in the Camp'.[91] Murray claimed that his best sleep of the day was during his afternoon nap, when he could still sense the stirring and rustle of other men and did not feel the loneliness that can often accompany despair.

Murray was the man who had complained that he was too hungry to care about sex, or to take any voyeuristic pleasure in the sight of white women in little more than their underwear. That was in August 1944. Not long afterwards his diary entries ceased but it would be another full year before his liberation. Dorothy Jenner, who had also made diary entries from the earliest days of her captivity, also stopped writing much at about this time. Internees almost everywhere slipped further into a daily quest to preserve energy and obtain food, and by then many more might have agreed with Murray's assessment. By the end of 1944 Jack Percival's diary had become not much more than an obsessive listing of food rations, shortages and spiralling prices. The vivid portraits of camp life had been replaced by lists of small servings of food and their likely energy content. Two days before Christmas that year, however, he sighted US bombers circling the camp. It was enough to cause Percival to pick up his pen again. 'It's Xmas eve tommorow', he wrote:

> we're being deliberately starved, our systems are so short on proteins that many of us can no longer control our urine, our children are crying for food, the aged are dying from starvation, men, women and children are fainting in the roll call and the 'food' lines from weakness – but now we feel that Santa Claus has really arrived.[92]

The Allied push back into the region had come too late for Harry Slocombe, who had died in his internment camp in March 1944.[93]

PART III

Freedom

I wanted to cry, to shout, to sing and jump around with joy; but I lit a cigarette and had a swig of brandy and tried to look as though being rescued after being three years a prisoner was quite an everyday event in a man's life.
Gordon Thomas, 'Rabaul 1942–45'

Today they came! Whole flights of silver, four-engined land-plane bombers, accompanied by fighters which sped around, over and under them like destroyers around battle ships. How long we have waited for such a sight, such a stimulus to morale! Three years into which has been crammed the grossest humiliation, mental torture for all and physical torture for some, starvation, living like pigs and trying to keep our heads above water as whites.
Jack Percival, Santo Tomas internment camp, diary entry,
23 December 1944

Instead of cheering and screaming, the emotions were so deep that they dumfounded us and we were completely silent. A golden silence fell over the entire ship. It was something transcendental. Something very memorable. That silence went on for the longest time possible. As we came alongside the wharf, the people down there sensed it too, and were equally silent. We moored. And snap. It was broken. We were all of us hugging and kissing people we had never seen before. Crying and laughing.
Dorothy Jenner, *Darlings, I've Had a Ball*, p. 223

6

LIBERATION

Gordon Thomas lit a cigarette and exhaled slowly when his Australian liberators arrived at Ramale Valley internment camp. This admission of feigned nonchalance is perhaps the most honest assessment of his emotional state in the entire memoir of captivity. Jack Percival, who often evinced a form of stoicism similar to Thomas but was an altogether more domesticated man, was understated but equally heartfelt: 'how long we have waited', he wrote. Percival's Santo Tomas was in fact one of the first internment camps to be liberated, in February 1945. Other internees were relieved only as the Allied forces successfully reoccupied territory the Japanese had controlled since 1942. Those on the islands of Java and Sumatra, for instance, had to wait until August or September 1945 for assistance to arrive. Liberation raised again some of the issues that had dominated the experience of capture and captivity for civilian internees. The view of the Pacific war as a racial conflict received renewed impetus when POWs and civilian internees were liberated and evidence of their suffering was carried around the world in newspaper articles and photographs. Journalists were also fascinated by civilian internment as a war experience shared by men and women in equal measure, and subsequently reported on the liberation of the camps with a heightened awareness of gender difference. Race and gender had been two of the principal lenses through which internees themselves viewed their captivity, and their responses to liberation also took such perspectives into account. The status of civilians during the conflict that preceded internment had frequently been ambiguous; years of detention had made their position, at least in regard to the Japanese, clear. But now relief and assistance were at hand, what obligations did their governments owe civilian internees, and what did internees owe them?

The approaching end of the war placed some internees in greater danger than they had been for much of their captivity. When their homes became battlegrounds as the Japanese invaded and occupied Allied territory, civilians had responded by assisting in the defence of their territory. Now that liberation was at hand after long years of captivity, civilians confined in internment camps again became vulnerable as the war front approached. It is often pointed out that a proportion of combat deaths are the result of 'friendly fire', the accidental killing of one's own troops. The residents of internment camps near the battle lines also ran the risk of surviving captivity under the Japanese, only to be killed by the bombs of Allied planes.

Those interned in and around Rabaul had become used to the bombing. They came to fear Allied bombing raids almost more than the wrath of the Japanese. From 1943, there were especially intense bombing raids over New Guinea. Concerned for their safety, the internees began to dig into the nearby mountain to create a safe haven from the bombs. The men of the camp created a maze of tunnels in the surrounding hills, reinforcing the walls and ceilings with logs. In an attempt to soften the floor, internees then lined the tunnels with coconut-palm fronds. Airless and dark, it was a depressing and unhealthy existence. As the war dragged on, the internees spent increasing amounts of time sheltering in the tunnels, sometimes for seven or eight hours at a time. The tunnels saved hundreds of lives but they could not save everyone. After one particularly intense raid beginning in February 1944, which continued for seven weeks, twenty-four of the camp inmates died.[1] There were many Japanese casualties too and the internees frequently emerged from the tunnels to discover the body parts of Japanese soldiers strewn along the barbed wire fences that surrounded their compound. Sister Catherine O'Sullivan, an Australian nun in her twenties, later described living conditions there as being 'under abuse from our enemies and under fire from our friends'.[2] Ultimately, repeated bombing raids destroyed the carefully built infrastructure of the camp.

Bombing raids in urban areas also proved hazardous. In January 1945, fourteen internees at Hong Kong's Stanley camp were killed in an air raid.[3] At Santo Tomas, internees were forced to seek shelter from shelling and bullets as the Japanese resisted the incoming Americans. About eighteen internees, mostly women, were killed in the last week of

Figure 12: *Tunnels dug into the hillside on the island of New Britain by missionary priests and brothers which sheltered internees during bombing raids by the Allies. Sister Catherine O'Sullivan described the situation as being 'under abuse from our enemies and under fire from our friends'.*

their captivity by Japanese shelling. Roy Stanford, describing the liberation of the camp, commented: 'Believe me, it was no joke to lie in bed at night and hear [the shells] passing overhead'.[4] Frank and Mary Merritt, and their daughter Jean, shared the dubious distinction of having what Jack Percival described as the 'most remarkable escape'. Hiding under the bed to shelter from the bombs, one penetrated the mattress but failed to detonate properly, only bruising Frank's thigh and 'whizzing between the heads' of Jean and Mary.[5] Another to escape serious injury was Dudley Rex, interned at Tha Phra Chandr camp in Bangkok. The camp was surrounded by Japanese military installations and subject to Allied bombing raids. In March 1945 Rex was struck. 'The explosion hurled me high into the air', he later recalled, 'and I landed back on Earth in a dazed condition'. His left ankle was seriously damaged and Rex still wore an iron on his leg in the 1950s. Rex pinpointed the location of this life-defining moment on a blueprint he compiled of the camp and its surrounds as part of his compensation claim. His annotation, in red, is succinct: 'Dudley R. Rex was blown up from this crater on 5/3/45'.[6]

Leonard Cowle, a young man in his early twenties, was not so lucky. He and several other Australian crew members of the SS *Nankin* had been captured by Germans in the Indian Ocean in August 1942. The merchant seamen had been handed over to the Japanese and spent the last six months of their internment in Tokyo. 'This particular period is the most vivid in my memory', one later recalled.[7] Members of the group discussed the repeated bombings that signalled the approach of the Allies and became pessimistic about their prospects of getting out alive. Cowle had long conversations with one of his close friends in which he appeared 'a little depressed' and feared that he would not see his family again. He was right to be concerned. Leonard Cowle was killed in an air raid on 25 July 1945, less than a month before Japan's surrender.

The Sacre Coeur nuns, also interned in Tokyo, witnessed the firebombing of the city. Sister Mary Hastings described the night their quarters were bombed and burnt to the ground as 'Hell', not a word a nun would use lightly. The nuns had been told to leave their windows open to prevent the glass breaking, which meant they could actually see the bombs falling. 'Everything was red', Sister Hastings recalled, painting a vivid picture of the sky, trees and grass all taking on the hue of fire. At the end of the raid, it became clear that the nuns' house was ablaze and they were forced to leave. They ran through the Tokyo streets covered in wet blankets 'because it was just like going out in a snow storm only it was fire that was falling on us. Our faces were scorched & our eyes filled with hot ashes'.[8] Alice Bowman's camp was at Totsuka, 24 kilometres from Tokyo, close enough to witness the city's incineration. She and her fellow Australians were speechless with shock at the spectacle, which looked like a 'volcano in violent eruption'.[9]

Some other members of the Sacre Coeur order had been interned at Nagasaki. They were just outside the range of the atomic bomb, but witnessed its explosion and after-effects at first hand. Sister Regina McKenna recalled the bomb's detonation causing everything to turn a golden yellow. 'It seemed as though the sun had burst and I was lost in its midst.' The nuns' internment house was virtually destroyed, but the sisters realised they had been blessed with a lucky escape. 'All the first day and night the mountains were on fire for miles and miles. Two-thirds of the population of Nagasaki are dead', Sister Regina McKenna wrote to a friend, in shock at the extent of the destruction.[10]

The nuns, such long-term residents of Japan, experienced the fire-bombing of Tokyo and the dropping of the atomic bomb on Nagasaki as an attack on their own home as much as an attack on the enemy. Sister Mary Hastings felt enormous sympathy for the Japanese victims of the Tokyo fire-bombing, who were 'a pathetic sight'. She was saddened to see homeless families walking the streets with the remnants of their households piled on a baby's pram or bicycle, 'despair on their faces, frightened children clinging to them'.[11] When describing the dropping of the atomic bomb on Nagasaki, Sister Regina McKenna referred to the plane she witnessed as an 'enemy' plane, an uncommon expression among internees who routinely referred to Allied planes as 'ours'. Although the Australian women interned at Totsuka were horrified at the fire-bombing of Tokyo, they still described 'scores and scores of, what were to us, magnificent American planes'. Nevertheless, once their freedom was assured, the nurses felt 'pity' for the peasants who worked near their lodgings. 'We understood something of their uncertainty for the future', Alice Bowman recalled.[12]

Despite the terrifying nature of bombing raids, liberation itself was a moment of joy and profound relief for the internees. The ABC's war correspondent, John Elliott, accompanied the US forces during their liberation of Philippines internment camps. Fearing that the Japanese guards would massacre civilians during the course of the American recapture of the Philippines, General Douglas MacArthur had decided to liberate the camps before conducting the final assault on Manila.

Figure 13: *Ramale Valley internment camp, September 1945: concert of welcome for Australian liberators and a celebration of freedom. The nuns had sewn the flag and the choir sang 'God Save the King' and 'Advance Australia Fair'.*

When the troops entered Los Banos internment camp, south-east of Manila, Elliott described the internees as 'delirious with joy' and their delight and gratitude as being 'one of the most touching things he had seen' during the long years of war.[13] The Americans were able to immediately provide the internees with their most desperately needed resource: food. Molly Jefferson was most grateful. Writing home on Red Cross airmail paper, a luxury compared with the scraps of paper scrounged throughout captivity, she told her family that 'we can't speak highly enough of the quality & variety of food we are being given by the American Army'. She listed with relish the great chunks of white turkey flesh served to the internees and the unaccustomed richness of cream, butter, cheese and bacon. 'Every day is Christmas day in the eating line to us now', she wrote, a sentiment that forms such a stark contrast to Percival's image only weeks before of men fainting in the food line from hunger.[14]

US forces were the first to announce liberation to most Australians interned throughout the region. Those in the New Guinea islands and on Borneo had the particular pleasure of learning about liberation from their own. After years of being a national minority in the camp, this was the Australians' moment in the sun. At Kuching, in north-west Borneo, mothers and children who had endured years of internment enjoyed an afternoon tea-party hosted by the crew of the Australian warship HMAS *Kapunda*.[15] Sister Berenice Twohill remembered sensing that peace had been declared because the regular air raids that had marked their captivity on the island of New Britain had come to end. The Japanese informed the internees that the war was over but the internees had to wait another month before help arrived. By this time, Gordon Thomas and his party had taken up residence in the valley. He described the anticipation among the internees about the arrival of the Australian army, and choir rehearsals for a song of welcome.[16] 'Then all of a sudden, one morning we heard this Cooee on top of the mountain . . . so we cooeed back', Sister Berenice remembered.[17] Her friend, Sister Catherine, remembered that the entire camp went 'wild' with rejoicing and cheering. In anticipation of this moment, the nuns had made an Australian flag – 'rather a patchwork accomplishment' according to Catherine – which was soon raised with a small ceremony. Despite the seventeen nationalities represented in the camp, all members sang 'God Save the King', followed by speeches and more singing of 'Advance Australia Fair'. 'Weren't we Australians proud of the fact that each one of the 17 nationalities in the camp could write confidently and reassuringly "*SAFE* in hands of *AUSTRALIAN* troops"', Catherine recalled. There was national pride but also a profound sense of relief. 'That night we went to bed for the first time in four years with a feeling of security', Catherine confessed.[18]

War correspondents seemed as eager as internees themselves to convey patriotism and reassurances about the internees' loyalties to and longing for Australia. The *Age*'s correspondent, reporting from China, assured readers that the internees had 'maintained their native cheerfulness and optimism' throughout captivity. 'We knew we would come out on top in the end," they said. "We knew the Diggers in New Guinea would not let us down."'[19] At Pootung internment camp, the teenage Joan Walker, whose father George had refused to broadcast for the Japanese, performed 'Advance Australia Fair' in the dining hall for assembled journalists. Members of the camp community had flown the Australian flag ever since the Japanese had withdrawn from camp. The entrance to a vegetable garden the internees had made during captivity was signposted 'Anzac Avenue'.[20]

Figure 14: *Nuns evacuated from Ramale Valley internment camp to Rabaul. On the far right is Australian Sister Flavia (Catherine O'Sullivan), who was in her twenties when she was interned along with her fellow sisters in the order of Our Lady of the Sacred Heart.*

The liberators of Ramale Valley, according to Sister Berenice, came 'slipping down the mountain'. Gordon Thomas, always conscious of racial difference, painted a more forthright picture. He thought that the liberating soldiers were fine specimens of Australian masculinity, who came 'striding down the steep pathway'. When the camp guards bowed to them, the Australians 'just brushed them aside without so much as an acknowledgement'.[21] Sister Catherine also wrote about the arrival of the Australian liberators as a return to a more civilised order. She made much of the gentlemanly behaviour of the Australian soldiers towards the nuns. As the soldiers lifted their hats, carried the nuns' bags and treated the nuns with 'civilized sincerity', it formed such a contrast to the women's previous treatment. 'Fine clothes and white gloves', Sister Catherine wrote of the Japanese officers whom she had encountered, 'do not make gentlemen'.[22]

This interpretation, of liberation as a return to civilisation, dominated press reporting of the internees' liberation. Reports from the islands of Sumatra, Java and Singapore, where there had been large concentrations of women and children, were especially concerned with their treatment. It had long been a feature of racial thinking in the West that the treatment of women was a marker of the standard of civilisation. 'Native' and indigenous women were often assumed to perform heavy manual labour from which civilised 'white' women had been freed, by both men and machines. Brutality and violence towards women were also thought to be a feature of 'uncivilised' peoples, despite their continuing existence in European societies. All of these assumptions about racial difference, and outrage that internment had violated them, permeated newspaper stories about the women's camps. There were claims that women had to 'work like coolies'. In some camps, refusal to perform work meant that women were stripped, flogged and burnt with cigarette butts. Other accounts emphasised the 'heaviest manual labour' women had to perform.[23] Nearly all major newspapers reported the story of the 'double 10th' at Changi, an incident in which the Japanese had detained and tortured over fifty internees about the possibility of a spy ring in the camp. Women and men had been arrested, and the mistreatment of white women and their interaction with men of colour provoked particularly intense outrage. Women were given 'no privacy, and shared cells with men of all races'. They were subjected to 'obscene insults and gestures by Japanese prisoners in the same cell'. White men attempted to protect their women but they were 'prohibited' from doing so.[24]

The outrage over Japanese treatment of white women did not prevent some journalists sexualising the female camp population. In some reporting of the crimes visited upon white women there is almost an element of voyeurism, or titillation at least. 'Women were forced to undress and go to the toilet in the presence of Japanese guards', one concerned reporter noted. Another described the female inmates of Changi as wearing 'costumes [which] varied from brassieres and shorts to an occasional smart white silk dress with a touch of colour saved from the wreckage'.[25] This sexualising of female internees was a natural corollary of concern expressed earlier in the war about the sexual vulnerability of women in a war zone. Internment had always been perceived as a site of sexual danger for women. Intense interest in the sexual fate of women in the camps moved like a shadow through reports written about them. Some women, such as a group of Australian army nurses interned on Sumatra, and the mixed group of army and civilian women transported from Rabaul to Japan, attempted to quell speculation by directly addressing the possibility of sexual abuse. At press conferences, they admitted pressure, and fear, but denied that they had been raped.[26]

If in some respects journalists sexualised female internees, there was also another, almost contradictory, impulse for internment to be perceived as somehow corrosive of femininity. Internment camps were ambiguous zones in the world of war. They were ambivalently placed in relation to the dominant understanding of war: the battlefield and the home front. The battlefield was usually thought of as a primarily masculine zone, the home front its feminine corollary. Internment camps did not fit easily into either realm. Internees had been removed from battle but remained in enemy territory, confined in camps that did not contain the refuge and nurture of a true home. Female internees had been placed dangerously close to the front and at the mercy of the enemy captor. Concern about the effects of such war experiences on women emerged almost by default, in repeated assurances about the liberated women's untrammelled femininity. Reports contained reassurances that despite women's experiences in camp, they were eager to return from the ambiguous zone of imprisonment to a fully feminine existence. One reporter interviewed women who had been interned in Java, Sumatra and Hong Kong and later travelled home on the SS *Tamaroa*. The reporter noted the 'unexpected interest that they took in trivialities' and insisted that what the female internees most wanted to talk about was hat fashions, hairstyles and the possibility of obtaining clothing.[27] Despite having been in a war zone, these were women embracing their return to femininity. It was a deliberate strategy to allay concern and to reassure relatives that war had not eroded their previous identities. The women from Rabaul who had been interned in Japan 'rouged and powdered their faces', and bought jewellery in Manila, 'to lessen for their families the shock of their appearance', according to the daughter of one of them.[28]

Despite the descriptions of sun tops and shorts as common camp attire, most women came by donated clothing relatively quickly and covered up for the cameras. The Ramale Valley nuns, reduced to wearing nightdresses by the end of their internment, retrieved habits they had buried at the start of their captivity in anticipation of its conclusion. They were photographed in white neck-to-ankle habits. It is often suggested that the camera's gaze is a male eye for a female body, but in the case of released internees and POWs, it was men's – not women's – bodies that were exposed for the camera.[29] Perhaps this was part of a tacit understanding that women must appear respectable to elicit true sympathy. At times the dominance of semi-naked men in these images makes them appear as if they are the visual manifestation of a facet

132

of captivity that words cannot express: that men have been somehow emasculated by their internment. The images of emaciated POWs in baggy shorts are legion. Civilian men too were photographed in this way. A brief film made after the liberation of Singapore reflects some of these concerns. The women appear smiling and demure, but the images of men emphasise the emaciated condition of their bodies. Most are shown without shirts and wearing pants that once fitted but were now greatly oversized, or loincloths. Hair is rough-cut and the styling crude. Untreated cavities and missing teeth are plain for all to see. This is internment as physical degradation.[30]

Yet a beginning of the antidote to that message also rested in images, as well as in words. The film also contains footage of white men watching Japanese dig. Masculinity and the racial order are restored at one and the same time here, and in the many, many photographs published in newspapers of Japanese soldiers and former guards labouring under the watchful eye of released prisoners and internees, almost always men. Words reinforced such messages. Ernest Doscas, originally from Perth, who had been Senior Agricultural Officer in Johore, stated on his return:

> Before leaving Singapore we had the satisfaction of seeing the Japs getting their share of humiliation and degradation which they issued to us in full measure. Our people had them out in large numbers doing town cleansing work.[31]

If, as Gordon Thomas told one reporter, 'Every humiliation was heaped on the whites to discredit them in the eyes of the natives', here was another message for them to absorb.[32] The Japanese were defeated and the white men were back in control. As Jack Percival put it, for some men, liberation signalled the end of 'trying to keep our head above water as whites'.[33]

Internees conscious of their captivity as a form of racial subjugation might have anticipated the moment of their freedom as the restoration of some kind of natural racial order but there were early indications that the world had changed. As the Japanese withdrew from Shanghai, for instance, some of the buildings that they had confiscated from foreigners at the start of the war were occupied by Chinese troops. The Chinese troops were not inclined to move on when the camp gates were opened and the foreigners emerged eager to reclaim their property. Keith Begley had sensed there might be trouble. He had proceeded immediately to Shanghai after his release from internment further north in Yangchow, to regain possession of the Salvation Army buildings in the city.[34] The China Inland Mission people had not been so lucky. In September 1945, when they approached their mission compound, they found it to be occupied by Chinese troops.[35] Reporting these developments, one diplomat, Keith Officer, sensed that change was in the air, although presumably even he could not have forecast just how dramatic that would be in China. In October 1945, he wrote:

> There was a very general appreciation of the fact that the old days were over and that the Shanghai of the future would have to be built on a new foundation, as a Chinese city where Chinese and foreigners worked in partnership to secure a common prosperity. There was a general realisation that months of hard and often disappointing work lay ahead before the goal was ever in sight, and that many difficult problems had to be solved'.[36]

In mid-February 1945, the secretary-general of the Australian Red Cross was mortified to receive a late-night call from a Sydney *Sun* journalist, claiming that the Australians just liberated in the Philippines had severely criticised the Australian Red Cross for not being on the spot to give them relief.[37] The next day he wrote to the prime minister, insisting that 'the Australian public expects certain definite action to be taken by its own National Society' and threatening to take the matter to the press.[38] The Red Cross had established a Standing Conference on POWs and Civilian Internees (Far East) in May 1944, and had liaised extensively with relatives associations and raised substantial funds for the relief of prisoners and internees. They felt that despite persistent lobbying and offers of help, they 'were caught unprepared though ready to act in regard to Australians in the Philippines'.[39] When the liberation of the camps began, the Australian government had almost no knowledge of how many of its civilians had been detained by the Japanese. Serious planning had been underway for some time in relation to the relief and repatriation of POWs, but civilian internees had always been tacked on as an afterthought. This was indicative of internees' position as citizens without service, who did not fit any of the accepted and broadly understood categories of wartime experience.

It was not from want of trying that Australian Red Cross representatives were not on hand to greet the liberated internees at the camp gates in Manila. The Red Cross had run a sustained campaign since at least mid-1944 to be included in the government's planning for evacuation, repatriation and assistance to civilian internees. The chairman, Dr J. Newman Morris, wanted the Australian Red Cross to be given auxiliary status by the government. Failing that, he wanted some official standing for his organisation and its inclusion in relief planning. He noted with some frustration and not a little longing the closer and more productive relationship with government enjoyed by his British, Canadian and American counterparts.[40] The Australian people also had a reasonable expectation that there would be some role for the Red Cross to fulfil. By June 1945, Australians had donated £2 380 000 pounds to the Red Cross's POW appeal. Despite the Red Cross ceasing to appeal directly, money continued to pour in. In many ways, it was an embarrassment of riches for the Australian Red Cross.[41] 'No Government can successfully avoid accepting voluntary aid organised by its people who expect and will insist on taking part in the relief of liberated prisoners at the earliest possible moment', Dr Newman Morris cautioned in late February 1945.[42]

The Red Cross was eager to help all Australians who had been held captive by the Japanese but in early 1945 were especially concerned about civilian internees. It felt that the army appeared to have concrete plans for the relief of POWs, but less certain ideas about the treatment of civilians. Initially, the army was keen to distance itself from any responsibility for the returning civilian internees. In March 1945, the minister for the army had informed the prime minister that the reception of civilian repatriates was not the responsibility of his department. The army, which had considerable experience in arranging for the reception of repatriated POWs, would be happy to offer assistance and advice without the burden of direct accountability. Curtin, however, continued to insist that the army's services would be required and used in conjunction with the Department of the Interior when the internees arrived back in Australia.[43] According to the Red Cross, the army was long on promises about civilian internees, but short on detail as to just what form the assistance would take.[44] In fact, there had been real limitations on the Australian government's capacity to secure representation for members of the national Red Cross in Manila. General MacArthur had rejected a request for Australian Red Cross representation, and allowed only the American society to operate. The Australian army sympathised with its own national society, which it considered would be able to 'render considerable service both for sentimental reasons and because of their particular familiarity with the needs and outlook of Australians'.[45] But the government also recorded its unwillingness to make official comment on the matter as it might be interpreted as criticism of MacArthur.[46]

In the meantime, Australian interests would have to be represented by the Australian Commander-in-Chief, General Thomas Blamey. Blamey visited the Santo Tomas internment camp in Manila in early March 1945. He assured Australian government ministers that he had 'heard many stories of heroic behaviour and fortitude' in the camp. 'On your behalf,' he continued, 'I expressed the anxiety of the Australian people for their welfare and assured them of a warm welcome when they reached their homeland'.[47] Ultimately, the Red Cross accepted that it was not the Australian government but the actions of General MacArthur that had impeded its efforts to provide relief for the Philippine internees.[48] The point still remained that planning for the repatriation and relief of civilian internees, as opposed to POWs, was alarmingly thin.

Perhaps mindful of the lack of representation specifically for Australians in Manila, in August 1945, when the camps of Shanghai were liberated, Australian representation was more effective. The Australian legation in China, based in Chungking and presided over by the Chargé d'Affaires, Keith Officer, an experienced diplomat, organised quickly. In September 1945 Officer reminded the British ambassador of his responsibilities towards Australians as the internment camps were liberated: 'This is for the purpose of putting on record what I know you are already cognisant of – namely that we look to you to do everything necessary for Australians, like other British subjects, in Shanghai'.[49] The Australian Red Cross was also quickly at hand, in terms of both staff to assist internees and with donations of food and clothing.

The internees had found their champion in Keith Officer. His efforts meant that internees released in China received some of the most extensive form of assistance of those released anywhere. 'I wanted to satisfy myself that everything possible was being done for repatriation, reinstatement of business and of people in their homes, here in Shanghai', Officer later said.[50] After the declaration of peace, Officer had quickly despatched his legation staff in order to develop an accurate picture of the state of internees in the Shanghai camps. A legation official, Mr Stokes, had visited the six internment centres in the city on his way back from the surrender ceremony in Nanking in early September 1945. The feeling that a long occupation was coming to an end was in the air of Shanghai. Despite a continuing Japanese presence, Stokes wrote that 'Shanghai is still in gala dress and there was a good deal of cheering as our party drove through the streets'.[51] He made a point of searching out the Australians and New Zealanders in the various camps, and reported that the internees appreciated the interest shown in their welfare.[52] 'A thousand thanks for coming & conveying my feelings of pride in the Australian Embassy of Chungking', Jean Armstrong wrote in appreciation to Mr Stokes soon after his visit to Yangtzepoo intern- ment camp. She had pinned a worn personal card to the top of the letter, which stated that she was the 'Edit'ress The Catholic Review'. The letter itself was written in lead pencil on brown wrapping paper, a sign of the continuing austerity of camp conditions. Jean Armstrong, who was fifty-three at the time of her liberation, described herself as a 'woman who has gone through Hell'. She was eager to ensure that former internees would be repatriated with some cargo space available for the household belongings they hoped to repossess after release from the camp. 'Formerly I was a worldly Australian citizen,' she wrote sadly, 'now I come to you "beaten & broke"'.[53]

The camp visits also convinced Keith Officer that Red Cross assis- tance alone would not be enough for the hundreds of needy internees Australian diplomatic staff had encountered. The legation estab- lished an office in Shanghai, where staff were available for interview each morning. The former internees responded by visiting in their droves. Even in late October 1945, staff still saw up to fifty visitors each morning.[54] Officer also had clear instructions that each civil- ian internee was entitled to an 'initial, non-recoverable cash advance', courtesy of the Commonwealth government.[55]

The diplomats took it upon themselves to be responsible for the wel- fare of internees while they remained in Shanghai. They understood that released civilian internees would face issues that POWs would not. In most cases, civilian internees were people who had lived and worked in the cities and towns in which they were captured. They were fac- ing the prospect of destroyed houses, businesses and livelihoods. POWs were waiting to go home. In many cases, civilian internees were already 'home', even if they were longing for a period of rest and recupera- tion in Australia. Officer recognised the dilemma that they were in. He noted in a report to the Australian government that about two- thirds of released internees actually wanted to stay in Shanghai. Some of this group had already returned to their prewar homes and apartments, but were finding it difficult to remain there without financial assistance because it was too soon to resume business and begin receiving salaries.

The homes of others had been occupied by the Chinese, commandeered by the American army, or so ruined by warfare that they were uninhabitable. The result for these people and those awaiting repatriation was that they were still in the internment camps where they were being rationed by the US army.[56] One of the camps was stated to be unfit for human habitation and four others were only a little better. Some internees were unwilling to repatriate because they felt it was in their best financial interest to remain and pursue assets lost or stolen because of the war. A substantial number had been employed by the Chinese government or semi-government bodies, such as the Shanghai Police, and they were owed considerable amounts for superannuation and unpaid salary.[57]

In recognition of this dilemma, Officer secured a building as a staging camp for Australian internees not planning to immediately repatriate. Keith Begley assisted him in the task and ably ensured the speedy removal of Australians out of internment camps into slightly more comfortable premises.[58] Once there, seventy liberated Australians decided to call their temporary home the 'Southern Cross Club' and hung a large Australian flag over the doorway.[59] Fred Drakeford, brother of the Australian Minister for Air, was appointed as manager until his departure. Former internees resided at the club until February 1946. This development had again marked the China internees out as fortunate. Dorothy Jenner had left Stanley camp by crouching in the bottom of a Japanese truck, despite the request of camp leaders that internees remain in their quarters. Her first nights of freedom were spent with an Indian family 'who didn't know me from Adam', and in a deserted church. Jenner eventually found her way to the British mission, which could offer floor space but no bed. Accommodation was in short supply in Hong Kong, which had been badly affected by bombing. 'Many of the prisoners stayed on in camp', Jenner reflected, 'because there was no where else for them to go until they were repatriated'.[60]

Once the location of internees had been determined, the government allowed anxious relatives who had not received news of their loved ones for at least three years to telegram them. The word limit on the cables did not allow for great statements of sentiment but the relief of anxious parents, wives and loved ones was palpable. Emily Payne, the mother of Salvation Army officer Nellie Brister who had been interned in Weihsien internment camp wrote simply: 'Thrilled with news. Looking forward your return, Love Mum'. Charles Thunder's wife was clearly delighted that he was alive and very keen to move on from the years of waiting and uncertainty: 'Thrilled News! What are your plans? I desire return to Peking. Love, Helen'. Mrs Doris Woodcroft tried to reassure her husband Ronald, who had been interned in Tokyo, that she had indeed written to him throughout the war, and to bring him up to date with family news: 'Have written fortnightly please get in touch with me as soon as possible. My father died Ronnie killed in action'.[61]

Some with relatives in high places received longer telegrams. Fred Drakeford received a 41-line telegram from his brother upon word of his release. The Australian chargé d'affaires was annoyed at the presumption of this. He asked External Affairs to remind the minister that there were no regular communications to or from Shanghai, and messages such as his were delivered by 'very over-loaded British Military Mission wireless service'.[62] Nevertheless, even in those confusing months when peace had finally been declared and governments around the world attempted to account for their dislocated citizens, connections still mattered. Within a few weeks Fred Drakeford flew out of Shanghai on a Catalina flying boat sent there expressly for that purpose. His sister-in-law and her adult son accompanied him on the journey. Keith Begley, who had been so helpful with setting up the Southern Cross Club, scored a seat to Hong Kong. Douglas Murdoch also managed to negotiate a seat for himself and his wife on the plane, despite some aspersions having been cast on the nature of his relationship with the Japanese only weeks before.[63] Other, less well-connected internees had to wait for the ships to come in.

Australian nuns of the Sacre Coeur order interned in Japan also benefited from connections in high places. Their Sydney-based superior, Mother McGuinness, was able to mobilise her networks to ensure that assistance reached the recently released nuns. Sir Mark Sheldon, prominent member of Sydney society, former chairman of the Australian Bank of Commerce and brother of the senior nun, Mother Mary Sheldon, paid for a shipment of six cases of goods, including warm clothing, medical supplies, shoes and food to be sent to the sisters in Japan. The prime minister agreed to allow the supplies to be sent on a navy ship.[64] Despite their years of internment the nuns, many of whom were quite elderly, considered Japan home and were not particularly interested in returning to Australia.

The desire of some released internees to remain in China was not one that army representatives, who had been despatched to Shanghai to arrange for their repatriation, could understand. It made them suspicious of the motives and loyalties of the people whom they were

139

Figure 15: *L to R: Jean Christopher, Methodist Mission Nurse (front); Joyce Olroyd-Harris (back), Matron of Rabaul Government Hospital; Kathleen Bignell (back); Dorothy Maye (front), civilian nurse. The women were captured in Rabaul and transferred to Japan. This photograph was taken in Manila on 4 September 1945, where they had been debriefed by Australian intelligence officers before returning home.*

there to assist. Despite the army's reluctance to become involved, the prime minister had decided that repatriation of civilian internees was indeed its responsibility. By early September 1945, the army had established three reception groups for liberated POWs and internees, based in Manila, the island of Morotai (now in Maluku, Indonesia) and Singapore.[65] The plan was for internees to stop at one of these posts on their return journey to Australia for a full and proper debriefing. This meant that before arriving in Australia, for instance, the Rabaul women interned in Japan stopped in Manila, where they were interviewed and debriefed by a reception team. The Australian government was particularly anxious to gather any relevant information about the wartime atrocities committed by the Japanese and the commission of other war crimes.[66]

An efficient administrator, Major H. W. Jackson, reported on Australian internees in the Shanghai area as part of his role with the 3rd Australian Prisoner of War Contact and Enquiry Unit. Jackson later reported he arrived with only sketchy information, and a presumption that there were about thirty-five Australian internees in the area.[67] The intelligence was incorrect. Jackson found himself required to collect information and compile nominal rolls on almost 300 individuals. He dutifully collected the names, dates of birth, next of kin and occupation of all former internees, and the records for this group of internees are among the most complete we have. He had to work with incomplete camp registers and the fact that many Australians were listed as 'British', and he attempted to follow up all leads.

By the time Major Jackson arrived, three weeks after the reoccupation of Shanghai, a large number of internees had already departed the camps without leaving a forwarding address.[68] A number of them had boarded the first available ships leaving Shanghai. By early October, thirty-six former internees had already left for Hong Kong. The army was keen to prevent any further departures for Hong Kong, and would have preferred released internees to travel home to Australia via Manila, where proper interviews with government officials could take place.[69] The unit spent months chasing after leads, 'not an easy task when it is realised that Shanghai is a city of six million'.[70] In November 1945, 105 people had still not been traced.[71]

Army officials were frustrated at the internees who had left the camps at the first available opportunity, before any government representatives had the chance to interview them. Owing to their civilian status, those internees who did feel inclined to leave Shanghai immediately felt no particular need to report to an Australian government representative before doing so. Service personnel, in the pay of the government and subject to military discipline, knew that there would be strict procedure to follow once they were released. Civilian internees, with no such formal relationship with government, did not think they would be beholden in any way. Their thoughts were of freedom, not of the need for a full debriefing.

Major Jackson was also critical of the motivations of those who he had been able to interview and who expressed a desire for repatriation. He clearly felt that most former internees who had chosen repatriation were planning only a short stay in Australia and wanted to return to their former lives in Shanghai. Keith Officer, a well-travelled diplomat familiar with expatriate communities, understood this; the army officials did not. Jackson wrote in January 1946 that 'Of the 155 persons already repatriated, it is a definite fact that the majority have gone to their respective destinations merely for a vacation until conditions re-adjust themselves here.'[72] He often made acerbic comments to the effect that 'Some people conveniently remember that they are Australians in order to receive welfare and repatriation benefits'. Before this they had let their passports lapse.[73] In late October 1945, Major Jackson interviewed Australian internees and forwarded their details back to Australia. He made a point of noting in the 'remarks' section of his list how long individual internees had been resident in China. Some individuals were relatively recent arrivals. Keith Graham, the doctor who won such admiration among his fellow internees, had lived in China for eight years before internment. The majority of the adults and nearly all of the children, however, had spent most of their lives in China.

The Fernandez family shows the complex nature of national ties. Roy I. Fernandez was born in Coonamble in New South Wales, grew up in a West Australian orphanage and went to China in his early twenties. There he met and married his Shanghai-born wife, Sybil. Their son had been born in Victoria in 1928 on a brief trip back to Australia. It had been difficult for the family to adjust to a relatively harsh life of farming in Monbulk in Victoria, after living for so many years in an apartment with servants. Roy, Sybil and Roy junior returned to Shanghai.[74] Their daughter Stephanie, eleven years old at the start of the war, had always lived in China.[75] Another family, the Turnbulls, shared a similar tendency to consider China home but retain Australian links. Eric Turnbull had been born in Shanghai in 1906 to an Australian father. The family's connections with Australia remained strong, with young Eric returning to Melbourne for his education at Wesley College, an elite boys' school. As an adult, Eric Turnbull again returned to Shanghai where he married a Russian woman. The couple's daughter was born in Shanghai in 1933. Despite their lifelong associations with China, both the Fernandez and Turnbull families re-established themselves in Australia at the end of the war. Eric Turnbull found work with the Shell Petroleum Company in Sydney, and his daughter attended school in the city.[76] The Fernandez marriage did not survive the strains of internment and the postwar struggle to re-establish life again and by the 1950s Sybil Fernandez was working in a music store in Sydney.

Long-term residence in China was also common among missionary families such as the Begleys, Stranks and Walkers. Missionaries usually returned to their country of origin in retirement. George and Jessie Walker, for instance, had spent twenty-seven years working as missionaries in India and China. Yet they did not return to overseas mission work after their repatriation to Australia, in large measure because George's health had been broken by his experience. He died in 1953. Jessie Walker continued working for the Salvation Army at its Sydney bookstore and managing the Sunset Lodge Retired Officers Home until her own retirement. She outlived her husband by many years, and died at the age of ninety in 1982.

It was certainly true that some of the Australians in the Chinese internment camps were Australian by adoption rather than birth. A proportion were Russians who had emigrated to Australia in the 1920s in the wake of the Revolution, became naturalised as Australians at that time, then travelled to China in search of employment in the economically depressed 1930s. Before the war, for example, Vera and William Marshall were known as Vera and Vladimir Mischenko. Vladimir had arrived in Australia in 1924 and became naturalised in 1930. He had served with the Australian military forces. In search of stable work in the mid-1930s, Vladimir travelled to China and found employment with the Shanghai Municipal Police. He met his Russian-born wife in Shanghai, and they married there in 1938. Marshall later claimed that he had attempted to rejoin the Australian army after war broke out in 1939, but his applications were rejected because the British authorities in Shanghai considered his services there essential. The Marshalls did not return to China once they had been repatriated from their Shanghai camp at the end of the war. By the 1950s, they were living in a flat in Ashfield in Sydney, and their son was attending Fort Street High School. Possibly in response to the Cold War climate of the 1950s, Vladimir Mischenko had changed his name by deed poll to William Marshall.[77] In spite of the army's queries about their sincerity, the fact remained that people such as the Marshalls were naturalised Australians who enjoyed a legal right to enter the country. Furthermore, conditions readjusted themselves in ways no one anticipated, forcing colonists out of China with the rise to power of the Communist Party. Many of the internees that Jackson had criticised as being 'Johnny-come-latelys' went on to spend the rest of their lives in Australia.

Army representatives were critical of the motivations, behaviour and loyalties of some internees. There were also tensions from within. Liberation allowed resentments that had festered away among internees themselves during the years of internment to break through. One

British resident, for instance, resented the continuing freedom of Alan Raymond who had made a name for himself with the activities of his Independent Australia League. Raymond had been spotted enjoying lunch with some Chinese friends, and an observer fulminated that for others who 'suffered the rigors and discomforts of internment during the war, it is galling to think that this man, who did so much to assist the enemy, should still be enjoying a full measure of freedom'.[78]

At a press conference in October 1945, Keith Officer assured journalists, and by extension the expatriate community in Shanghai, that 'everything necessary will be done' to punish those who had collaborated with the Japanese.[79] Despite these assurances, diplomatic staff knew that they needed concrete evidence to secure a conviction and could not be seen to provide knee-jerk reactions to community suspicions and innuendo. The Australian legation was acutely aware that 'there is considerable resentment amongst . . . Australians over the failure to take action against known traitors', but urged External Affairs to make sure that they followed correct legal procedure.[80] There had been disquiet in the Southern Cross Club about an Australian man who had been suspected of collaborating with the Japanese enjoying its facilities. 'The rest of the inmates resent his presence', a staff member informed Chungking, to which the chargé d'affaires responded by insisting that the onus was on former internees to 'produce enough evidence, as a group or individuals, to warrant our ejecting him from the club'.[81] The official line did not prevent individual representatives of the Australian government making clear to suspected collaborators like Raymond their personal opinion of his wartime activities. When one of them went to Raymond's house to visit his elderly mother, they reported, 'her son met me at the door with outstretched hand, which I pointedly ignored'.[82]

Even though Australian diplomatic staff in China shunned the likes of Alan Raymond, they had in most cases shown themselves to be deeply sympathetic to the needs of released internees. In this, Australians interned in China were fortunate, because almost everywhere else their relief and repatriation were organised by representatives of the military forces from Australia, the United Kingdom or the United States. As Major Jackson's frustrated criticisms demonstrate so clearly, the ambiguous place of civilian internees meant that army personnel were sometimes not quite sure how to respond to the specific needs of released internees. In some instances, this translated into a lack of sympathy for them. The homecoming experiences of civilian internees would underscore this fact, as the Commonwealth government also struggled to deal with the welfare and repatriation needs of its citizens so adversely affected by war but without the benefits that service alone could confer.

7

HOMECOMING

In the same month that members of the Merritt family were photographed at Sydney's Central Station upon their return from Santo Tomas, the Commonwealth government informed them that £750 (double the average annual male wage at the time) had been deducted from their account at the Bank of New South Wales for the costs of their repatriation. Mary Merritt considered that her war experiences, which constituted a daily interaction with 'the enemy' and suffering at their hands, had placed her 'in the front line' of the war. More tellingly, she also argued that to differentiate between the experiences of civilian internees and military POWs was to make a specious distinction:

> I cannot see why civilian prisoners-of-war should not be transported home as are soldier prisoners-of-war. The only difference between soldier prisoners-of-war and us is that our soldiers imprisoned by the Japanese received during their internment a sum equivalent to the pay received by Japanese soldiers, and we received nothing. I would have thought that our Government would be willing to help reinstate us.[1]

Mary Merritt's husband Frank also wondered how the federal government could turn a blind eye to the sufferings of Australian citizens affected by war: 'It does not seem fair that Australia which is funding 12,000,000 pounds for a lot of foreigners who have suffered the horrors and ravages of war is treating so meanly its own nationals who have suffered just as horribly'.[2] Mary Merritt went public with her complaints. In May 1945, she addressed a meeting of the AIF Women's Association at the Melbourne Town Hall. If she had been aware before embarking how much repatriation would cost her, Mary Merritt told the audience, she probably would have stayed behind in the Philippines.[3] Well into the 1950s she was still furious about what she saw as the Australian government's parsimony and unsympathetic attitudes towards former civilian internees.

Quibbling over repatriation costs is ostensibly a small issue, but it does expose the tensions around issues of citizenship entitlements, sacrifice, service and government responsibility raised by the war experiences of civilian internees. The Merritts felt aggrieved precisely because they believed government-funded repatriation from a Japanese-run internment camp was their right as Australian nationals. Partly in response to their complaints, the initial decision to bill released internees for their repatriation costs was reversed and subsequently all former internees were entitled to be returned to Australia at government expense.[4] The federal government also entered into an arrangement with the Australian Red Cross to provide hostel accommodation for repatriated civilian internees – Australians and other nationalities – who had no families or friends to support them upon return. Thus in the immediate postwar years the support for the majority of former civilian internees was decidedly short-term. While the government approached the question of internees' homecoming in terms of the immediate needs of accommodation and clothing coupons, it posed more complicated questions for internees themselves. They were acutely aware that 'official' information about their captivity would be in short supply and some took it upon themselves to bear witness to the suffering of fellow internees who would not be coming home.

Internees from the Philippines prompted the first extended consideration of issues surrounding the repatriation and welfare of civilian internees. The Americans were understandably eager to repatriate the internees to their home countries. They were also concerned about how much this repatriation would cost. British and Commonwealth embassy and legation officials in Washington were soon aware of General MacArthur's request that their governments guarantee to the US Treasury the cost of each individual internee's repatriation. MacArthur had estimated the cost to be US $275. The British agreed and the Australians followed suit, with the proviso that each internee would sign an undertaking to repay the repatriation costs.[5] In early March 1945, Prime Minister John Curtin sent a telegram to General MacArthur, conveying his thanks for the safe recovery of Australian civilian internees. He guaranteed to refund the US Treasury for the cost of their repatriation, and included a request that MacArthur obtain from each repatriate a signed undertaking to repay the cost of repatriation. MacArthur replied that it had been his 'great privilege' to liberate the internees.[6] Despite Mary Merritt's pride in General MacArthur's commendation of the war she and her fellow captives had endured, it was his suggestion that she pay to get herself home.

When it came time to repatriate individuals, matters proceeded with great haste. 'It was of first importance to get the ex-internees out of the Islands and away from those unpleasant surroundings as quickly as possible', one sympathetic official later commented.[7] A volunteer group of British ex-internees had drawn up evacuation and repatriation lists for British subjects and the US army relied on this information. The offices of the British Consulate-General did not reopen in Manila until mid-April 1945, by which time most of the internees had left the islands. A group of about 300 released internees had sailed for Australia aboard the *David C. Shanks*.[8] Those ex-internees who were repatriated to Australia were not asked to sign an undertaking to repay their repatriation costs. As a British consul official was to comment several months later: 'Embarkation was carried out in inevitable haste and the humanitarian principle of getting as many people out as quickly as possible tended to overshadow the desirability of efficient tabulation'.[9]

When the former internees arrived in Australia, the US army sought to rectify its original error. The ship carrying the internees docked at Townsville, where the 'scantily-clad' internees entered a harbourside shed full of tables laid out with donated clothing. Disappointed at their exclusion from proceedings in Manila itself, the Australian Red Cross was fully involved with the released internees once they reached Australian shores. The Townsville branch organised the clothing depot and lunch for the internees. Each adult internee received a donation of £5 from the Red Cross. They also received a small white card with a message of sympathy and welcome from the governor-general and his wife, the Duke and Duchess of Gloucester. 'We followed with anxiety the privations and hardships which you all experienced at the hands of our barbarous enemies – the Japanese – and we were distressed at our impotence to help you.' Despite the colourful opening, the message continued in a more traditionally bland regal style: 'We trust that now assisted by the wonderful Australian climate and looked after by Her most kindly people you will soon all regain your health and recover from your privations'.[10] After changing their clothes, reading their messages and eating lunch, the internees boarded trains bound for Brisbane and further south. The Red Cross had decided that owing to the 'short-age of time' and unspecified 'other circumstances' that a reception was inadvisable. The public was not admitted to the railway station. Those internees not fortunate enough to have relatives in Sydney to meet them and offer them shelter were taken by a special train to a Red Cross hostel. Almost one-third of the original group proceeded on to this hostel accommodation at Mount Victoria.[11]

On the journey from Brisbane to Sydney, officers from the US and Australian armies had boarded the train and demanded the internees sign a promissory note guaranteeing repayment of their repatriation costs. The Red Cross was 'at a loss' to explain this 'extremely inconsiderate' behaviour.[12] So too was the Minister for the Interior, Joseph Collings. Collings was appalled at the idea of traumatised internees dealing with such matters the minute they landed on home soil. He informed the prime minister of his feelings on the matter:

> Bearing in mind that the ex-internees have been in confinement for a long period and have suffered severe privations as well as being deprived in many instances of their all, I feel that in the case of Australians the Commonwealth Government should meet any claims received from the United States Government.[13]

The Australian army appears to have authorised the actions of its US counterpart despite a note of caution struck by its own representative in the Philippines the previous month. Lieutenant General F. H. Berryman reported in March 1945 that the released internees still showed considerable evidence of the strain through which they had passed, and would require careful and considerate handling on arrival in Australia.[14] It was not a message appreciated by Australian-based army officers, who remained officious with liberated internees once they reached home soil.

Initially at least, the government appeared most willing to help with the former internees of Australian nationality and to offer British, American and Dutch internees at least temporary refuge in Australia on humanitarian grounds. Officers in the External Affairs Department thought in August 1945 that 'arrangements made for the handling of recovered civilian internees should err on the side of making too much rather than too little'.[15] This was before the end of the war, when they believed the numbers of Australian civilian internees to be fewer than 300, which was about one-fifth of the final total. In a tribute to the prime minister's known sympathy for the internees, the Chairman of the Red Cross Committee on POWs, Arnold Johnson, stated on the day John Curtin died:

> In our dealings with the Government Departments at Canberra we found a very strong desire that everything possible should be done to assist these people; the Prime Minister took a personal interest in it and gave instructions that we were to receive every possible help and that all regulations governing admission of persons into Australia, such as Immigration, Quarantine and Customs Laws were to be administered with the utmost sympathy.[16]

Although there were indications of compassion, there were other signs that whites were to be the subject of preferential treatment. Before the final Japanese surrender, an instruction issued to units who might encounter internees in the course of their reoccupation of British, American and Dutch territory stated that they were authorised to distribute on behalf of the Red Cross a cash gift to released internees who were 'white people of British descent & white citizens of the USA'.[17] Moreover, senior government figures had already become concerned before the end of the war about the potential for humanitarian repatriation programs to contravene Australia's strict immigration policies. After the repatriation of internees from the Philippines, but before the liberation of camps elsewhere in Japanese-occupied territory, the Minister for the Interior expressed his concerns to Acting Prime Minister Ben Chifley. It was essential, Collings suggested, that the Commonwealth government retained the right to determine who entered Australia. Accordingly, the government should examine carefully the cases of those released internees who were not of British nationality, or 'where the ex-internees are not of pure European descent'.[18] The Minister for the Interior was determined to maintain the integrity of the White Australia policy, whatever the circumstances.

Perhaps Collings had been alarmed by a Red Cross report on the repatriation of internees from the Philippines. This report had expressed some reservations about the racial composition of the group. This might explain the reluctance of the Red Cross to allow the public into the railway station in Townsville. The Red Cross representatives had also been most concerned that there were undefined 'personal reasons' why it would be inappropriate for released internees to stay overnight anywhere other than Red Cross hostels in New South Wales. Accordingly, they had kept the internees moving, first from their ship in Townsville to waiting trains bound for an overnight journey to

Brisbane. On arrival in Brisbane, the internees were treated to a lunch at the Union Jack Club or in private homes, but were soon on their way again, aboard another overnight train to Sydney. The reasons for this haste became clear at the report's end:

> For confidential information, it must now be mentioned that there was a considerable number of women of foreign origin who had only acquired British nationality by marriage.
>
> Unfortunately many of these were coloured, many of the children were also coloured, several could only speak broken English and several were definitely undesirable in other ways. They were not acceptable for billeting in private houses.[19]

This was confirmation for the government, if any was needed, that the repatriation of internees contained the potential to breach the White Australia policy.

In the lead up to liberation, several government ministers and department heads had expressed concern about the potential for non-whites to enter Australia as part of humanitarian relief programs after the conclusion of hostilities. Discussion centred on the mixed-race populations of Netherlands East Indies and non-white British subjects. The government was concerned as early as June 1945. At a planning conference held in Melbourne, government representatives noted that there were about 50 000 civilian internees in Java and Sumatra, 'all of whom would be classified as Europeans by Dutch authorities'. 'In actual practice,' the conference minutes continued, 'many would not be regarded as Europeans on British standards'.[20] It was duly noted that most non-Europeans would not seek respite in Australia but the potential for a conflict with the White Australia policy had been noticed. The Minister for the Interior was especially concerned for Australia to retain control of people they admitted to the country in the wake of war. One of the 'complicating factors' in planning relief programs would be that '[p]arties of repatriated prisoners may consist of all types – British subjects of purely European origin, British subjects by marriage, persons of various European nationalities etc'. The conference also agreed with his suggestion to the prime minister that the Commonwealth government be furnished with the following information as territory was liberated from the Japanese: 'Where nationalities other than British are concerned, or where the ex-internees are not of pure European descent, particulars are to be separately furnished for consideration by the Commonwealth Government as to whether they will be admitted to Australia'.[21]

When it came to issuing instructions to army personnel involved in the repatriation of Australian civilians, there was veiled but easily understood reference to the enforcement of the White Australia policy. Administering officers were told that: 'The broad test to be applied is – "is the applicant in a real sense a member of the Australian community"'.[22] Army officers on the ground were nervous about their limited knowledge of the vagaries of Australian immigration law. They were aware of the importance of maintaining the White Australia policy but knew that policing racial boundaries was a tall order. In late September 1945, the army requested urgent advice regarding the repatriation 'policy particularly racial and financial aspects' in relation to liberated civilian internees. They received confirmation that any white British subject was welcome in Australia but 'facilities should not be granted for Asiatics to be evacuated to Australia'. There may well be 'exceptional cases' but these would require separate consideration.[23] 'No action need be taken in regard to white Netherlands subjects', customs and immigration officers were advised when the occupants of liberated Netherlands East Indies camps began to filter into Australia, but they were also reminded that non-whites would be required to complete certificates of exemption and their arrival reported.[24] After the Netherlands East Indies legation complained of racial discrimination against non-whites, immigration officials adopted a procedure that ostensibly treated all Indies evacuees in the same way on arrival but kept track of the numbers of Indonesians and Eurasians entering Australian territory.[25]

Despite the Red Cross constantly offering help and assistance to the government in relation to civilian internees in the planning stages, their attitude to such programs changed once caring for the former internees became a reality. The Red Cross had been delighted to be consulted at a series of conferences with various government departments about the reception and aftercare of liberated civilian internees.[26] It was during these negotiations that the Red Cross had agreed to accommodate liberated civilian internees of all nationalities at their hostels, most of which were situated in New South Wales. Destitute Australian released internees certainly stayed at the hostels but most of the residents were either British or Dutch. By July 1945, the number of residents at the Mount Victoria hostel still came to a total of seventy, a much greater number than anticipated. The Red Cross began to lobby the high commissioner for the United Kingdom that these people were the responsibility of his government. 'You will agree', the standing conference was informed, 'that we cannot turn them out in the street'.

The residents were aware of the reluctant help they were given at the hostels. An elderly Australian woman who had spent the war interned in China, Dorothy Hood, was eager to leave the hostel at St Mary's after a month's residence. She described the hostel as being '50 miles [80 km] from Sydney with *no space bad food*'. Dorothy Hood also sensed she was less than welcome. She described the Red Cross as 'anxious to get rid of us all here'.[27] The Red Cross had approached the Far East Relief Association who had agreed to pay for the former internees' medical, dental and optical services. Such services 'were not even a moral obligation of the Red Cross', Arnold Johnson, chairman of the POW (Far East) Committee insisted.[28]

In May 1945, the federal government had decided to cover released internees' 'initial' medical, dental and optical costs on arrival in Australia. The period of 'initial' treatment was never defined, and the Red Cross was to be responsible for any ongoing requirements.[29] Apart from the Red Cross's reluctance to take on the long-term treatment and care of destitute internees, there were other problems with the execution of the government's plan. In the latter half of 1945, the government received constant advice that there was a desperate shortage of medical personnel and that public institutions, such as the Royal Naval Hospital at Herne Bay, were unable to treat civilian internees. By October 1945, the Department of Social Services, which had assumed responsibility for the released internees, had printed a 'Form of Undertaking to Repay'.[30] 'Although the Commonwealth Government will bear all expenditure in the first instance, the greater proportion will be recoverable', Social Services advised the Treasury in 1946.[31] It would seem that the message that the government should 'err on the side of making too much [effort] rather than too little' had become lost within the year, as medical facilities came under pressure and government departments attempted to balance their budgets.

Internees themselves had no impression of receiving even any 'initial' treatment at government expense. When Kathleen Bignall returned from Japan she was more or less 'left to her own devices'. This was in distinct contrast to the army nurses with whom she had shared her captivity and who were cared for in hospitals at the government's expense. This was 'very wrong', according to one of Kathleen Bignall's daughters, because it meant that she and her sister were left to rehabilitate their mother at a time when they were also responsible for their own small children. Kathleen was still suffering from nervous anxiety, the after-effects of malnutrition, beriberi and was nearly blind in one eye from a slapping, and her daughters found it difficult to nurse her because they had no experience in dealing with such illnesses. 'Once the excitement of being home was over', one daughter later reflected, 'it was difficult for two inexperienced girls to cope – but cope they did, and Kathleen was happy'.[32]

Despite the difficulties of caring for people who had been malnour-ished for years, most families were of course eager to be reunited with their relatives who had been released from captivity. George Walker and his wife Jessie had been interned with two of their children; another two had returned to Australia before the outbreak of war. One of them, Jean, worked as a nurse at Queen Victoria Hospital in Melbourne. She took the first train to Sydney after hearing that her family had flown into Australia from China on a military plane. 'I did not recognize the tiny old lady as my Mother', she later recalled, 'and the usually bright & outgoing, now quiet and subdued man, as my Father'.[33] Other families were similarly shocked at the condition of their relatives. In Brisbane, for instance, a small crowd gathered to welcome internees returning from Hong Kong aboard the hospital ship *Oxfordshire*. Eighty-seven of almost 300 released internees were carried down gangplanks on stretch-ers, and 'people who had come to cheer were too stunned by the con-dition of internees and could only raise gasps of horror'.[34]

Some released internees, who had either witnessed the death of their colleagues and friends before internment or watched as their fellow inmates succumbed to illness and starvation, chose to write to bereaved families. This was both a human courtesy and, at times, necessary con-firmation of a death for families who had received no official word. One survivor of the incident at Yala in southern Thailand, Reginald Strat-ford, wrote to the wife of his friend, Keith Craigie. 'Your husband and I were very close friends', Stratford assured Rose Craigie, describing for her the circumstances in which her husband went missing. 'I am sorry to be the bearer of such sad news, but I can assure you I did everything possible for your husband.'[35] On receipt of this news, Rose Craigie wrote to the prime minister in October 1945 and again the following Decem-ber seeking official confirmation of Keith's death. 'I am sure you will realize my distressing position', she pleaded.[36] Another bereaved wife, Lilian Evenson, also wrote to the government after she received a let-ter from a Catholic priest who had been in the same prison camp as her husband, Albert. Shortly afterwards, she read in *Pacific Islands Monthly* that he had been executed. Lilian Evenson claimed that she received no official word from the government about her husband's fate until May 1947, when she was informed he had been presumed dead since May 1944.[37]

Violet Kentish had known since 1943 that her husband, Methodist missionary Reverend Leonard Kentish, had been plucked from the waters of the Arafura Sea, immediately to Australia's north, by a Japanese seaplane. He had been working on Goulburn Island, 400 kilometres east of Darwin, and on the day he was captured was aboard a naval patrol boat, on his way to the mainland. The boat was bombed and its survivors machine-gunned by the Japanese; Reverend Kentish was the only man actually taken prisoner. The last time he was seen alive, Reverend Kentish was drinking from a flask the Japanese pilot offered him as the plane flew off in a northerly direction.[38] After the Japanese surrender Violet Kentish still had no official word about her husband's fate. 'I know that Len is not beyond God's love and care wherever he may be', she wrote to the Minister for the Navy, 'but you will understand because we are only weak humans, the heartache and longing for one we loved so much'. The mother of three young children, Violet Kentish both desired and dreaded confirmation of her husband's death. 'I feel sure that you will do something in this matter if it is at all possible', she concluded.[39] It was another year before she received official confirmation of her husband's execution by the Japanese in May 1943. A confidential report from the Australian army revealed that during his internment at Dobo, on a small island in the Banda Sea, Reverend Kentish had been almost starved and bashed so severely that his nose was broken and he could barely see. When the island was reoccupied by the Allies, his body was recovered by the War Graves Unit, transported to Ambon and buried there in the internees' cemetery.[40]

The news was alarmingly thin for the wives and children of the civilian men from New Guinea, almost 200 in total, who could not be located on the island of New Britain once it had been liberated from Japanese occupation. Perhaps in an effort to comfort them, Gordon Thomas wrote an article for the *Pacific Islands Monthly*. He described last seeing the men in June 1942. In journalistic fashion, Thomas attempted to provide quick pen-portraits of men who he had known for many years. He described their physical condition and attitudes to captivity. Perhaps this was some comfort for families who were waiting in vain for news of their loved ones. But how much solace might Mrs Gascoigne, waiting anxiously for news of both her husband and son, have taken in the news that her husband had 'faded away to a shadow but was cheerful' and that her son 'was a comfort to him'?[41]

For almost all of the anxious relatives of Australian civilians who had been trapped on the island of New Britain, there was to be no joyful reunion. The Department of External Affairs had anticipated hundreds of Territorians being released from internment camps. They created a prisoners' welfare section and set up a well-equipped office in Sydney. The staff employed remained idle.[42] Most of the men had been dead since 1942, when the *Montevideo Maru* was sunk. They left behind at least 175 widows and dependent children.[43] Other close relatives were also at a loss. The grandmother of Herbert Bowman, a medical assistant at Rabaul in his mid-twenties, was devastated. Herbert was actually her daughter's illegitimate son but 'I brought him up from a babe. As my own son', the elderly Mrs Bowman wrote. He was a 'kind helpful lad, both as a companion and help in the home'.[44]

Shocked relatives and the mouthpiece of the Pacific islands white community, the *Pacific Islands Monthly*, demanded a full government enquiry into the failure to evacuate civilians from Rabaul. Their argument was that the civilians ought to have been evacuated once it became clear – forty hours before the fall of Rabaul – that the Japanese would invade New Britain. They claimed that ships were waiting in the harbour at Rabaul that could have been employed to evacuate the civilians who remained behind. 'Those men should not have been prisoners of the Japanese', the editor of *Pacific Islands Monthly* insisted.[45] Years later, one *Montevideo Maru* widow was still expressly critical of the wartime Labor government. Mona Bruckshaw, wife of the Chief Clerk of the Department of Public Health in Rabaul, complained that 'it was the fault of the then Labor men in Canberra' that civilians had not been evacuated. 'They need not have died poor men' another wrote, criticising the government's failure to evacuate.[46] The loss of life was regarded not only as a personal tragedy for the families concerned. Committed to the pioneering and colonialist presence in the Territories, *Pacific Islands Monthly* considered the loss of senior bureaucrats, businesspeople and farmers as an economic tragedy for the Territory.[47] Among the dead were the Government Secretary, Harold Page (brother of Australia's former deputy prime minister, Earle Page); the Territory's Crown Law Officer since 1922, the Hon. Gerald Hogan, MLC; the Territory's Senior Magistrate, F. W. Mantle; the Director of Public Works,

C. R. Field; and P. Coote, manager of Burns Philps operations in New Guinea.[48]

Those connected with the civilian men lost on the *Montevideo Maru* were angry at the government for its failure to evacuate civilians before the Japanese occupation and frustrated by the delay in receiving official confirmation of their deaths. Other situations also arose in the postwar years where the government's actions incurred the wrath of the families of civilian internees and of the former internees themselves. The Philippines repatriation scandal would not be the last time that the Australian government decided that internees had incurred their own expenses in captivity and that the government had settled accounts only on their behalf. In peacetime, such logic ran, costs should be recouped. This was a 1940s version of 'user pays'. It resulted in some former internees receiving constant and cruel reminders of the years in captivity. Internees in China, Japan and Bangkok had received small cash advances during their internment from the Swiss protecting power. In this they were fortunate, because most other camps had no such access. The internees had used this money to buy small items from the camp canteen and had signed notes promising that they would repay the funds once the war was over. Many of them probably completely forgot about the rectangular sheets of thin paper they signed each month. It is a testament to the powers of bureaucracy that, in light of all the lives and assets lost during the course of the Pacific war, the Australian government was in the late 1940s in receipt of the individual slips of paper that some internees had signed each month before receiving their allowance from the Swiss. In the postwar years these slips were used as evidence upon which the Commonwealth Investigation Service, the predecessor of ASIO, followed up former internees in their workplaces and homes and insisted that the money be repaid to the Commonwealth. Sometimes the activities of its officers seemed to fly in the face of the Department of External Affairs's own policy that where repayment of the advances might involve undue hardship, recovery would not be pressed.[49]

The recovery of relief money was evidence that there were advantages to be had from loyal and long-standing service to an employer or religious order. Tin-mining companies whose employees had been captured while at work in Siam and Malaya forwarded the money owing to the government on behalf of their employees with barely a moment's hesitation. The same was true of the Sacre Coeur order, which gladly repaid to the government the money that had been given to its nuns interned in Japan. Members of the China Inland Mission, the Salvation Army and the Methodist Missionary Society who received relief payments from the Swiss during the war also had their costs covered.[50]

Individuals fared less well. People whose lives had so clearly been interrupted by internment – families who were now living in bedsits in Manly, men working as drovers at the Newmarket saleyards or driving timber jinkers – were pursued for the debts they had incurred while interned by the Japanese. Violet Farmer, a widow in her sixties, was pursued for a debt of £600 she had incurred in a Shanghai internment camp. She had the Red Cross write to the department, telling them that she was 'a very worried and unhappy woman with reason for being concerned about her future'. Even the Department of Social Security wrote on her behalf, saying that she had been on unemployment benefits for two years and was 'not in a good financial position'. Still the debt was not waived. Three years later, her son, a fruit-picker in Innisfail, was contacted to see if he could settle his mother's debt.[51]

Isaac Uroe, who had been interned in Shanghai, said in 1950 that the bill for £166 'came to me at the most inappropriate moment, as a shock. Having mother & family to support I am absolutely lost having no knowledge how to squeeze blood out of a stone. I have no property and no assets of any type'.[52] Lionel Roope, also interned in Shanghai, stated that his debt:

> was a great surprise, as the relief advances during my internment in Japanese prison camps were for the occasional purchase of peanut butter and other bread spreads in the Camp's canteens. I felt certain that the Government would bear the expense for us (from the Swiss Consulate there) as prisoners of war. If not, then we must certainly be described as 'self-supporting' prisoners of war.[53]

Roope's investigating officer noted that Roope's wife had moved out, taking their baby with her, but leaving behind two other children aged three and two years. Roope's mother looked after the children during the day while he worked. The officer thought repayment of the debt would 'create great hardship on Roope', who he thought to be 'a good living man who is presently extremely worried over his domestic troubles'. Yet Roope was contacted twice more by the Department of External Affairs. An annotation in the margin of the file eventually conceded defeat: 'The mother can't pay so it looks as if the whole lot will have to be wiped'.[54]

Others pursued for the debt were more overtly hostile. Judah Whitgob fulminated in 1950:

> Surely being interned as a loyal British subject . . . losing every stitch of clothing, and all belongings and losing one's job besides the inhuman treatment we suffered in camp should be sufficient, and the Government should try and rehabilitate us instead of charging us for loans whilst being interned.

'It is the principle not the actual cash which counts', he concluded. 'And paying for being interned is hard.'[55] Family members pursued for repayment of money owed by those still absent overseas also protested. Oswald Goulter was from a large family of seven children in Colac, Victoria. Some of his siblings worked on Aboriginal missions in New South Wales, but Goulter had taken his missionary ambitions further afield. After completing university education in the United States, Oswald Goulter joined a missionary society and spent most of his career engaged in mission work in China. After release from internment, Goulter remained there. External Affairs, seeking repayment of the comfort money he had received, pursued his many siblings to help settle the debt. One brother protested directly to Prime Minister Menzies:

> It seems very hard that one who has given not only thirty of the best years of his life but his meagre salary also for so noble a cause should be called upon to repay what in his case was absolutely necessary to keep body and soul together during those 4 1/2 years of enforced semi-starvation. I know that you Sir, as a Christian Gentleman are deeply interested in Church and Foreign mission work. I wish, therefore, on his behalf, to appeal to you to use your influence in having this debt remitted if possible.[56]

The plea fell on deaf ears.

Despite the protests of most people who were pursued, the Department of External Affairs was dogged in its effort to recoup the money. It enlisted the help of intelligence officers, who visited the workplaces and homes of former internees, interviewing them about their financial affairs. They delved into private affairs, in one case unearthing a long-held secret about illegitimate birth.[57] One former internee lost his job after his employer became suspicious about the visits and inquiries of federal agents.[58] Sometimes the efforts to press people into settling the debts endured for years. There was the capacity to waive the debt in hard cases, but the Department of Finance pressed for settlement. Frank

159

Hooley, a man in his sixties married to a younger Chinese woman, with four children to support, was pursued for years. Many times the External Affairs people who interviewed him felt sympathetic to his plight – the family were clearly living in poverty – but they did not receive permission to waive the debt.[59] It is somewhat of an irony that the files that contain the details of many of these cases are titled 'Protection'.

These protests of former internees, and of concerned family members on their behalf, remained private objections to the pursuit of government policy. Mary Merritt had revealed herself as willing to go public with her objections to the government's decision to bill her for repatriation costs from the Philippines but in this she was very unusual. Most internees remained reticent, at least in public, about their war experiences. Those who did draw attention to the war experiences of civilian internees did so not to highlight the contradictions it posed for ideas of citizenship, but rather to explore internment as a test of faith. After his return from the Ramale Valley camp, for instance, Reverend James Benson conducted lecture tours for the Australian Board of Missions. The Methodists, who had lost ten missionaries on board the *Montevideo Maru*, needed to glorify the work of the lost in order to recruit workers for the present.[60] The leaders of the Methodist Overseas Mission were acutely aware that they had lost male missionaries in the prime of their life: the oldest was only forty-four. 'We find our ranks depleted,' the General Secretary of the Methodist Overseas Mission pleaded, 'out of this loss must come an upsurge of missionary passion . . . this is the task of young men'. The pressure was on the faithful. At a memorial service to the missionaries held in December 1945, Rev. Harold Chambers asked of his congregation:

> Will you be among the first-fruits of this harvest to go forth as they went forth, and, though not to die, perhaps (although that were an alluring prospect to the fully-consecrated soul) yet to sacrifice and serve abroad for him?[61]

In the late 1940s George and Jessie Walker, who had long service in China before their internment, used their internment experience as the foundation for spiritual campaigns. Their personnel folder in the Salvation Army Heritage Centre contains the handbills and flyers for lectures and campaigns they conducted before George's health failed. The advertising promised that they would be 'Dressed in Chinese, Sing and Speak in that Language'. The lecture titles promised dramatic revelations: 'Sick, Starved, Bashed and Bombed' and a special meeting for women: 'Tears, Trials and Triumphs'. The emphasis was largely on the Christian message – 'With my Bible in a Jap Camp' – but George Walker clearly wanted to emphasise compassion and forgiveness too. One night he lectured on the subject 'Should We Forgive the Japanese?'. The text of the lecture is not reproduced, but it would seem unlikely that a senior Christian missionary would call for retribution.[62]

8

LEGACY

In 1957, aged forty-three, Gwen Kirwan described the legacy of her internment in Changi. She had the greatest difficulty holding down office jobs because of their requirement for 'so much figure work'. 'At times my mind becomes a complete blank', she confessed. Gwen Kirwan also experienced black-outs, depression, severe headaches and the inability to handle, at times, the simplest of jobs. She thought these symptoms were probably due to head injuries she had received during a particularly harsh beating while she was interned. Gwen Kirwan's colleagues at work, and her boss, often noticed her mistakes and lack of concentration. They did not know that there were times when her 'mind melts into soft black velvet. I find myself in this engulfing mass, struggling desperately to push it aside and come back to clarity of mind and vision'.[1] Gwen Kirwan's statement of her continuing anguish almost a decade after her release from internment is perhaps the most eloquent and moving in an extraordinary and unexamined archive of testimony from Australian civilian internees about their war experiences. Her evocative description of the 'engulfing mass' that threatened to overwhelm her is the plea of a woman traumatised by war. What we would now call post-traumatic stress disorder was a consequence of internment that some internees wrote about openly in the 1950s; others were more reticent. They detailed the more mundane but still destabilising legacies of internment: financial insecurity, unemployment, compromised masculinity. Continuing ill-health could also be a constant drain on household finances, particularly in an era when medical care did not attract government rebates and was a cost borne entirely by individuals.

'Trauma' itself is a loosely defined and much-debated concept, one that challenged Freud and continues to confront analysts as a pathology unusual in its literality. There does seem to be general agreement among psychiatrists that traumatic symptoms include:

> a response, sometimes delayed, to an overwhelming event or events, which takes the form of repeated, intrusive hallucinations, dreams, thoughts or behaviours stemming from the event, along with numbing that may have begun during or after the experience, and possibly also increased arousal to (and avoidance of) stimuli recalling the event.[2]

The flashbacks, insistent memories and dreams that so disturb the traumatised individual are usually key events or anxieties directly and explicitly related to the traumatic episode. Trauma's core lies in the reception of the event, which is 'not assimilated or experienced fully at the time, but only belatedly, in its repeated possession of the one who experiences it. To be traumatized is precisely to be possessed by an image or an event'.[3] This delay between the traumatic event and its return, which Freud described as 'latency', also means that knowledge of the event has not been fully possessed by the individual. Some civilian internees, for example, did not experience 'panic attacks' or other symptoms of trauma until many years after their liberation. Eve ten Brummelaar, a Dutch woman interned in the Netherlands East Indies who later migrated to Australia, recalled: 'Around 1973, I discovered that some outwardly normal situations could plunge me, quite suddenly and without warning, into an acute state of anxiety'.[4] Cathy Caruth has further suggested that trauma is a 'symptom of history' and that the traumatised 'carry an impossible history within them, or they become themselves the symptom of a history they cannot entirely express'.[5] This tension between the assimilated and unexpressed elements of an individual's past is reflected in Eve ten Brummelaar's description of feeling like 'two totally different persons. One a cool, calm and collected woman, looking with amazement and disdain at this other creature going to pieces for no apparent reason'.[6]

Considering this notion of an unexpressed history, theorists and psychiatrists working in the area of trauma and memory often note the importance of witnessing, or having another person listen, which then enables the traumatised individual to move from the sense of isolation imposed by the experience of trauma and to begin the process of recovery. Dori Laub, a child survivor of the Holocaust, has written about 'the imperative to tell' and considers that 'no amount of telling ever seems to do justice to this inner compulsion'. For Laub, it is the '"not telling" of the story that serves as a perpetuation of its tyranny'.[7] For traumatised people to recover, their stories must be told in order for them to integrate the experience into their life history, autobiography and personality.[8] It is through witnessing and speaking about and of the past that the impossible history of a trauma is realised. The impossible becomes possible, the history becomes just that, the past, fully incorporated into the present rather than returning insistently and unbidden to it as an alternative reality.

Witnessing can only occur when there is a receptive audience for the tale one has to tell. This insight is particularly useful when it comes to understanding the difficulties former civilian internees faced in the postwar world. The trauma they had experienced was linked to a specific historical event and their fears and anxieties were frequently literal replays of traumatic events endured during their internment. Yet opportunities for discussing and absorbing the meaning of those experiences were limited in a postwar society that discouraged people from dwelling on the past.

In 1952, an opportunity for civilian internees to describe (we might say witness) their wartime experiences came from an unlikely source. In that year the Menzies government established the Civilian Internees' Trust Fund. The fund, created in the wake of the peace treaty with Japan, oversaw the distribution of money from frozen Japanese assets among Australian civilians or their dependants who had experienced 'distress or hardship', leading to a 'permanent disability', as a result of their internment during the war.[9] In its ten years of operation, the fund distributed over £44 000 to eligible applicants.[10] Hundreds of Australians wrote to the trustees, not confining themselves to the official forms that allowed them only a small space to describe years of pain.

The entreaties that make up this archive reveal the continued suffering of some internees long after the war was over. The applications demonstrate the difficulties that doctors, the trustees and former internees had in articulating the mental anguish that resulted from internment in the days before psychiatrists called such symptoms post-traumatic stress disorder. They also show that for some individuals the anomalous place that civilian internees occupied in dominant narratives about war, the nation and sacrifice compounded their sense of having experienced an 'impossible history' for which it was difficult to find an audience in the 1950s. If the blue foolscap forms that applicants completed acted as a kind of witnessing for lonely and distressed internees, the archive that they now constitute provides historians with the opportunity to bear witness for them. Opening up the folded pages of the forms often reveals further letters attached with a rusted pin, some of them making up a correspondence that occurred into the early 1960s. They are often written on the small notepads of an earlier era, in uneven hands that wrote with random capitalisation and underlining.

The applications to the fund demonstrate that there was no homogeneous traumatic experience and that the same event or occurrence did not traumatise everyone equally. One missionary nurse who had been interned in China when she was in her mid-forties, Rose Rasey, worked as a nurse in Tasmania after she returned to Australia. She wrote breezily: 'I have not suffered any "hardship". If, in the future, the secondary anaemia which I have had since internment, prevents me from earning my living I know that my heavenly father will, in some way, meet the need'.[11] Similarly Robina Thompson, vice president of the Australian and New Zealand Association in Singapore before her internment in Changi, concluded after reading the application form that it would be unfair of her to claim money that others might need more than she did. Widowed and living in Melbourne, Mrs Turnbull reported that she was 'not in "dire distress"'.[12] There were internees who also recognised that there were, and would always be, competing memories of captivity under the Japanese. Not everyone shared the same internment experience; some took longer to reconcile themselves to their wartime experiences than others. Jean Gittins, the daughter of a wealthy Hong Kong family who spent the war in Stanley and later migrated to Australia, recognised this in her memoirs. Gittins felt that many of her fellow internees would 'vouch for the truth of my presentation . . . those who still harbour bitter memories may feel that it is over-restrained'.[13]

In contrast to Gittins's memories of Stanley, another woman, who had been interned in Shanghai along with her three-year-old son, reported constant suffering since war's end. By 1953 she had spent four separate periods in Paramatta Mental Hospital, tormented by 'acute mania'. She had twice received electroconvulsive therapy. All of the doctors and psychiatrists reporting on her case pointed to the patient's three-and-a-half-year internment as the cause of her mental instability. The woman's husband wrote on her behalf: 'She is avoiding discussion on the life in the camp in general. Dr Mahon expressed an opinion that she might have been bashed or assaulted by Japanese causing extreme mental depression.'[14] An Adelaide-born man, interned in Changi, had by 1947 been admitted to that city's Parkside Mental Hospital under the South Australian *Mental Defectives Act*. His doctors considered that the 76-year-old's 'present mental illness was probably aggravated (if not caused by) his suffering at the hands of the Japanese'.[15] Betsy Barnes, who had been interned in Changi, told the trustees that she lived in the Melbourne bayside suburb of St Kilda but suffered from 'nerves' and was 'unable to take a position in the city or anywhere where there are crowds'.[16]

Depression, anxiety, 'nervous' disabilities, tensions and breakdowns were all words that former internees used to describe their continued suffering. 'Trauma' was not a word in common usage in the 1950s, and neither internees nor their medical practitioners used it to describe the legacy of their war experiences. Eva Russell, Melbourne-born but a long-term Shanghai resident before her internment, described in layperson's terms the process that Freud identified as the 'latency' inherent in trauma:

> People who had 'physical disabilities' didn't live to tell the tale – and . . . the 'disabilities' we suffered were 'mental' – and therefore not visible to the naked eye. People say 'you want to forget internment camp' – how can we, when these so very 'personal' things keep cropping up? . . . Who can, therefore, say when and where results of those years of internment will strike us?[17]

Eva Russell raged against the restrictive terms of the fund but other former internees merely noted with sadness the anxieties that plagued their daily lives. Clara McLeod stated that she was a 'nervous wreck' as a result of her internment in Singapore. The postwar years had not been kind to her; in the 1950s both she and her husband were unemployed and living in a tent in Queensland. 'Starvation and mental torture has left its mark on me for life and made me a broken wreck', she told the fund.[18] Hazel Trimble, whose husband, a Gallipoli veteran, had died in their Philippines internment camp, described herself as suffering from 'periodical nervous debility and collapse directly due to the hardships and malnutrition suffered in camp'.[19] Alice Mayes claimed to have suffered a 'nervous breakdown' during the war when the Japanese searched her home in Shanghai and stole her possessions. Since war's end she had been 'unable to do any work in particular as I lose my memory often & have to rest in bed for some days. Dr Nordioni said there was no medicine he could prescribe for a cure'.[20]

General practitioners and psychiatrists who wrote to the fund on a patient's behalf often attributed physical symptoms to unspecified 'nervousness'. Sybil Fernandez had married her now-estranged Australian husband in Shanghai before the war. ('I can assure you that Mr Fernandez's family arrived in Australia before 1843 and we are not "New Australians"', she insisted.) In relation to her internment, she stated:

> I cannot claim that I am incapacitated by loss of any limbs through the Japanese – and I know I only survived because I was healthy and strong when we started our imprisonment. I know too that I have not come out of those bad years of starvation and fear without any marks or trace of the ordeal. When the gates of our camp were opened by the Americans I was flat on my back for six weeks because my heart was behaving very strangely, and it has been the same ever since.[21]

The doctor's certificate that Sybil Fernandez included with her application stated that she still suffered from 'palpitations and pains in the chest' and that there was 'a large nervous element in her condition'.

Many former civilian internees continued to experience pain and discomfort long after doctors could find a continuing physiological reason for its occurrence. Dorothy Hood, for example, had suffered from persistent vomiting and insomnia since her internment in Shanghai. By the 1950s her marriage had also broken down, she was living in Sydney and was now over seventy years old. Her long letters to the fund are full of pleadings and a sense of injustice, written in smudged blue ink on fine sheets of pale paper, replete with much jabbing and underlining. She informed the fund that she was 'nervous and unable to sleep & vomit[s] nearly every day'. The doctor who treated her stated that she had lost 30 kilograms while an internee and that 'there has been persistent vomiting & insomnia for a very long time probably of neurologic origin. Nothing could stop her vomiting sometimes. Luminal and morphine injections were sometimes useful to induce her to sleep'.[22] Irene Spicer, the mother of alleged collaborator Alan Raymond, was another ageing internee who lived at the New South Wales Home for Incurables. The medical officer at the Home reported that:

> When an internee she is reported to have suffered much in the way of beatings and kickings by the Japanese, & she constantly complains of pains in her back & right kidney. These pains are not related to

her cerebral tumor, & her constant suffering & obsession with them is undoubtedly due to ill-treatment during her internment.[23]

While some former internees experienced the legacy of camp life as repeated behaviours and pains that recalled actual events and illnesses of captivity, for others the trauma appears to have been of a more abstract nature. For them, internment represented the transition from privilege to poverty, and it was a loss that was keenly felt. Some of the most 'nervous' people who wrote to the fund were those who had once led a very different life in expatriate communities or British colonies, and now found themselves relatively impoverished. One perceptive doctor, who treated an Australian businessman who had previously enjoyed great success in the Philippines, described this situation in the following way:

> I am sure that his period of three years as an internee of the Japanese was an enormous factor in his present state of health. For a man aged more than seventy, his physical condition is satisfactory, but from a mental and emotional point of view, he is not able to rehabilitate himself.
>
> Prior to his internment, I believe he conducted a prosperous business in the Far East, but since returning to Australia he has been unable and incapable of successfully carrying out even small projects.
>
> I was a P.O.W. in German hands for three years, and even with health and youth on my side, I, like many of my friends, found rehabilitation not easy. With this in mind, I am sure a man in his late sixties, who returned from some degree of affluence to nothing, would have an almost impossible task.[24]

The man about whom the doctor wrote continued to struggle with depression and poverty for the rest of his life. When he died in 1961, his second wife wrote to the fund and told them that in the final months 'he was back in the past where one simply could not reason with him at all. He was pathetic & he relived those awful years of his internment more often than I care to recall'.[25]

Women widowed after their husbands died during internment or shortly after, or who remained responsible for the support of young children with the added burden of a permanently sick or incapacitated husband, were particularly vulnerable. Alice Ishoy, for example, was an Australian woman who had married a Dutch planter, then spent the war years interned in a Javanese village. 'Everything we possessed had been taken from us', she told the Trustees, 'we had to start life again "from scratch" when the war ended in 1945'. Her husband's health had

been ruined by his time as a POW; Indonesian independence termi-
nated their dreams of returning to the plantation lifestyle. In 1957 they
were living on a heavily mortgaged farm in Queensland and Alice Ishoy
had only 'just recently been in hospital because of nervous disorders'.[26]

The Kirwan and the Ishoy marriages had survived internment and
the stresses of separation, internment and the loss of the husband's
bread-winning capacity in the postwar years. Others had not. Family
breakdown or breakup was another of the unfortunate consequences of
war with the Japanese. During his time in Changi, Harold Murray noted
his 1944 wedding anniversary in his diary and reflected:

> Was married on this day in 1920. Well a lot of water has run down the
> rivers since that day and a family that arose from that event are now well
> scattered over the Globe. When, if ever? We will again be a family group
> it is hard to say and by the look of things now the chances of me been
> [sic] there are not very bright.

Murray did, in fact, survive his internment but 'passed away in his sleep'
in 1954. He did live for a time with his son, his daughter and a sister,
but did not live with his wife, Georgina, again. [27]

The Murrays may well have been separated before the war, given
Harold's reference to the water which had 'run down the rivers' since
1920, but internment had an immediate and direct impact on another
family. Zena Canning had sailed from Shanghai with her two daughters in December 1941, intending to return to Australia. The ship,
whose route to Australia included a stop in the Philippines, arrived at
Manila just in time to coincide with the Japanese invasion. Its occupants were transferred to internment camps. Zena Canning and her
daughters spent the remainder of the war in Santo Tomas. In September 1942 her husband Jimmie mistakenly believed that she would be
among a party of Philippines internees fortunate enough to be repatriated to Shanghai. He later described filling every room of their house
with flowers, how he had 'the boy cooking an enormous dinner, and
everything was ready for you'.

> At that time, I had a bicycle, and I went to the Customs Jetty at 3 p.m.
> a tremendous crowd were waiting, and we waited until 9.30 p.m. before
> the Manila people were brought ashore, imagine the confusion, I was
> running up and down in the dark searching for you, never for one minute
> did I dream that you were not aboard . . . finally I ran across Jimmie
> Campbell and his wife. I asked where you were as I could not find you,
> and then they told me you had refused to come back. I think that was

the greatest shock I had in my life . . . they told me you did not come back because I had not written to you . . . I did not go home for three days. How people sent letters to Manila I have never found out, I only know I tried every way.[28]

The Cannings' war did not end happily. Zena and her daughters remained in Santo Tomas; late in 1942 Jimmie Canning was interrogated in Shanghai's Bridge House prison for sixty days before his release to hospital and ultimately Lunghua internment camp. There he formed a relationship with another woman and fathered a son, whom he assured Zena was an 'absolute double' of their own daughter. In September 1945 Jimmie Canning wrote to his wife asking for a divorce and stating that 'he would rather not see the children again, but remember them as they were when you left [Shanghai]'.[29] While there appear to have been marital difficulties before the war began, for this family the confusion and chaos of invasion and internment in 1942 exacerbated an already unstable situation, altering the course of their lives forever.

Internees suffered the legacy of a difficult war, but so did the widows and dependants of those who did not return home. Historian Joy Damousi has pointed to the necessity of extending studies of the impact of war to the families of servicemen. This should also be the case with internees. Some of the women evacuated from Rabaul were pregnant at the time. The children were born in Australia but they were never to see their fathers. Irene Davies gave birth to her daughter Diane five weeks after the fall of Rabaul, and was almost immediately required to return to work so she could pay her medical expenses. Olive Coomber, whose husband Arthur died on the *Montevideo Maru*, said that she and her two sons had lost 'security, love and companionship and a Fathers guidance and Comradeship' when he did not return once the war had ended. Janet Eglinton had no children and felt that her husband Abel's death meant that she had lost 'everything that marriage stands for'. Nellie Simpson eagerly awaited the return of her husband, the Rev. Thomas Simpson, from Rabaul. The Simpsons already had a daughter and they had a son born after Nellie left Rabaul, but Thomas Simpson never learnt of his existence. 'We lived in hope of a reunion until the end of the war,' she wrote in the late 1950s, 'when at last we had news, and realized that our family life would always be broken'.[30]

Elizabeth Hurst was not herself interned, but spent the war concerned about her husband and missionary parents who were detained at Stanley in Hong Kong. She had been evacuated from Hong Kong in 1940 with her son. In 1953 she wrote that 'I am still feeling the strain of the years when my 3 nearest relations were interned in Stanley camp'. It was a difficult time in Elizabeth Hurst's life: her mother, the last surviving member of the trio liberated from Stanley, had recently passed away. She was desperate for some assistance from the Civilian Internees Trust Fund. 'Sorry that having to live in the bush with no electric light and pumping my own water . . . And with a son aged 13 years to bring up on child endowment and my widow's pension is not hardship enough for your Trust fund', she wrote bitterly.[31]

The non-white wives of Australian men who had died during their internment also faced an uncertain future. Efigenia Quark's husband William, originally from Bundaberg in Queensland, was working as a sales manager for Lever Brothers soap company in China in the early 1940s. Captured in Canton, William Quark died during the first year of his internment. Efigenia Quark was Chinese. Fortunately for her, their son was serving in the Australian army and arranged to have her repatriated to Australia when the war had ended. The Department of Immigration agreed, 'provided you accept responsibility for her maintenance whilst she is here'.[32] The path was less smooth for other similarly placed widows. A mining engineer originally from Broken Hill, Luke Teddy, had married a Malayan-born Indian woman who was much younger than himself. Teddy almost made it to the end of his internment in Changi but died a month before the camp's liberation of beriberi and high blood pressure. His wife, Alberta, had taken on the burden of Teddy's nationality and spent the war interned in the women's section of Changi prison. Upon liberation, she was 'left bereft and in the position of having to earn her own living for the first time in her life', according to a well-intentioned but slightly condescending Australian employer who wrote to the fund on her behalf. By 1957 Alberta Teddy was working as a servant – 'quite a difference from being mistress in her own home & her own staff' – but was 'a Christian & a most refined & modest lady. She is completely Western, having absorbed those cultures & ways of living'.[33] Although she continued to serve in, rather than direct, a Singapore household, Alberta Teddy received a higher than average grant from the fund.

Gwen Kirwan was the most eloquent of the correspondents for whom internment represented not just the loss of freedom but the loss of their status and position in life. She provided the trustees with detailed descriptions of her prewar life in Singapore 'where we had a home and a business of our own'. Health problems and increased competition from 'Asian businessmen' in the postwar period meant that the Kirwans failed to re-establish their 'once-flourishing livestock and fodder business'. The family migrated to Brisbane. By the mid-1950s her husband was in his seventies and, according to his wife, an 'old, frail and broken man'. Their previously privileged life in Singapore was now a distant memory. It is significant that Gwen Kirwan's experiences of 'black velvet' and the 'engulfing mass' happened when she performed menial work, her daily reminder of all that she had lost as a result of the war and her much-reduced circumstances.

Others were faced with constant material reminders of the war. James Benson, who had established a mission at Gona, on the Papuan coast, in 1937, opened his account of captivity with a reflection of the difficulties of homecoming to an area that had been a war zone. Reminders of the war were implicit in the landscape. Benson described bomb craters, the burnt-out fuselage of a crashed plane and, a kilometre and a half out to sea, the wreck of a 10 000-ton Japanese transport. From his window, Benson could see the 'bleached ribs' of the carrier on the 'jagged teeth' of a reef. His account opens the morning after a night of heavy rain. The heel of a boot had emerged from the sand. Careful digging by Benson and his companions revealed the remains of an Australian soldier, who had fallen and been buried by the drifting sands. 'It is a strange experience', he wrote, 'to come home to a battlefield'.[34]

In New Guinea the battle was over but in China it continued apace. Henry and Frances Collishaw, long-term Salvation Army missionaries in China, returned there in 1947. It was a difficult time: they were caught in a frightening siege in their Shanghai apartment block and Frances Collishaw's health had been impaired by her internment by the Japanese. Continued civil conflict and the growing popularity of the Communist Party also undermined their missionary work. In November 1949 the Collishaws returned to Australia and, while putting on a brave face, spoke about the 'unprecedented discouragement' in their missionary field. 'Owing to the expected upheavals resultant from the civil war', the *War Cry* reported, 'Salvationists who have suffered the privations of internment camps during the Japanese occupation now see one Corps after another, the work of years of painstaking and faithful service, come under the spell and disabilities of internal conflict'.[35] The victory of the communists in China in 1949 spelt the end of Salvation Army missionary endeavour there. Within a year Henry Collishaw, 'broken in health', had retired from active service. He died at the Sunset Lodge Retired Officers' Home in Sydney in 1958. Frances Collishaw survived a little longer and died in 1970 at the age of eighty-five.[36] Like the Collishaws in China, former internees who had lived in other colonial communities such as the Netherlands East Indies and the Philippines were also unable to re-establish their pre-internment life, in part because of the independence movements that the Japanese occupation had nourished.

The material losses that Australian civilians sustained when the Japanese military invaded their country of residence were enduring memories and a bitter reality, particularly in the first decade after the conclusion of the war. The peace treaty with Japan, signed in 1952, contained no provision for property lost or damaged in countries occupied by Japan during the war, neither did the treaty provide for the satisfaction of claims for personal injury. Numerous former internees wrote to the Commonwealth government for many years, including lists of long-vanished household possessions, carefully valued and for which they wanted reimbursement. The loving and fastidious descriptions of all they had lost – lacquered tea-sets, embroidered linen, wedding silver, fur coats, silverware sets designed to sit on dressing tables, blackwood trays with silver handles, crystal wireless sets, carved jade lamps – seem to conjure up a colonial life at the very moment it was swept away. One woman had left Australia in her late twenties to work as a 'special cable stenographer' in Hong Kong and had met and married her husband there. 'I lost everything I owned in the world when the Japanese took Hong Kong', she wrote.[37] James Ellis, interned in Rabaul, felt that his case for compensation was one of 'extreme righteousness'. The loss of his property in Rabaul as a result of enemy action meant that Ellis was 'compelled . . . to recommence my life with a bitter struggle for rehabilitation'.[38]

Leonard and Florence Stranks, a Salvation Army missionary couple who had spent the best part of their married life in China, felt that internment in their mid-fifties struck particularly hard. They lost all of their possessions in China, and their retirement plans had to be put on hold as they attempted to rehabilitate their finances.[39] George and Jessie Walker, fellow Salvationists, found themselves in a similar position. They had been in China for twenty-five years. George Walker died from a heart condition in the early 1950s, and his widow had to supplement her small superannuation from the Salvation Army with part-time work. She lived in a garage. 'In a word,' she wrote, 'WE LOST EVERYTHING'.[40]

Internment and its after-effects seem to have been particularly pronounced among the elderly and the young. As well as losing most of their financial possessions, the elderly had access to only the most basic medical care during their internment at a time in their life when they needed the best. One internee was already a widow in her mid-fifties at the time she was interned in Hong Kong, and was totally incapacitated within a decade of her release. In 1958 she was living at the Convalescent Home for Women in outer-suburban Melbourne, or staying with friends.[41] The parents of children interned felt that they had missed essential vitamins, minerals and nourishment at a critical stage of their development. When Gwen Kirwan made application to the fund, she included a photograph of her son taken not long after his release. 'How could the small bodies grow, bones & teeth become strong?' she asked.[42] Others who had been teenagers during their time as internees later reflected that, despite the best efforts of the adults to continue classes for the children, their education had suffered. Ian Begley, interned as a teenager in China with his parents, felt 'the most significant set back for me personally was the lack of effective high school education leading to a school leaving certificate'.[43]

Those about to enter the work-force felt their prospects had been compromised; some with established careers felt that internment had curtailed their capacities. Jean Armstrong, who had been a journalist in Shanghai before the war and author of the memorable phrase 'worldly Australian citizen', was completely unable to return to her former occupation. She claimed that she had been 'beaten and held in terror for months before internment, both hands [were] permanently injured'.[44] The letters she wrote to the fund attest to her disability. Those that are handwritten were composed by a shaky hand, each letter laboriously formed. The typewritten correspondence is in equal disarray – the paper has been loaded unevenly into the machine, the ink blurs, typographical errors mar the text. For a former journalist, whose stock in trade was words and communication, these letters are the sign of a life derailed by illness and mistreatment. In the early 1950s, an intelligence officer visited Jean Armstrong, who was living alone in a rented house in Brisbane. He was there to inquire whether she could settle the debt she owed the Commonwealth for money lent to her during captivity. Any discussion of internment, according to the officer, caused her 'acute distress'. He concluded that she was 'unable to restore herself to normality and her condition is somewhat pathetic'.[45] The debt was waived.

Two other journalists who had spent the war interned, Jack Percival in Manila and Dorothy Jenner in Hong Kong, received diametrically opposed treatment from their employers. When liberated by American

Figure 16: *Jack Percival, far right, six months after his release from Santo Tomas. Percival was in Japan as part of the Occupation Forces, and back at work as a war correspondent for the* Sydney Morning Herald.

forces in February 1945, Percival immediately cabled his employer, the *Sydney Morning Herald*. The paper proudly published his message on the front page of its newspaper:

> I hold card No. 11, issued Sydney, authorizing me send ordinary rate and urgent rate messages to 'Herald'. Have been interned. Again in business. Appreciate renewal of business relations.[46]

The same edition ran a long article written by Percival about the liberation of civilian internees in Manila, and many other reports in the days that followed.[47] A quick return to work was Percival's conscious choice as the best road to recovery. 'What I had to do was get cracking as soon as possible,' he later recalled, 'to pick up where I'd left off. I knew work was the best thing for me'.[48] At the time, when arguing for immediate resumption of his war-correspondent duties, he told his manager 'I know myself. When I get wound up I've got to stay wound or bust'.[49] Percival (along with his wife and son) accompanied General Douglas MacArthur as a war correspondent and reported for the *Herald* on the

175

US occupation of Japan, remaining there for the next three years until his employer recalled him back to Australia.

Dorothy Jenner received no such welcoming reception from her employer, Associated Newspapers. On her return to Australia in spring 1945, she offered the Sydney *Sun* copy about her experiences during internment in Hong Kong but there was no space made available in the paper for her. Jenner's bitterness was palpable in her reflections on the treatment she received. It was all very well, Jenner suggested, for Associated Newspapers to send her off as their staff war correspondent in 1941 'with great hurrahs', and for her to behave with 'dignity' during her long internment, but it amounted to nothing once hostilities were over. 'I then arrived back in Australia to be dismissed as a mental case, without even being given the opportunity to speak for myself', Jenner complained. She was convinced that it was only because she was a woman that the paper felt able to treat her so appallingly. 'I can promise you that had I been a man, my reception would have been totally different. They thought that as I was merely a woman they could get away with such behaviour'.[50] Jack Percival's immediate posting with MacArthur's forces to report on the occupation of Japan, straight from internment at Santo Tomas, during which he had lost one-third of his bodyweight, would seem to bear her out.

Internment had put paid to Jean Armstrong's career as a journalist, and caused Dorothy Jenner's employers to think that because she was a woman, and hence more fragile than a male internee, that the strains of captivity had compromised her professional abilities. Most women internees did not have careers, however, and on the whole it was men who complained most bitterly about their blighted prospects and destroyed careers. Herbert Conn was only in his mid-twenties when he was interned by the Japanese. At the time of his capture, Conn had read for his Second Marine Engineers Ticket and expected to progress further through the ranks. But a war spent working in railway yards at Kawasaki and in flour mills at Nisshin had left him with fibrositis and nervous dyspepsia. By the 1950s, he 'just about live[d] on stomach powder'. In what appears a particularly cruel twist of fate, the only employment Conn could find was working on the railways. 'The internment ruined my career', he wrote, '[I am] now only a railway fitter which is a backward step and no future'.[51] Alexander Grimpel, interned in China, complained before his captivity he had been 'an officer manager and accountant'. Bad health since release had forced him to accept lesser positions in clerical work. In a further blow, his wife had been compelled to work in a factory to, as he put it, 'alleviate our position'. 'I have not had a decent job in six years,' Herbert Kirwan told the trustees, 'am penniless and depend on my wife & young son to keep the home going & educate the youngest boy'.[52]

Lesser positions, working wives: there is a sense among these men that it is their masculinity itself which had been compromised by internment. For some, this extended to their very bodies. Men commented upon their physical weakness and incapacity as a result of internment. 'Prior to internment I was a strong and healthy man', dredgemaster Walter Blaikie informed the fund, but after release from Changi he 'was almost blind . . . due to malnutrition'.[53] Allister Greig pointed out that his physical deterioration was so dramatic that he had actually figured in postwar publicity about the camps. 'I was one of the first to be photographed after release', he stated, 'and was exhibited in the Dept. of Information displays in all Cities of the Commonwealth. I actually weighed 97 lbs, 6st 13lbs [43.7 kg] – was 14st 10lbs [92.7 kg] before interned'.[54] In her memoirs, Dorothy Jenner painted a vivid portrait of the effects of internment on her body: 'When I went into Stanley Camp in January 1942, I had black hair and weighed around ten and half stone [66 kg]. When I came out almost four years later, my hair was dead white and I weighed less than six stone [38 kg] . . . Nothing could conceal the fact that I was an awful looking, thin dame'.[55] Women sometimes commented in their applications to the fund about the number of pounds they had lost in captivity; for men it was common enough to be routine. Samuel Warren who was interned in northern China with his wife and three children clearly felt that internment had undermined both his bodily capacities and ability to perform in employment:

> I am quite unfitted to hold positions of employment which by reason of earlier training and experience I should be eligible to hold. This means I have had periods of unemployment and also that I have to accept employment where rates of pay are low as, and even lower, than basic standard. Also I am quite unable to do anything in the way of heavy or manual labour. While only fifty two years of age I am more like a man in his late sixties.[56]

Similar feelings were expressed by James Hope, originally from Camperdown in Victoria but with a twenty-year career in the Malayan rubber planting industry behind him. Although a civilian, he was taken out of Changi and sent to work in the coal mines in Japan. This aggravated a gunshot wound in his leg and gave him a skin condition. In the postwar years, he could not resume his rubber planting career because it required a lot of walking, and dermatologists recommended that his skin condition would be aggravated in the tropics. As a consequence, Hope had purchased 'virgin scrub land' on the Victorian coast.[57]

In an echo of the post-World War I soldier settlement schemes, some men used the capital they had left after the disruption of war and internment to begin again by taking to the land. And like earlier veterans, many of them found themselves unsuited to and unprepared for the demands of hard farm-work. Apart from their physical incapacities, many of those who chose this path were already well into middle age. For some, it seemed like the only choice left. Ernest Henty had spent most of his adult life working on tea and rubber plantations in Ceylon and Malaya. At the end of the war, his former employer would not take him on again, considering him too unfit to resume work in the tropics. 'In other words,' Henty wrote bitterly in the early 1950s, 'I was old enough to risk my life when the Japanese overran Malaya but was useless when all the danger was over'. At the age of fifty, newly married and with a baby daughter, Henty began dairying in the Margaret River region of his native Western Australia. He described this as 'a bush farm which gives a return entirely inadequately to our needs'.[58] Another man interned in Kuching had also bought a farm in Western Australia in the hope that it would provide for himself and his family. A younger man than Henty, he thought that 'the outdoor work may be more healthful'. Yet he too found the mortgage payments crippling, the farm unproductive and his ill health an added burden.[59]

Some former internees inscribed these new homes with memories of the old. Ernest Henty named his Margaret River property Tanah Merah, 'red ground'. John Bryant was a long-term resident of Borneo who briefly returned there after the war. By the 1950s he was back in Australia and had established a farm in South Queensland named Bukit Sapi or 'Cow Hill'.

Most of these men who established farms were fortunate in that they had wives, and some, as in the case of John Bryant, children who helped them in the attempt to make the land bear fruit. Others felt that health difficulties that presented barriers to employment had also blighted their marriage prospects. Herbert Crocker, not even twenty when he was captured aboard his merchant ship, suffered greatly with nervous disability following his release from a camp in Japan. In 1953, he stated that 'I am desirous of being married but feel insecure due to the ailments from which I suffer and which result in frequent loss of work'.[60]

178

Malcolm Macfarlane, who had survived the incident at Yala, claimed the loss of his marriage prospects when seeking compensation from the Siamese government at the end of the war.

Some civilian internees exhibited symptoms of trauma but others articulated their longing for that which is so critical to recovery from trauma: a willing audience to hear them out. The assessors of Malcolm Macfarlane's compensation claim considered him to be a 'neurotic' but his obsessive repetition of the details of his captivity and the long 'statements' he typed out about the course of events suggested the need for a different kind of hearing.[61] On one occasion in the 1950s, when Macfarlane was in Broken Hill, he discovered that he was staying at the same hotel as the prime minister, and promptly wrote him a letter detailing the particulars of internment and had it delivered to his room. Marie Wahlstrom-Lewis, whose husband was formerly a health inspector in Shanghai, was one individual who expressed her frustration at the way civilian internees struggled to receive a hearing within government and bureaucratic circles. Her husband had died within five years of their release from internment in China, leaving her a widowed mother, not yet thirty years old, of four children. She complained:

> All my efforts to obtain some small measure of our family rights, which were taken away by the war, has only resulted in one official Department passing the buck on to another Department, and I am getting very tired of it, I do not want anything for myself, but I do want something for the children, even if only sufficient for a deposit on a small home, to give us some measure of security. It is not easy for a woman with 4 young children to entertain ideas of remarrying.[62]

Marie Wahlstrom-Lewis's difficulties were not merely bureaucratic. Civilian internees struggled to find an audience because they found themselves in a highly ambiguous position when it came to common understandings about war, sacrifice and suffering. Civilian internees had personally suffered hardship, privation and loss at the hands of the Japanese but were not military personnel in service of their country. Their relationship to discussions about national sacrifice was, in the 1950s, tenuous at best.

Marie Wahlstrom-Lewis was one of the few internees to mention her frustration; but others might have felt that the fund was an organisation that would, at last, hear them out. There had been other occasions on which internees had expressed their anger and disappointment at their equivocal position in the eyes of their government, particularly during the repatriation process. The Commonwealth government had heard frequently from Mary Merritt, the disgruntled Philippines repatriate, in the decade after her liberation from Santo Tomas. By the early 1950s the Prime Minister's Department described her as 'one of our chronic complainants'.[63] Yet far from merely complaining about her situation, Mary Merritt also detailed the dissolution of her marriage – her husband and daughter now lived in Canada – and her own precarious mental health: she had suffered a 'nervous breakdown'. From the financial details she supplied to the fund, Mary Merritt did not especially need the comparatively modest grants they distributed. She did seem to need the opportunity to be heard out, to tell her side of the story, to act as witness to a past that continued to cause her grief and sorrow.

There is a sense too that some of the most persistent applicants to the fund, alongside some of the most perfunctory and reticent, shared a deep loneliness and sense of isolation owing to their traumatic war experiences. Gwen Kirwan's letters appear to have been written without her husband's knowledge, in the calm of night after she had attended to his needs and those of her two sons. She never mentions other internees in her correspondence. Some single and divorced men had their mail returned unclaimed from boarding houses and Salvation Army shelters, signs of an rootless postwar life. Although he had once been married and fathered seven children, and worked as a dredgemaster in Siam before his internment, by the 1950s Frederick Hall was in his seventies and living in a miners' hostel in Captain's Flat, in New South Wales.[64]

Support was strongest for people whose ties in internment pre-dated their captivity. The nurses from Rabaul are a case in point. They had belonged to one of three groups: the Administration Hospital in Rabaul, the Methodist Mission or the Australian army. Alice Bowman, a government nurse, acknowledged that in captivity there had been tension between the various groups, but in freedom they sought solace in each other's company. 'There had been periods in Japan when some of us were scarcely on speaking terms with others in our group', she wrote in her memoir. 'Yet now, we frequently sought out one another's company'.[65] The widows of the New Guinea civilians who perished on the *Montevideo Maru* were also a well-connected group. As people with social connections before the war, and a shared identity as 'Territorians', they appear to have supported each other through crisis. There were particularly active groups in Adelaide and Sydney, the home of the New Guinea Women's Club. Lorna Hosking, whose husband, Herbert, had been the medical officer at Rabaul, emerged as the spokeswoman for Adelaide women. She wrote to the fund on behalf of other women insisting on the need to help them: 'this lass is ill at present and in very real need so that any financial assistance would be both a moral as well as material uplift'.[66]

Sympathetic families were also a help. The widow of Norman Holt, who was murdered at Yala in 1941, received unrelenting support from her father, W. P. Beahan. Beahan was a frequent correspondent to his local members and prime ministers both during the war and afterwards. He fought for his daughter to receive some compensation for all the war had cost her. 'It is a job for a woman to kick off on a new life & keep a son 12 years of age', he once remarked.[67] Beahan tried to pull every possible string. His local member was reminded that Mr Beahan had been a member of the ALP and a participant in factional battles. 'I have marked for a lot of men in the Labour movement, but got nothing in return but love'.[68] Beahan wanted his loyalty rewarded by serious attention paid to the claims of internee widows such as his daughter. He described the incident at Yala as 'wanton destruction by savages'.[69] He made sure that other widows and families of the Australians murdered there were kept informed about the progress of negotiations about compensation, and forwarded them copies of any reports he received about the incident.

The details that applicants supplied to the Civilian Internees Trust Fund about their former lives, their experiences of internment and the difficulties they faced in postwar Australia as they struggled to find a place after years away read as more than merely factual responses to questions on a bureaucratic form. The overwhelming impression left by this correspondence is that former internees experienced the process of describing their immediate past as both a painful and cathartic act. The litanies of suffering both within the confines of the internment camps and in the immediate postwar years are a measure of the limited opportunities former internees had to act as witness to their own painful, and often traumatic, past. There is a palpable sense that former captives had now themselves discovered that elusive captive audience for which they had been searching. A faceless bureaucrat or a board of trustees with the power to dispense once-off financial aid did not constitute an end to the suffering or recovery from trauma. But for some, the process of witnessing had begun.

In the 1950s civilian internees often complained of experiences, feelings and symptoms that would, later in the century, come to be seen as typifying post-traumatic stress disorder. By drawing on psychoanalytic approaches to trauma, it becomes clear that former civilian internees did not merely suffer from incomplete, or inaccurate, diagnoses of their symptoms. These models suggest that an initial traumatic experience can be compounded, and indeed often relived, if the traumatised individual is unable to bear witness to his or her own past. Postwar Australian society offered stoicism and fortitude as antidotes to the sufferings wrought by war; encouragement to express grief and trauma were the hallmarks of a later period.[70] The broader cultural injunctions to 'get on' with life and not dwell on the past are sometimes manifest in internee letters. This attitude is reflected in a letter written in the early 1950s by Joan Dodwell (née Walker), who spent her childhood in China as the daughter of George and Jessie Walker. After detailing the suffering she endured in camp, and the legacy of contracting polio, Joan Dodwell reassured her reader that despite her 'long "tale of woe"', this was 'not my present outlook on life'. 'I am trying very hard to forget the hardships and privations which I was called upon to endure and enjoy the years ahead of me with my husband and family in a wonderful country.'[71] Yet four years later, the brave optimism of this letter had been replaced by a more bleak and fearful tone. Time had not healed the wounds of Joan's internment. Her doctors considered that Joan suffered from constant 'emotional and nervous tension'. Childbearing had aggravated an internal injury suffered when in camp and brought forth constant reminders of those years. The letter contains much more detail than previous correspondence about the work women were required to perform in camp. Joan Dodwell felt no compulsion at this time to crack hardy: 'Each confinement has worsened my condition', she wrote.[72] The broader, public exhortation to reticence in the immediate postwar period is the reason that the archive created by the trust fund is so extraordinary. For it offered both the chance to view feelings rarely expressed in the 1950s, and it established an audience, of sorts, for the war stories of civilian internees. This offered civilian internees a chance to articulate their own war histories and an opportunity to express and thus begin to incorporate them into the present.

9

COMPENSATION

Kathleen Bignell had lived in the islands north of Australia for almost thirty years. She described herself as a 'widow', then a commonly used term by women whose marriages had failed but who felt disinclined to dwell on the details. (A memoir written by Mrs Bignell's daughter makes clear that her mother was separated, rather than widowed, at this time.) In the late 1930s she was the proprietor of the Rabaul Hotel, and was awarded an MBE for her bravery during the volcanic eruption of 1937 that had so devastated the township.[1] By 1942 she had been declared bankrupt, and had decided to pitch in to the war effort by running a soldier's convalescent home on the site of her latest business venture, a plantation at Kokopo, New Britain. Out of a sense of duty to the soldiers she nursed, Kathleen Bignell ignored the evacuation order for women and children. During this time, she also sketched the grave sites of Australian servicemen killed at Rabaul. Within months, Kathleen Bignell was captured by the victorious Japanese and soon transferred to Japan, where she spent the remainder of the war years in captivity. Apart from her own captivity, war brought further tragedy to the Bignell family. Her son Charles, also taken prisoner in New Guinea, boarded a different ship, the *Montevideo Maru*. Her son-in-law was also killed in action.

The language Kathleen Bignell used to describe these events reflects not only her grief, but also her sense of sacrifice for the nation. She felt that her actions during the Japanese invasion of New Guinea, the damage to her property there and her labour carried out during internment, constituted a direct contribution to the country's war effort. She demanded compensation but this was driven by financial necessity as much as any firm notion of wartime service. In January 1946, four months after her release from internment, she was living in a garage without electricity or running water. 'The future under these circumstances is not very pleasant to face', she wrote.[2] She was also seeking compensation from the War Damages Commission for losses at her Warenvulu plantation on New Britain. 'I feel sure you will assist me to have my claim paid, or rent for my New Guinea property or something to allow me a feeling of independence & freedom after the years of imprisonment', she pleaded with the Department of External Territories.[3] Kathleen Bignell was under the misconception that part of her property was used as an internment area for Japanese captured in New Guinea, and she hoped the government might pay her some rent. In mid-1946, the Department of External Affairs set her straight. Her property was not a camp, she was assured, it was 'utilised as a garden for the production of food crops, as the result of its close proximity to a Japanese camp'. As she was still uncompensated and still suffering the ill effects of long internment on a semi-starvation diet, this admission that her land was being used to feed Japanese prisoners seems breath-taking in its insensitivity. One wonders how much heart Kathleen Bignell took from the government's justification that 'the clearing of plantation areas for the growing of crops to permit prisoners of war to be self-supporting, will in the long run save time and money for the owners when they return'.[4] By the 1950s, she and her daughter were living together in New South Wales and were both in receipt of pensions, but had 'taken in sewing to augment' this money.

Some of Kathleen Bignell's sense of injustice might have also had a well-spring in grief. The loss she felt at her son's death was expressed poignantly at war's end in a correspondence she entered into with the Australian army over the loss of her sketchbook. Throughout her captivity, Kathleen Bignell had carefully preserved her sketches of war graves at Rabaul and reluctantly handed them over to interested army officers during her intelligence debriefing after liberation. She never saw them again and discovered their loss at about the time she learnt of the fate of her son, for whom she had been 'eagerly waiting'. In an angry letter to the army, written in October 1945, she said of the sketchbooks: 'They are of value to no one but myself and the mothers of the men who died for whom I tried to draw the resting place of their sons'.[5] Although Kathleen Bignell had drawn the graves of other women's sons, she had no illustration, no grave to tend, no 'resting place', for her own son.

Now these too, like her son, were lost. 'The sketches were of places which meant a great deal to me and my family now that my son has gone', she wrote sadly in early 1946. Perhaps it was this loss, this sacrifice for her country, that compelled her to press her other claims.

Even given these circumstances, Kathleen Bignell's language reflects her belief in the war service she herself had performed. Significantly, in correspondence she always referred to herself as a 'prisoner-of-war', never as a 'civilian internee'. She described her work with the soldiers as 'supply officer for ASC 2/22 Battalion at Rabaul in an unofficial capacity'. Claiming compensation from the Australian government, she stated: 'I only ask for the same privileges that the soldier POW's should have [including] the POW pay during our years of working for the Jap'. She considered that 'overwork, felling trees, carting coal etc etc in starved condition' while a civilian internee in Japan was a sacrifice for her country in wartime and that she should be duly compensated.[6]

In the early postwar years the Australian government's attitude towards assisting and compensating former civilian internees was an effort to blend pragmatism with compassion, with the ultimate aim of limiting expenditure for the Commonwealth. Internees had not been serving members of the armed forces and neither they nor their dependants were entitled to any long-term or continuing repatriation benefits. This caused resentment among some former internees: 'Civilian Internees . . . lost their homes, personal belongings and still suffer ill-health no less than POWs', one former internee complained to the local member of parliament in 1953. 'The Japanese treated all their prisoners the same', another woman who had been interned in the Philippines complained, 'they starved us and ill treated us all whether we were civilians or military men, and no one who went through that ordeal from 1941 . . . can boast that they are free of any mark'. Lionel Buttfield, who married his first wife Phyllis in Santo Tomas internment camp, felt his civilian internee status disadvantaged him in his search for work on repatriation to Australia. 'I experienced great difficulty in obtaining permanent employment', he complained, 'on account of ex-servicemen preference act (being only a Civilian Internee)'. Another objected that 'there is no machinery for ex-internees to receive free medical treatment as exist for ex-servicemen. I incurred quite considerable medical expenses on return to Australia'.[7]

What were the consequences for former civilian internees like Kathleen Bignell of returning to a society in which the citizen–soldier was the dominant figure in accounts of sacrifice in wartime? This dominance did not merely occur in cultural or commemorative forms. The extensive benefits available to returned servicemen and women have led Stephen Garton to suggest that a 'welfare apartheid' developed in twentieth-century Australia, one which distinguished and privileged those who had served over those who had not.[8] This 'welfare apartheid', when coupled with changing attitudes to the state in the twentieth century, left civilian internees in a highly ambiguous position. Warfare in the twentieth century transformed 'the conception of the state from an entity that protected the rights of all citizens', American historian John Bodnar has argued, 'to one that had distinctive obligations to some citizens whom it had hurt or punished'.[9] In the immediate postwar years, the dilemma for former civilian internees was that they felt hurt and punished, but could find no arm of the state willing to assume distinctive obligations for them. Their war experiences prompted a consideration of what, if any, responsibilities the nation–state bore towards its citizens who chose to live beyond its borders and then unwittingly suffered owing to their nationality when confronted by the nation's military enemy. The case of civilian internees became not so much a question of citizenship 'rights' as it did a matter of charity – and accordingly, it invoked familiar issues of discretion, judgement and contingency.

The government was keen to keep at arm's length those who might be construed to have performed a 'service', of a sort, for the nation. This was an open-and-shut case for civilians resident in countries outside of Australia. It was less clear for civilians who lived in Australian external territories. A case in point relates to the actions of civilian nurse Sister Dorothy Maye during the attack on Kavieng, on the island of New Ireland, in January 1942. Major Edmonds-Wilson recommended her for an OBE 'for her gallant and heroic action during the air raid on Kavieng'. 'Although a civilian nurse', he wrote:

> Sister Maye was completely at the Coys. Disposal . . . when she quietly attended the sick and wounded, while under enemy fire she assisted . . . with all operations and then immediately volunteered to alone accompany the wounded down to Lamacott Mission, knowing that in case of an enemy landing no succour from my troops would be available.[10]

For her troubles, Sister Maye was captured by the Japanese and interned at Rabaul and Japan for the remainder of the war. The army supported the recommendation for Dorothy Maye's OBE, and her name was included on a list of individuals forwarded to the prime minister for periodical awards for distinguished services rendered during the operations

Figure 17: *Dorothy Maye, greeted by family on her return from internment in Japan. Recommended for an OBE for her bravery during the Japanese invasion of New Ireland, the Minister for the Defence declined to make the award owing to her civilian status.*

in Malaya, Timor, Ambon and Rabaul.[11] The Defence Department approved all those listed except for Dorothy Maye. This was despite the Minister for the Army's comment that 'I know of few more outstanding cases'.[12] John Dedman, the Minister for Defence, argued that Maye's 'actual status at that time', being neither a member of the forces, a full-time uniformed representative of the Red Cross or other philanthropic body nor a recognised uniformed press correspondent, meant

187

that she was ineligible for the award. He felt that it would be 'wrong in principle' to give Maye retrospective accreditation or attachment to the forces, mainly because this would have 'implications in relation to the position of other civilians in the Territories who may have rendered services to the forces during the war'.[13] The Department of External Territories seemed to agree with him. Despite several reminders from the Prime Minister's Department in the late 1940s, the matter was left to rest. Dorothy Maye, who returned from Japan with a 'nervous condition' which meant she could not return to nursing until 1947, ultimately received an OBE for twenty-five years' service in the territory.[14] Her bravery during the Japanese invasion of Australian external territory remained officially unrecognised.

Part of the difficulty former internees faced lay in their appeals to a state that privileged the claims of ex-servicemen and women. Although Dorothy Maye never asked for any acknowledgement, other former internees hoped to win sympathy, and perhaps concessions, from the government, by association with the much-vaunted concept of service. Civilian women who had been interned in the same camp as well-known nurse POWs Vivien Bullwinkel and Betty Jeffrey, and civilian men who had been in the camps adjacent to the nurses, never failed to mention this in their correspondence with the government.[15] Similarly, men who had served in the First AIF were at pains to point out their record. Their claim to service had already been established, despite the fact they spent the next war interned as civilians. 'I would ask the Trustees to consider my 1914/18 service (I possess the 1914 star)', one man noted, despite the fact that this bore no relevance to his position in World War II.[16]

Internees were at a disadvantage in their efforts to be heard because they were civilians with war grievances but no war service. Their sacrifices arose directly from the Japanese invasion of their homes, the destruction of their livelihoods, their internment during the war and from extended absence from Australia. Dorothy Hood returned home to Sydney in April 1946 to discover that she was unable to resume control of her home. During the war, the Rose Bay house had been rented out to an ex-serviceman, his wife and three children for what she considered to be a peppercorn rent. She demanded to know how a seven-roomed house in Rose Bay with verandahs, a double garage and extensive gardens 'became let at a rent less than I used to get from my garage' in the prewar years. Legislation protected the tenants, who could not be asked to vacate the premises until one year had elapsed since the soldier's discharge from the army. This is the reason that Dorothy Hood and her husband, both of whom were aged and ill from the effects of internment, were forced to endure their humiliating tenure in a Red Cross Hostel outside Sydney. 'I fear there is little sympathy for the land lords,' Mrs Hood wrote, 'but we are *prisoners of war* far *worse* than x service men . . . if you knew how it would bring tears to your eyes. Please help me to get back my house as soon as possible'.[17]

The English wife of Geoffrey Scott-Settle, the Australian mining engineer tortured in Siam when a sword was inserted in his arm for four days, attempted to remind the government that most Australians had been spared the horrors of front-line warfare. Her husband had not. Mrs Scott-Settle believed it only right that her husband should receive some compensation for all he had suffered. It was unfair in a country 'where they pride themselves on voluntary service and no conscription', and most people had been 'spared Blitz and front-line atrocities' that 'men who have been nearly ruined physically and often mentally too – should have to carry on against overwhelming difficulties of rehabilitation'.[18]

Others tried to insist that the distinction between servicemen and women and volunteer civilians was an arbitrary and in essence meaningless one during the invasion and occupation of their former homes. The Kirwan family typifies this response. Gwen Kirwan had been placed in solitary confinement for eight days during her internment, and later testified at war crimes trials that Japanese sentries had beat her with a stick, and one in particular had kicked her in both breasts and her lower stomach. Her husband Herbert, a successful Australian businessman in Singapore prior to the war, was thirty-five years his wife's senior. Internment had been particularly hard on the elderly. By the 1950s Herbert Kirwan was in his seventies, and stated that he suffered from 'stomach ulcers, gall-bladder trouble, mental depression, skin cancers, appearance so bad that I cannot get a job even when I try'.[19] He was therefore totally dependent on the efforts of his wife, Gwen, who was also trying to support their two young sons. Gwen Kirwan tried to make a case to the government that her husband's actions during the invasion, often under the direction of colonial authorities, constituted a form of service. She detailed how her husband had been directed by the colonial government to join the Medical Auxiliary Service and wrote:

> His job was to collect [blood] donors and drive them through shell-fire
> & bombing to the G[eneral] H[ospital] where transfusions were badly
> needed, & then to take them home again. I don't have to tell you what

a ghastly job it was to drive day & night around Singapore in the midst of war . . . I still have his M.A.S. badges and can send them to you at any time. Would it not be the happiest thing in the world for us if my husband could get an army pension?[20]

Mrs Kirwan, and others like her, often mentioned their husbands' service in World War I or in volunteer forces: in the Kirwans' case, Herbert Kirwan's long-standing membership of the Singapore volunteer forces as an instructor in small arms. The reply was always the same: 'I regret to inform you that your husband is not eligible to receive an Australian war pension as he did not serve in the Australian Forces during the late war'.[21] Service was almost the only way in which citizens or their dependants could become entitled to repatriation benefits. Although civilian internees had withstood the pressures and demands of warfare, invasion and internment, ultimately they could not construct their sacrifices and sufferings as service to the nation.

Some volunteers actively resisted the distinction drawn between themselves and ex-servicemen. Claude Coats, a teacher from Adelaide who had enjoyed a successful career in the Malayan Education Department before the war, is one example. In the postwar years, Coats's identity was firmly that of a liberated POW, despite his official designation as a civilian internee. When he tried to claim from a POW trust fund he was advised to contact the fund created for civilian internees, and was 'unhappy about doing this . . . [I am] a member of the R.S.L'. He had been told, unequivocally by the government, that he was considered to be a civilian, yet 'as servicemen, we find it difficult to regard ourselves as such'. Coats felt that this meant it was difficult to get assistance from any source.[22] A power station engineer in his early thirties who served with the Hong Kong volunteer forces, Robert Cherry, found himself in a similar position. He, like Coats, had tried seeking repatriation benefits from the Australian government but had been turned down because he was not in the AIF. Similarly, the British government had refused to compensate him through their Private Chattels Scheme (War Damage) because Cherry had been born in New South Wales. In the early 1950s, Cherry complained: 'It seems I have fallen between two stools and have no one to appeal to'.[23] Herbert Crocker, who had been a member of the merchant navy when captured at sea by Germans and handed over to the Japanese, also considered himself a POW. For official purposes, however, members of the merchant navy were civilian internees. When applying to the POW trust fund in the 1950s, Crocker was told to look elsewhere. Crocker registered his disgust: 'It would appear that such persons, who, during the war were regarded as members of the forces, and who were subject to equal perils of war, with much less self-armament or protection, are to be completely disregarded'.[24]

Despite these protestations, all three men were in receipt of some help from British sources. Those who had served with the various volunteer forces and with the merchant navy under charter to the British Ministry of Transport were entitled, for varying amounts of time, to pensions from the UK government. Cherry, for instance, who had been hospitalised with tuberculosis for two years after his liberation from camp, received a war disability pension at a 50 per cent rate from the Hong Kong government.[25] Australian crew members of the SS *Nankin*, Herbert Crocker's vessel, also received part-pensions from the British government for a few years in the early postwar period.[26] Yet by 1957 Herbert Crocker had his small pension of 10 shillings per week stopped 'as they say he should be over the effects of the prison camp life now', his mother wrote.[27]

Internees who had been resident in Malaya immediately before the war were entitled to receive some compensation from the War Damage Commission established by the Malayan government. Most felt that they received a fraction of what they had lost. John Wardell, a Changi internee who was born in Melbourne but had lived in Malaya since his discharge from the First AIF, claimed that he received only a third of what he asked of the commission. Another interned in North Borneo scoffed that despite the loss of 'all [his] private goods and chattels' the payment he received was 'just sufficient to pay for half a car'.[28] Others were still waiting. Frank Salmon, a dredgemaster who also spent his war in Changi, complained in 1952: 'Big concerns have been paid, and Heads of big concerns, who bolted for safety on the approach of the Japanese troops, but men like me who stuck to their job get nothing but a few illuminated letters from the Commission'.[29]

There was one group for whom an exception was made. They were civilian internees who had been captured in New Guinea or Papua, the dependants of civilians who had lost their lives during the occupation of New Guinea, and the dependants of Australian civilians captured in Australian mandated territories who had died during their internment. These people were entitled to receive benefits under the New Guinea Civilian War Pension Scheme. This scheme entitled eligible recipients to 'pensions, medical benefits, children's education allowances, furniture grants and remarriage gratuities as the same rates and under the same conditions as would apply under the Repatriation Act to a member of the forces'.[30] It is worth noting, however, that this legislation was passed almost two years after some of these affected civilians returned home. From May 1947 the Australian government gave and continues to give full entitlements to civilians captured within the borders of its external territories, and it was also prepared to pass on these entitlements to the dependants of those who died as the result of internment.[31] These provisions covered approximately one-fifth of those who had been interned, and their dependants.

The majority of former internees were forced to accept that they would receive no continuing benefits from the government in the immediate postwar years and, for those who were not resident in the Territories, no compensation for the destruction or confiscation of their property and assets by the Japanese. Former internees and their dependants with links to Australian external territories were eligible to receive compensation from the Australian War Damage Commission for their property that had been destroyed as a result of enemy action. Those who had the misfortune to be outside Australian territories, and to have their property there destroyed as a result of enemy action, did not receive any compensation from the Australian government. Alexander Grimpel, who had been interned in China along with his wife and daughter, corresponded with the Controller of Enemy Property for over a decade in an attempt to get some compensation for the losses his family had sustained. Mr Grimpel claimed £750 (sterling) for himself and £500 for his daughter, Lily, in 'the hope that you will do justice to your subjects who were deliberately robbed of their personal belongings and had to be replaced at a great sacrifice'. The Grimpels were to be sorely disappointed. They were informed in September 1951 that the terms of the peace treaty negotiated with Japan 'do not extend to property lost or damaged in countries occupied by Japan during the war, nor does the Treaty provide for the satisfaction of claims for personal injury'.[32]

There was one exception to this general case. Siam, one of the few independent nations in the region, had itself declared war on the Allies. Accordingly, the Australian government negotiated a separate peace treaty with Siam. Article VIII of that treaty contained provision to compensate Australians 'detained or interned by the Government of Siam or their agents or subjects' for 'any loss or injury sustained by them' as a result of detention or internment.[33] The dependants of any Australians whose death was caused by the Siamese government or its agents were also eligible to claim compensation. In the late 1940s, the British Commonwealth–Siamese Claims Committee was established to arbitrate claims by individuals and companies against the Siamese government. Some former Australian civilian internees received generous grants from this fund. John Hugh Hughes, a shift engineer for a mining company, had attempted to flee Siam and enter Burma during the chaotic days of December 1941. He and his party of fellow Australians and British were arrested and detained by Siamese troops for almost a month before they were interned in Bangkok. The claims committee awarded him over £2000 compensation in August 1948, a sum that would have paid Herbert Crocker's pension for seventy-seven years.[34] A few years later, Geoffrey Scott-Settle received £6502. Now happily settled after a peripatetic postwar life marred by illness – 'we love Tasmania and everything connected with it, even the bracing weather we have up here in the mountains' – Scott-Settle and his wife were delighted to receive the money. Mrs Scott-Settle was so moved that she invited the Delegate of the Controller of Enemy Property, a senior Canberra bureaucrat, to dinner: 'If ever you should be this way "incognito" for a holiday or fishing – you are more than welcome to our humble fare'.[35]

The one avenue which remained open to all former internees was the funds available from Japanese assets in Australia. After concluding the peace treaty negotiations, in 1952 the Menzies government announced that it would use a portion of these assets, £25 000, to create the Civilian Internees Trust Fund. Simultaneously, and using the same funds, the government also created a £250 000 trust fund for ex-POWs. Given that there were 1500 civilian internees and 22 000 POWs, the civilians received a generous proportion of the available funds. POWs were obliged to prove their continuing disablement as a result of imprisonment but not required to give details of their financial situation. The terms of the funds for civilian internees were different and allowed greater discretion to the trustees to determine who would be eligible for the grant and the type of grant they would receive. Former internees had to provide evidence that they were 'suffering distress or hardship as a result of loss of limb or other permanent disability (physical or mental) directly referable to the conditions of internment'. Applicants also had to include information on their marital status and the number of children they had, and fill in a page detailing their financial position. The same information was to be supplied by dependants of a deceased internee, and they had to prove that the internee died during captivity or, if the death occurred after release, that it was directly referable to the conditions of internment.[36] A further £20 000 was voted to the fund in 1957 and distributed to existing applicants and any new cases that arose from renewed publicity.

Unsurprisingly, the trustees were not swamped with applications. By January 1953, only 200 of the eligible 1500 civilian internees or their dependants had made a claim.[37] The ex-POWs and their dependants were also slow off the mark: only 3000 of the 22 000 had applied. The Department of External Affairs was quick to offer an explanation: 'the restrictive nature of the terms of the Trust as stressed in the advertisements, has precluded many enquiries', its secretary informed the Prime Minister's Department in March 1953.[38] The primary concern of the Trustees, however, appears to have been a desire to police the boundary between civilian internees and POWs. They were most concerned that those former internees who had made a claim would receive more than they were entitled to. Their major worry was that civilians and, most especially, the widows of civilian internees would be seen to receive a more handsome compensation payment than military POWs. Brigadier Blackburn, the chairman of the fund, wrote to the prime minister:

> If . . . these people receive a substantial grant, it may be claimed in certain quarters that they are better treated than the dependants of deceased servicemen, who, apart from their pensions, have received only £32 from the distribution of Japanese assets.[39]

Yet this would be true for only the minority, widows in receipt of the New Guinea Civilian War Pension. Most internees received no other continuing rehabilitation benefits from the government. As one former internee who spent the war at Santo Tomas and Los Banos camps in the Philippines reminded the trustees: 'There is no machinery for ex-internees to receive free medical treatment as exists for ex-servicemen'.[40] The prime minister was less worried than the trustees, and his department was less parsimonious and more inclined to be generous to people who had suffered. Had the trustees considered that some former internees had disabilities 'accentuated by their experiences'? Perhaps they should be 'treated with sympathy' and given 'the benefit of the doubt'? The trustees were also advised to be less strict about the asset clause: the financial position of an applicant should be 'not necessarily important, unless financial disadvantage is the only claim'.[41]

Some former internees considered the fund to be miserly. John Bryant, who was in his late forties when interned in Borneo, thought £25 000 was a 'paltry sum'. He waived his right to claim on the fund in order that those more deserving and needy should receive assistance.[42] Others thought that the terms of a grant, most specifically the essential requirement that former internees have a permanent disability, were unfair. 'Although my mother lost no limbs,' the daughter of one internee wrote, 'I know that she still has nightmares and sleepless nights'.[43] Reverend James Benson suggested that none of the Australians rescued from his Ramale Valley camp could claim to be permanently incapacitated. This was because the weak had already died: they were unable to survive the harsh conditions of internment. Benson objected to the proviso that he would only be eligible to receive a grant if he were a 'decrepit, broken down doddering invalid!!'. Next war, Benson insisted, he was going to get himself a job administering one of these funds.[44]

There were also former internees who thought that deprivation and suffering were so innate to the internment experience that they barely warranted description. 'I do not think their [sic] is any need for me to describe the hardships we went through', wrote former jockey Clive Whalan. 'We can thank our Lord that after our experience we came out alive and with out loss of limb. I think we suffered enough distress and hardship as we lost all our possessions and when released came back to our homeland penniless and received no help from any funds or associations'.[45] Whalan had been interned in Sumatra, where conditions had been particularly harsh. Allister Greig, a South Australian engineer in his mid-forties who lost half his body weight when interned in Changi, responded to the question about continuing hardship with the following terse note: 'no one who experienced internment can ever be the same'.[46]

Others were obsessed with the detail of their medical conditions and thought piling on lists of their disabilities would obviate the need to have left the internment camp without a leg in order to receive a grant. The wife of one young man who had been captured at sea and interned in Changi stated that he was unable to confront the task of writing about his time as an internee. Yet she was fully versed in the detail of his lasting ill health, possibly because she bore the burden of his care:

> As to disabilities, he has not lost a limb, but is a terrible sufferer: through war causes and he is getting steadily worse, as regards his nerves. Here is a list of his disabilities: Malaria (BT), neurocirculatory asthenia, injury left parietal region of head with traumatic headaches; chronic appendicitis with associated dyspepsia; . . . conjunctivitis, injury left foot,

folliculitus . . . I think if anyone is entitled to a share he is. He was physically fit before he left here, now he is a wreck with failing eyesight.[47]

The former editor of the *South China Post*, Queenslander Richard
Cloake, who spent the war interned in Hong Kong, was aware that
applications to the fund had been slow.

> I am making this application, however, in the hope, however faint, that
> the scope of relief from the fund will be broadened. I read that applica-
> tions on the present grounds are tardy and I suggest that this is because,
> as in my case, the losses of most internees were material rather than phys-
> ical.
>
> As such, however, they were very real and they are still being felt.
> Many caught (like myself) in essential jobs lost all their possession and
> nearly four years' earnings through the accident that they were not in
> the forces. I feel that at least some nominal recompense should be made
> to those who seek it and I am raising my small (probably futile) voice to
> that end.
>
> I do so, believe me, very respectfully and diffidently, but I believe that
> internees seemingly overlooked by both Britain and Australia have a
> genuine case.[48]

One Salvation Army missionary interned in China agreed: 'civilians
chief injury was the material losses as well as the physical and mental
suffering of the time'. He was also inclined, as Claude Coats had been,
to point out that POWs received full pay, full medical treatment upon
return and in a material sense had lost only their kit. 'Prisoners of war
only suffered physically'. Civilians, in contrast, 'usually *lived* in the foreign land', lost all their assets, received no pay during internment and
no rehabilitation. 'Is it no more reasonable that seeing the fund is from
seized assets of former Japanese residents in Australia, that it should
come to folk who lost *their* assets in China or Japan', he concluded.[49]
'It is hard not to feel a bit bitter about the whole business', a woman
interned in China complained, 'as the Japanese just walked in to our
homes and confiscated everything. We lost our homes, furniture and
valuables and they have never been forced to repay us'.[50]

Some former internees, and their dependants, interpreted the terms
of the fund as imposing a means-test upon their eligibility and were
appalled at the distinction thus drawn between themselves and former
POWs. 'What exactly is meant by "cash on hand"', one applicant wrote.
'Sometimes I have in purse £5 sometimes 5/–.'[51] Lorna Hosking, eligible

to claim as the dependant of a deceased internee, wrote to the fund on behalf of herself and other 'New Guinea' widows:

> I was bitterly disappointed when I received this form & realized there is to be a means test & 'investigation'.
>
> It is now 11 1/2 years since our group had to abandon our husbands & our homes, & all have had enough courage & determination to establish themselves & their families. Many had to work very hard to do this & deserve the recognition that a payment from this fund could give.
>
> All have told me that they would greatly prefer an equal allocation to all & be spared the humiliation of filling in this application form.
>
> I will enquire of my local Federal member the reason for the Civilian Fund being administered in this way instead of the method used for its military counterpart. So you need not waste any more of it on postage to me.
>
> Yours faithfully,
> Mrs L. Hosking.[52]

Frank Merritt, who had protested a decade earlier about being billed for his repatriation costs, commented that: 'The terms under which Australian ex-internees may claim compensation are without precedent in other countries and are astonishing to say the least'.[53] He too objected to the conditional and contingent nature of grants made under the terms of the fund. The widows of the men lost in New Guinea were appalled at the invasive questioning. 'The military widows had none of this dreadful business', Mona Bruckshaw complained, 'but were just given their money . . . Before last Christmas'. When providing details of her marriage, she further commented that she had been given away by the then Administrator General Wisdom – 'It was all quite in order'.[54] Lily Banks, widow of a New Guinea man, thought that 'all this questioning is ridiculous – for a few pounds'. In the end she resorted to sarcasm: 'I do not know the colour of my grandparents eyes'.[55] Another former internee objected so strenuously to the 'means test' that he let his application lapse rather than 'undergo this further humiliation'.[56] The trustees never bothered to advise him that since printing the forms, they had decided on the advice of the Prime Minister's Department to make their decisions 'without regard to the applicant's financial status'.[57] And indeed, those claimants who simply ignored the financial questions were not taken to task.

An element of judgement did enter the trustees' decisions, and applicants were sufficiently versed in the language of welfare to identify elements of 'charity' when they saw them. 'I appeal for justice not charity', one applicant stated.[58] 'The loss of my breadwinner has meant that I must work hard,' Edna Greenwood wrote to the secretary of the fund, 'but I cannot claim to be in the extreme need of charity'. 'I felt that I was a candidate for compensation, rather than a supplicant for relief', complained another.[59] Means-testing, when combined with questions about marital status and the need for evidence from doctors and psychiatrists, caused some to question the equity of the arrangement. 'I can only conclude with "Let right be done"', wrote Amy Westwood, 'I have faith and I am not asking for charity but I feel I have a legitimate claim'.[60] 'I thought that perhaps some consideration might be shown to all of us who were interned', wrote one who had been interned in Changi, 'we were interned through no fault of our own'.[61] Some applicants who had fallen on hard times pointed to the expense of obtaining doctor's certificates: 'I have not had much time or money to go running to doctors', one separated mother of two told the Trustees.[62]

Sometimes the trustees' decisions did seem harsh. They were inclined to give generously to the widows of men captured in the external territories, even when recipients like Lorna Hosking withdrew her claim in protest at the means-testing. She still received a basic £50 grant. Former internees themselves were not always so fortunate. Robert Roope, who had worked before the war as a stenographer to the engineer-in-chief of the Shanghai Power Company, was denied any grant. In his still-perfect script, written on note paper from Long Bay gaol where he had been detained for failing to pay a maintenance debt for his children while unemployed, Roope detailed how his ailments arising from internment had prevented him from finding work. Roope's faith that the prison doctor would forward a medical certificate proved unfounded; the fund's administrators did not receive it and denied him any grant. The stigma of imprisonment in his home society seems to have militated against Roope receiving any consideration, despite his life being so clearly affected by internment by the Japanese.[63]

There is a sense among some former internees who corresponded with the fund that they deserved compensation and reparation for all they had suffered, and a corresponding frustration that they could find no state or department of government willing to hear them out. As victims of war, former internees felt entitled to compensation from the state. But which state, which office, which department? Five years after his release from internment in China, James Lewis died at the age of forty-six from the after-effects of malnutrition and abuse. He left behind a young widow and three children; the fourth was born two weeks after his death. His wife, Marie, wrote that she expected to live at least another forty years, and that she was 'beginning to doubt if this will be long enough to see some measure of justice given my children'. She despaired about 'the wreck that circumstances have made of my life'.[64] Another former internee wrote: 'I paid rates and taxes all those years' and deserved some compensation for wartime suffering.[65] Ruby Taylor, the former employer of alleged collaborator Wynette McDonald, stated that she had lost her business and all her worldly possessions in China:

> I lodged my claim for these with Canberra on my return to Australia thru Senator Cooper. My opinion is that 'Japan' should pay me for all this. I don't expect my Government or China to pay me but I do expect my Government to see that Japan does pay me. I returned to Australia without a penny after three years internment.[66]

The former internees who wrote to the fund thinking that it would reimburse their stolen, confiscated or destroyed assets were to be sorely disappointed. When the fund closed in the 1960s, the average grant for successful claimants was £140, but this did not settle the claims for the loss of businesses, homes and livelihoods.[67] Throughout the fund's decade-long operation, the trustees always remained anxious that the public not perceive that civilian internees were receiving more than their military counterparts. This continued despite the Prime Minister's Department's advice that they should relax a little and give applicants the 'benefit of the doubt'. At times, they appear to have been insufficiently sympathetic to people who had endured a difficult war. At one point, the chairman of the fund, Brigadier Blackburn, expressed frustration that most of the applicants were old anyway and that:

> The question arises in the mind of some of my co-trustees whether it is intended in cases such as these a substantial grant should be made for what, after all, is little more than a failure of health common to most of us as the years overtake us.[68]

One former internee, who was one of the few civilian men to be liberated from Rabaul, had a trustee write in the margins of his application '"stress" complaints indeed!'[69] The Treasury in fact considered that 'in comparison with ex-prisoners of war . . . ex-internees and their dependants have been well treated'.[70] The mother of one young man interned in Japan, whose postwar years had been blighted by continued mental instability and unemployment, was told when she enquired again in the early 1960s whether there might be some further money available to assist with his rehabilitation that her son had already 'receive[d] grants totalling £142.17.6 which is an amount in excess of the total per-capita payments to each ex-serviceman'.[71] Yet the man himself had written to the fund stating that 'the amount granted certainly assisted me and was received with gratitude but in the intervening years my condition has not improved and as each year proves that I am not going to "outgrow" these disabilities, I fear for the future and my old age'.[72]

The records of the Civilian Internees Trust Fund clearly demonstrate that internees felt they had some entitlement to compensation as Australian citizens who had suffered as a consequence of their nation's involvement in war. George Walker's daughter, Joan Dodwell, expressed her confusion over how to interpret a war spent as a civilian internee in the following way:

> I was not fighting for my country (as much as I would like to have been) when taken prisoner by the Japanese, but I am an Australian and I did lose all but what I arrived home in, & that was donated by the Australian Red Cross, & at the age of twenty had to start my life in Australia with no assistance from my parents who had also lost everything they possessed. I have since lost my Dad whom the Japanese took away from me for 3 years, and whom I blame for his death.[73]

Others even disputed the definition of what constituted war service and contested the right of former servicemen and women to be the most well-rewarded beneficiaries of repatriation benefits. The administration of the Civilian Internees Trust Fund showed that those in power saw former internees' receipt of a grant as a privilege rather than a right; this reflected older attitudes of philanthropy and charity. Former civilian internees, however, had just as much difficulty re-establishing themselves and adjusting to life post-captivity as demobbed servicemen. Sybil Fernandez wrote:

> It is hard not to feel a bit bitter about the whole business as the Japanese just walked into our homes and confiscated everything. We lost our homes, furniture and valuables and they have never been forced to repay us. A lot of us lost a lot more than that, and coming back here, and finding no decent place to live within a reasonable price, and having to start life anew trying to earn a living in place where if you are over 30 years of age you are too old for most jobs, even though you might be quite capable. It has not been easy at all.[74]

And what of those few, comparatively privileged internees who had been captured in Australian external territories and were entitled to both the New Guinea Civilian War Pension and to receive compensation from the War Damage Commission? The War Damage Commission considered that Kathleen Bignell's claims for the values of her property in New Guinea prior to the war were 'fantastic'. In 1947, her claim was assessed at one-third of the value she requested. Owing to her bankruptcy in 1939, the sum total of her compensation was paid to the New Guinea trustee.

At this time, Kathleen Bignell was also informed that she would now receive the Civilian War Pension. In June 1947, she wrote to the Department of External Affairs. The war had clearly become, to her, one long continuum of loss:

> The Repatriation Commission evidently consider that 2/6 a week was all my son was worth to me before he gave his life for his country.
>
> I also, on two occasions 1937 & 1942 have willingly given all that had in life to offer & also 3 1/2 of the best years of my life –
>
> Now I am just as much as a prisoner with starvation & privation facing me.
>
> I am not allowed to return to New Guinea to try & start again . . . I am thus compelled to starve in Australia on 2/6 a week.
>
> I am unfit for work and have been laid up for over a month in my tent with cold & pleurisy from exposure. Dr & medicines £2-18-0.
>
> Please do something for me. I feel absolutely desperate over this final blow.[75]

Living in a tent, financially insecure and unwell, Kathleen Bignell felt that she was still 'just as much a prisoner' as she had been in Japan. Her complaints did have some effect. From 1947, instead of the 2/6 a week (which would have taken nearly six months to cover her medical debt), as one of the few civilian internees entitled to some form of ongoing compensation, she received the slightly more generous widow's pension as the dependant of her son who had been killed in the war. She never did return to New Guinea. Kathleen Bignell died in December 1955, ten years after her release from internment. The only assets that made up her estate were the recent pension payments that had remained uncollected owing to her death.

CONCLUSION

The relative invisibility of civilian internees in Australian commemorations of the Pacific war is linked to the centrality that the POW experience has come to hold in the cultural memory of that conflict. In one sense, civilian internees are simply swamped by the numerical preponderance of POWs. After all, there were 1500 civilian internees compared to 22 000 POWs. This book suggests that the reasons for the virtual absence of civilian internees from celebrations of Australia's experience of the Pacific war rest on more than mere numbers alone.

The official and community ambivalence to civilian internees in the 1940s and 1950s did not lend itself to their early incorporation into national commemorations of sacrifice and suffering during World War II. Although there were common concerns expressed by internees – resentment about the distinction between themselves and POWs, the sense that internees did not fit in common ways of understanding sacrifice and suffering – they never developed into any form of public activism. In the years since then, the paucity of extensive support networks among former internees has compounded this reticence. Former civilian internees have been far less likely than POWs to form networks of 'fictive kinship'. The term is Jay Winter's, and he defines these networks of fictive kin as 'families of remembrance', usually constituted by survivors who share a common, often traumatic experience.[1] Returned POWs moved quickly to establish precisely these sorts of memory communities. Civilian internees, many of whom could not return to their former homes owing to political developments in the postwar world, dispersed more widely and rapidly in the years after their release.

The bonds of fictive kinship are important not just for individual well-being, but for the way in which a group deals with the public representation and understandings of its wartime experiences. Such networks frequently occupy the 'space between individual memory and the national theatre of collective memory choreographed by social and political leaders'.[2] Former POWs and their associations have been singularly successful in opening up that space, and in opening up new ways of incorporating their war experiences into national commemorations of Australians at war. Former civilian internees have not enjoyed these bonds to the same extent; neither have their experiences shared that public prominence. Collective memories are not simply forged through the top-down direction and organisation of remembrance campaigns. They tend to coalesce around the intersection of public pomp and communities of remembrance. Civilian internees have not fared well in either of these arenas, and they remain relatively invisible in government-sanctioned commemorations of the Pacific war. The most cohesive communities before internment – the religious orders, the missionary organisations – were not by nature given to big-noting their suffering for public-political purposes. They were more likely to point to internment as a test of faith.

There is one prominent war experience to which the Japanese-run internment camps have always stood in uneasy and awkward relation. The Holocaust, and the horror of state-sanctioned murder, stands astride both public and academic discussion of forced detention. There are parallels between types of imprisonment, but the contrasts are more stark than the similarities. Civilian internees of the Japanese found themselves in internment camps through circumstance rather than design; they numbered in the hundreds of thousands not the millions; their deaths were most often from starvation, disease or neglect rather than as a result of a planned program of extermination; most of them survived rather than perished in the camps. The difference was put most succinctly by a distinguished Dutch jurist, B. V. A. Roling, who sat in judgment at the Tokyo War Crimes trials in the late 1940s: 'Japan wanted to expel the colonial powers from Asia. But there was no plan to exterminate all Europeans.'[3] Consequently, there is no word for the war experiences of civilian internees of the Japanese that even comes close to the power of 'Holocaust' or 'Shoah'. Those who were executed in European concentration camps had been persecuted on the grounds of religion, race, sexuality or political allegiance. These elements of persecution, of deliberate genocide, have led survivors and their communities to search for meaning in the madness, to seek explanation in the realm of the metaphysical and sacred.

There exists no single, powerful word like Holocaust to which a survivor of a Japanese internment camp can lay claim. This is worth mentioning because the difficulties in naming the war experiences of civilians interned by the Japanese, the lack of consensus, the lack of *gravitas* which even some survivors of the camps have themselves perpetuated, actually says a great deal about the personal and broader cultural dilemmas faced in bearing witness to this war experience in peacetime. If military service has circumscribed national discussions about sacrifice in wartime, and thereby caused the war experiences of civilian internees to be largely overlooked, the Holocaust has become the international benchmark for the trauma of internment in war and its scale and depth may well have beleaguered internees' attempts to find a place for their histories.[4] Comparison, insidious by any measure, was almost inevitable and it began early. War correspondents reporting on the liberation of the camps commented on their similarity or difference to Belsen, which had immediately entered the cultural lexicon as a reference for suffering and inhumane treatment. The AAP's special representative in Singapore, for instance, informed his readers that 'Sime Rd was not another Belsen or Buchenwald, but certain periods of the imprisonment were hard and bitter'.[5] In the postwar years, some internees, when corresponding with the Australian government, resolutely referred to their places of detention as 'concentration camps', almost as an act of defiance.

The one exception to the general neglect of this issue in Australia relates to civilians interned in the Pacific island territories Australia had administered under a League of Nations mandate since the early 1920s. Gordon Thomas once remarked of the civilian men who had been left behind in Rabaul that the 'iron of injustice had entered their souls'.[6] The same could be said of their descendants, people who had ties as members of the Australian colonial community in Rabaul. The civilian men who died on the *Montevideo Maru* have received attention in part because their families did form networks of 'fictive kinship'. These descendants have been active in organising memorials in Rabaul, publishing memoirs and other accounts and, more recently, running websites.[7]

Although they were already commemorated in New Guinea, the civilian men from the mandated territories became the first civilian internees to be recognised by a war memorial on the Australian mainland. A plaque commemorating the *Montevideo Maru* tragedy was opened in Ballarat as part of the privately initiated Australian ex-POW memorial in February 2004. Nevertheless, despite the *Montevideo Maru* constituting one of the most dramatic losses of Australian lives in a single incident in World War II, it remains a story peripheral to mainstream commemorative activity.[8] The five Australian men who survived internment in New Guinea, and the ten Australian nuns who were also interned there and liberated at the conclusion of hostilities, have received far less attention.[9]

The case of internment in New Guinea is interesting because, unlike the other locations where Australian civilians were captured and interned which were British, American and Dutch possessions, New Guinea was nominally Australian territory. The families of those Australians interned in New Guinea, and the few who survived their internment there, have always spoken in particular terms about the claims of this group. Theirs was a language of responsibility and belonging. During the war, the New Guinea Women's Club had written to the Minister for External Territories, pleading for the release of their men. They described the New Guinea internees as 'Pioneers of Australia's Territories' who had proved 'so vital in the defence of the Australian main land'. Most significantly, they referred to the New Guinea internees as 'the only civilian prisoners captured on Australian soil'.[10] This is a powerful phrase, but it is one that the Australian government has never appropriated or adopted.

After the war, the Australian government tacitly acknowledged responsibility for the fate of civilians captured in Australian territories, by granting extensive benefits to them.[11] This has rarely attracted any publicity or attention; neither did the civilian recipients of the $25 000 compensation payment that the Australian government paid in 2001 to Australians detained, imprisoned or interned by the Japanese in World War II. Some former internees have even been presented with medals. In 1999, Joyce Coutts (née McGahan), one of the government nurses captured in Rabaul and transferred to Japan, received a series of medals at a quiet ceremony at her nursing home. Aged ninety, Joyce Coutts accepted the Australian Prisoner of War Commemorative Medal, the International Prisoner of War Commemorative Medal and

International World Peace Commemorative Medal. She also received a Certificate of Appreciation from the federal government.[12] It was a far cry from the early 1940s, when the Department of Defence had denied an OBE to Dorothy Maye, who had also nursed soldiers under fire in New Guinea. In the twenty-first century, civilian internees receive compensation and certificates but still no official commemoration.

Although the New Guinea internees and their descendants could be considered a relatively privileged group of internees, given their entitlement to particular forms of welfare, the Australian government has never shown much willingness to draw attention to their experiences or to commemorate their sacrifices. Relatives shocked by the virtual elimination of the prewar male community demanded a full government inquiry into the failure to evacuate civilians from Rabaul. The government would not consent. There may well have been military and strategic reasons for the Australian government not wanting to revisit the Japanese occupation of New Britain. In the immediate postwar period there were also broader, international tensions around the issues of imperialism and colonialism that militated against any extended consideration or commemoration of the fate of civilians in colonial possessions. The end of World War II saw a new emphasis on self-determination in international forums such as the United Nations, and a concomitant disdain for older languages of colonialism. In the context of the Cold War, of course, 'self-determination' for many countries was an entirely contingent process, but the dawn of the post-colonial era made prewar notions of possession and pioneering in relation to external territories somewhat obsolete.

Yet the Australian 'Territorians' – as those with an interest in New Guinea and its surrounding islands called themselves – were determined to re-create their prewar life, which was an essentially segregated community in which whites sought to control the activities and labour of indigenous peoples. Committed to the pioneering and colonialist presence in the Territories, the community's mouthpiece, the conservative *Pacific Islands Monthly* magazine, was expressly critical. Editorials chided the 'spiritless ranks' of the Chifley Labor government, and argued that the Minister for the Territories did not support their community. The minister allegedly 'hated' the Territories's European population, who were 'sturdy individualists'.[13] His government was also accused of possessing a 'positive passion for sometimes ill-considered "reform"'. The Labor government was making an 'attempt to socialise New Guinea'.[14] Although the Labor government did indeed offer the people of New Guinea a 'New Deal', and took steps to abolish the indentured labour system, reforms were limited and for many years after the war under both ALP and Liberal governments Australian colonialism merely assumed a new guise in New Guinea.[15]

Although there are many issues here, it is interesting to note the alignment of civilian internees with a colonialist community clearly out of step with contemporary international developments in race relations and self-determination. Already in 1946, the language used by Territorians sounded dated, the remnant of a bygone era. Yet in the postwar period the Australian territory of Papua and the formerly mandated territories of New Guinea became Papua New Guinea, and the United Nations granted Australia 'trusteeship' of the Territory until its independence in 1975. It might just be possible that the public commemoration of civilians captured on 'Australian soil' could bring unwelcome attention to this continuing colonialist blind spot in Australian foreign policy.

The absence of civilian internees from commemorations of the Pacific war in Australia is a multi-faceted phenomenon. The numerical preponderance of POWs might begin to offer an explanation, but it is actually POWs' status as citizen–soldiers that ultimately ensures their commemorative visibility. Civilian internees have stood in awkward relation to the links between service, sacrifice and nation, and their confinement to camps that did not readily fit the division between front and home front that has dominated war talk compounded this ambiguity. Furthermore, in the postwar era the Holocaust has assumed centrality in American and European narratives of trauma and war, and internees of the Japanese have struggled to confront the dominance of that particular historical experience of detention and suffering. Apart from the staggering scale of the Holocaust tragedy, and its program of planned annihilation, one of its special horrors was that the killers were members of an industrialised European society. They were 'civilised', white representatives of a society not dissimilar in many ways from others in Western Europe. In this sense then, it is not just the extreme suffering of the Holocaust's victims but the actions of its perpetrators as representatives of a European culture corrupted and perverted by prejudice that has driven public discussion. The tortures and abuse endured by some internees of the Japanese were, in contrast, assumed to be easy to explain according to popular racism of the day: they were the actions of an 'uncivilised' Asian race that had now shown its true barbarism. The cultural 'otherness' of the Japanese captor has driven voyeuristic speculation and licensed xenophobia, but has stifled more sensitive debate about the meaning of suffering and the legacy of captivity. An additional explanation for the commemorative invisibility of civilian internees is more speculative. As reminders of the colonialist and imperialist past, in an era when self-determination was the preferred course for previously colonised nations but one not always followed, former civilian internees held the potential to bring blind spots to the light.

The final words belong to former internees and they remind us that, however awkwardly internees were placed in relation to prominent concepts of war, sacrifice and nation, the personal costs of internment were keenly felt. Ian Begley, the son of Salvation Army missionaries, spent part of his adolescence interned by the Japanese in a mission school compound at Yangchow, a village on the Grand Canal north of Shanghai. In December 2003, he described his feelings about compensation and commemoration as follows:

> I shall always be grateful to the Australian Government for the grant of $25,000 paid to former internees. Sadly we had to wait 55 long years for that compensation. In the mean time, both my parents and my elder sister [who were also interned] had died. Only my brother and I remain to reflect on what might have been. For too many years Australia has been oblivious to the fact of civilian internees. This is understandable in the light of the experiences of the Diggers in Changi and the Burma Railway and the heroic work of Sir Edward 'Weary' Dunlop. Whilst there have been a few small accounts published, the conditions faced by military POWs and civilian internees cannot be compared . . . It has taken a long, long time for recognition – and, as far as I know – there has never been any commemoration. However, that does not lesson the personal, emotional cost to a teenage lad, who was a prisoner during the years of his important growth and development.[16]

One of the first internee stories in this book was about the Merritt family's outrage about the Australian government's intention to charge them for their repatriation from a Philippines internment camp. It was an early indication of an ongoing dilemma about how civilian internees were placed in relation to the way Australians understood war. Years later, Mary Merritt reflected on her time as a civilian internee in more personal terms. 'We very nearly did not come out of that internment camp alive', she wrote of her family's time in Santo Tomas camp in the Philippines.

> Every night, towards the end, when I kissed my daughter good-night I wondered if she would be alive in the morning. Only those who were interned under similar conditions could understand how long it took to put the war and the Japanese out of our minds.[17]

NOTES

Introduction

1 Susan Sontag, *Regarding the Pain of Others*, Penguin, London, 2003, p. 21.

2 A key compilation such as *Australians: Historical Statistics* lists internees *within* Australia and Australian prisoner-of-war statistics. It makes no mention of the estimated 1500 Australian civilians held in Japanese-controlled internment camps throughout the Asia–Pacific region. For statistics see 'Statement "A": Analysis of the Total Number of Australian Civilian Internees by Location of Internment' in CITF, Final report: Covering the Operations of the Trust 1952–1962, 29 October 1962, Typescript, NAA series B512/1, box 1. The exception to the general ignorance relates to civilians captured in New Guinea. See A. J. Sweeting, 'Civilian Wartime Experience in the Territories of Papua and New Guinea', in Paul Hasluck, *The Government and the People 1942–45*, series IV, vol. II, Australian War Memorial, Canberra, 1970, pp. 668–708; Hank Nelson, 'The Troops, the Town and the Battle: Rabaul 1942', *Journal of Pacific History*, vol. 27, no. 2, 1992, and 'The Return to Rabaul 1945', *Journal of Pacific History*, vol. 30, no. 2, 1995; Patsy Adam-Smith, *Prisoners of War: From Gallipoli to Korea*, Viking, Melbourne, 1992; Margaret Reeson, *A Very Long War: The Families who Waited*, Melbourne University Press, Melbourne, 2000. See also Prue Torney-Parlicki, '"Unpublishable Scoops": Australian Journalists as Prisoners of the Japanese 1941–5', *Journal of Australian Studies*, no. 66, 2000, pp. 180–9.

3 Stephanie Sherwood, *Growing Up as a Foreigner in Shanghai: Recollections*, Mini Publishing, Sydney, 2004.

4 'Courage and Caring: Mrs Colonel Edith Begley promoted to glory', *War Cry*, 1 September 1989, p. 4.

5 'German New Guinea', colonised by the Germans in the 1880s, had been occupied by the Australian military since 1914. After the conclusion of World War I, the territory continued to be under Australian military administration until the formal granting of a C Class mandate by the League of Nations in 1921. The Territory of New Guinea then transferred to civil administration. See Roger C. Thompson, 'The Formation of Australia's New Guinea Policies 1919–1925', *Journal of Pacific History*,

vol. 25, no. 1, 1990, pp. 68–84. See also John Dademo Waiko, *A Short History of Papua New Guinea*, Oxford University Press, Melbourne, 1993, pp. 82–107.

6 Donald Denoon with Stewart Firth, Jocelyn Linnekin, Malama Meleisea and Karen Nero (eds), *The Cambridge History of the Pacific Islanders*, Cambridge University Press, Cambridge, 1997, p. 255.

7 This is how his journalist colleagues described him to an intelligence officer who had made inquiries in 1941. See R. Powell, Lt Col General Staff, Eastern Command to Director, Security Service, Canberra, 17 July 1941 in NAA, A367, C70868, Percival Jack. See also Pat Burgess, *Warco: Australian Reporters at War*, William Heinemann, Melbourne, 1986, pp. 99–105. For biographical details on Jack Percival (1907–1988) see Torney-Parlicki, '"Unpublishable Scoops"', p. 181.

8 Christopher Thorne, *Allies of a Kind: The United States, Britain and the war against Japan, 1941–45*, Hamish Hamilton, London, 1978, pp. 3–5.

9 For a full listing of civilian internment centres see Van Waterford, *Prisoners of the Japanese in World War II: Statistical History, Personal Narratives and Memorials Concerning POWs in Camps and on Hellships, Civilian Internees, Asian Slave Labourers and Others Captured in the Pacific Theater*, McFarland and Company, Jefferson NC and London, 1994.

10 Miriam Kochan, *Britain's Internees in the Second World War*, Macmillan, London, 1983; Margaret Bevege, *Behind Barbed Wire: Internment in Australia during World War Two*, University of Queensland Press, Brisbane, 1993; Yuriko Nagata, *Unwanted Aliens: Japanese Internment in Australia*, University of Queensland Press, Brisbane, 1996; Bill Bunbury, *Rabbits and Spaghetti: Captives and Comrades, Australians, Italians and the War 1939–1945*, Fremantle Arts Centre Press, Fremantle, 1995; David Dutton, *One of Us? A Century of Australian Citizenship*, University of New South Wales Press, Sydney, 2002; Cate Elkner et al., *Enemy Aliens: The Internment of Italian Migrants in Australia in World War Two*, Connor Court Publishing, Bacchus Marsh, 2005; Kay Saunders and Roger Daniels (eds), *Alien Justice: Wartime Internment in Australia and North America*, University of Queensland Press, Brisbane, 2000; Klaus Neumann, 'A Doubtful Character: Wolf Klaphake', <www.uncommonlives.naa.gov.au>, accessed 30 November 2005; Christine Winter, 'The long arm of the Third Reich: internment of New Guinea Germans in Tatura', *Journal of Pacific History*, vol. 38, no. 1, June 2003, pp. 85–108; Anthony Kaukas, 'Images from Loveday: internment in South Australia, 1939–45', *Journal of the Historical Society of South Australia*, no. 29, 2001, pp. 47–57; Kay Saunders and Helen Taylor, 'The enemy within? The Process of internment of enemy aliens in Queensland 1939–45', *Australian Journal of Politics and History*, vol. 34, no. 1, 1988, pp. 16–27.

11 Australian Red Cross Society: Civilian Evacuees from the Philippines, encl. In J. Newman Morris to Prime Minister, 14 April 1945, in NAA, MP742/1, 282/1/731.

12 NAA, B2455, Merritt Frank Leslie. Service Record, B13/0, 1934/7225, Merritt.

13 Mrs Mary Merritt to Minister for Information, 4 June 1945, NAA, A1379/1, EPJ1108, Merritt (Mrs) Mary Bertha.

14 For further biographical details about Dorothy Jenner (1891–1985) see Bridget Griffen-Foley, 'First Lady of the Airwaves', *Eureka Street*, June 2005. See also Dorothy Jenner, *Darlings, I've Had a Ball*, Ure Smith, Sydney, 1975, p. 164.

15 Jenner, Dorothy Gordon. Papers 1921, 1938–47, including correspondence and prisoner-of-war camp diaries: ML MSS 5184, Microfilmed as CY Reel 2690, War Diary, 20 December 1941 (Jenner Papers).

16 Jenner Papers, Diary, 25 December 1941.

17 Jenner, *Darlings, I've Had a Ball*, p. 213.

18 Thomas to Civilian Internees Trust Fund, 28 November 1952, in NAA, B510 No. 294, Thomas, Edward Llewellyn Gordon.

19 Ibid.

20 Alan S. Walker, *Medical Services of the R. A. N. and R. A. A. F. With a Section on Women in the Army Medical Services*, Australian War Memorial, Canberra, 1961, pp. 441–55; Catherine Kenny, *Captives: Australian Army Nurses in Japanese Prison Camps*, University of Queensland Press, Brisbane, 1986; Jan Bassett, *Guns and Brooches: Australian Army Nursing from the Boer War to the Gulf War*, Oxford University Press, Melbourne, 1992, pp. 133–52; Waterford, *Prisoners of the Japanese in World War II*, pp. 207–8. The women were interned at Yacht Club II, Yokohama and Totsuka in Kanagawa.

21 This group included A. Chauncy, A. Evenson, A. Cameron, H. J. Badger, W. Korn, C. Ostrom, J. Beaumont, Bachmann [initials not known], K. A. Sherwood, Wheatley [initials not known] and a missionary; see *Pacific Islands Monthly*, November 1945, p. 7.

22 For a complete list of civilians missing in the Territory of New Guinea see NAA, A518, EQ16/2/1. The Our Lady of the Sacred Heart Nuns were Sr Flavia (Catherine O'Sullivan), Sr Borgia (Mary Kelly), Sr Adela (Kathleen McGrath), Sr Philomena (Philomena Bryant), Sr Editha (Jessie Macrae), Sr Michael (Ivy Macrae), Sr Immaculata (M. Mazengarb), Sr Felicitas (E. McFadden), Sr Berenice (Dymphna Twohill), Sr Marcella (Ellen Hyndes).

23 Information on Gordon Thomas's library is contained in his claim for war damages in NAA, SP24/1, 890, Gordon Thomas.

24 'How Rabaul's civilians met their fate', *Pacific Islands Monthly*, November 1945, p. 15.

25 Gordon Thomas, 'Rabaul 1942–45: An Account of four years as a prisoner of war of the Japanese', ML MSS 1425 Thomas, Gordon, Papers, pp. 2, 21.

26 Hank Nelson, 'Measuring the Railway: From Individual Lives to National History', in Gavan McCormack and Hank Nelson (eds), *The Burma–Thailand Railway: Memory and History*, Allen & Unwin, Sydney, 1993, p. 23.

27 Apart from works already cited, see for example Hank Nelson, *P. O.W: Prisoners of War Australians Under Nippon*, ABC Enterprises, Sydney, 1985; Joan Beaumont, *Gull Force: Survival and Leadership in Captivity 1941–45*, Allen and Unwin, Sydney, 1988; Adam-Smith, *Prisoners of War*; Stephen Garton, *The Cost of War: Australians Return*, Oxford University Press, Melbourne, 1996; Michael McKernan, *This Pain Never Ends: The Pain of Separation and Return*, University of Queensland Press, Brisbane, 2001.

28 The earliest and most influential Dutch study is D. van Velden, *De Japanse Interneringskampen voor burgers gedurende de tweede wereldoorlog*, J. B. Wolters, Groningen, 1963. For a Dutch study written in English see Esther Captain, 'The Gendered Process of Remembering War Experiences: Memories about the Second World War in the Dutch East Indies', *European Journal of Women's Studies*, vol. 4, 1997, pp. 389–95. For studies of civilian internment, see A. V. H. Hartendorp, *The Japanese Occupation of the Philippines*, Bookmark, Manila, 1967; Lavinia Warner and John Sandilands, *Women Beyond the Wire: A Story of Prisoners of the Japanese, 1942–45*, Michael Joseph, London, 1982; Joseph Kennedy, *British Civilians and the Japanese War in Malaya and Singapore, 1941–45*, Macmillan, London, 1987;

Margaret Brooks, 'Passive in War? Women internees in the Far East 1942–45', in Sharon Macdonald, Pat Holden and Shirley Ardener (eds), *Images of Women in Peace and War: Cross-Cultural and Historical Perspectives*, Macmillan Education, London, 1987, pp. 166–78; Lynn Z. Bloom, 'Till Death Do Us Part: Men and Women's Interpretations of Wartime Internment', *Women's Studies International Forum*, vol. 10, no. 1, 1987, pp. 75–83; Shirley Fenton Huie, *The Forgotten Ones: Women and Children Under Nippon*, Angus & Robertson, Sydney, 1992; Bernice Archer, 'The Women of Stanley: internment in Hong Kong, 1942–45', *Women's History Review*, vol. 5, no. 3, 1996, pp. 373–99; Bernice Archer, '"A Low-Key Affair": Memories of Civilian Internment in the Far East 1942–1945', in Martin Evans and Ken Lunn (eds), *War and Memory in the Twentieth Century*, Berg, Oxford, 1997, pp. 45–58; Frances B. Cogan, *Captured: The Japanese Internment of American Civilians in the Philippines, 1941–45*, University of Georgia Press, Athens, Georgia, 2000; Theresa Kaminski, *Prisoners in Paradise: American women in the wartime South Pacific*, University Press of Kansas, Lawrence, Kansas, 2000; Bernice Archer, *A Patchwork of Internment: The Internment of Western Civilians Under the Japanese, 1941–45*, Routledge Curzon, London, 2004.

29 Bernice Archer, *A Patchwork of Internment*, p. 8.
30 Gerald Horne, *Race War: White Supremacy and the Japanese Attack on the British Empire*, New York University Press, New York, 2004, p. 4.
31 *Sydney Morning Herald*, 27 April 1939, p. 9.
32 Peter Stanley, 'He's (not) coming south: the invasion that wasn't', in Steven Bullard and Tamura Keiko (eds), *From a Hostile Shore: Australia and Japan at War in New Guinea*, Australia–Japan Research Project, Australian War Memorial, Canberra, 2004, pp. 3–57.
33 Liz Reed, *Bigger Than Gallipoli: War, History and Memory in Australia*, University of Western Australia Press, Perth, 2004.
34 Penny Summerfield, 'Gender and War in the Twentieth Century', *International History Review* xix, no. 1, February 1997, pp. 3–15; Marilyn Lake and Joy Damousi, 'Warfare, History and Gender', in Joy Damousi and Marilyn Lake (eds), *Gender and War: Australians at War in the Twentieth Century*, Cambridge University Press, Cambridge, 1995, pp. 1–20; Miriam Cooke, 'WO-Man: Retelling the War Myth', in Miriam Cooke and Angela Woollacott (eds), *Gendering War Talk*, Princeton University Press, Princeton, 1993, pp. 117–204; Margaret Randolph Higgonet et al. (eds), *Behind the Lines: Gender and the Two World Wars*, Yale University Press, New Haven, Connecticut, 1987.
35 Although see E. Binks, *Through Japanese Hands For Three Years 1942–45*, Richard Whelvell (Bolton) Ltd, Lancashire, c. 1946; James Benson, *Prisoner's Base and Home Again*, Robert Hale, London, 1957; Alice Bowman, *Not Now Tomorrow*, Daisy Press, Sydney, 1996; Neil Begley, *An Australian's Childhood in China under the Japanese*, Kangaroo Press, Sydney, 1995; Audrey Begley-Bourke et al., *Separated For Service*, Salvation Army, Melbourne, 1994; Sherwood, *Growing Up as a Foreigner in Shanghai*.
36 Sheila Allen, *Diary of a Girl in Changi 1941–45*, Kangaroo Press, Sydney, 1994. There were reprints published in 1999 and 2004.
37 See, for example, AWM, 3DRL/7925, Papers of HR Slocombe Civilian Internee and AWM, PR87/188, Papers of Harold Leslie Murray, Civilian Internee, Changi, Sime Rd.
38 AWM, PR000015, Percival, Jack Papers.

1 Casualties of war

1 Gordon Thomas reported Page's efforts in 'How Rabaul's citizens met their fate', *Pacific Islands Monthly*, November 1945, pp. 9, 66. The advice given to Page is from War Cabinet Minutes, A2670/1, 36/42, cited in Hank Nelson, 'The Troops, the Town and the Battle: Rabaul 1942', *Journal of Pacific History*, vol. 27, no. 2, 1992, p. 215.

2 Lionel Wigmore, *Australia in the War of 1939–45*, series one, Army, vol. IV, *The Japanese Thrust*, Australian War Memorial, Canberra, [1957], 1968, pp. 392–418. Nelson, 'The Troops, the Town, the Battle', pp. 212–14.

3 ML MSS 1425, Thomas, 'Rabaul 1942–45', p. 7.

4 Dorothy Jenner, *Darlings, I've Had a Ball*, Ure Smith, Sydney, 1975, pp. 185–9.

5 Berenice Archer, *A Patchwork of Internment: The Internment of Western Civilians under the Japanese 1941–45*, Routledge Curzon, London, 2004, pp. 33–6.

6 Broadcast noted in the diary of Bishop of New Guinea, Philip Strong, in David Wetherell (ed.), *The New Guinea Diaries of Philip Strong 1936–1945*, Macmillan, Melbourne, 1981, p. 65. Women and children from New Ireland flew out of Rabaul on 28 December 1941: Margaret Reeson, *A Very Long War: The Families Who Waited*, Melbourne University Press, Melbourne, 2000, p. 14.

7 Department of Veterans' Affairs, Australians at War Film Archive 0177, Berenice Twohill, transcript p. 120.

8 The nurses from the Namanula hospital were Alice Bowman, Joyce Olroyd-Harris, Joyce McGahan, Mary Goss, Grace Kruger and Jean McLellan. Dorothy Maye was stationed at Kavieng. The Methodist Mission nurses were Mavis Green, Jean Christopher, Dora Wilson and Dorothy Beale. The six AANS nurses were Lorna Whyte, Kathleen Parker, Marjory Anderson, Daisy 'Tootie' Keast, Eileen Callaghan and Mavis Cullen.

9 Wetherell (ed.), *The New Guinea Diaries of Philip Strong*, entry for 16 January 1942, p. 69.

10 Ibid., entry for 27 January 1942, p. 76.

11 Thomas, 'Rabaul 1942–45', p. 2.

12 E. C. Rowland, 'Faithful Unto Death', in Theo Aerts (ed.), *The Martyrs of Papua New Guinea: 333 Missionary Lives Lost During World War II*, University of Papua New Guinea Press, Port Moresby, 1994, pp. 55–7; Tony Matthews, 'Missionary Martyrs: Second World War 1939–1945', *Wartime*, no. 21, 2003, pp. 13–15; Robert Willson, 'A Canberra nurse who became a martyr', *Anglican Historical Society Journal*, no. 14, October 1992, pp. 37–41.

13 Wetherell (ed.), *The New Guinea Diaries of Philip Strong*, entry for 28 January 1942, p. 76.

14 James Benson, *Prisoners' Base and Home Again: The Story of a Missionary P.O.W.*, Robert Hale, London, 1957, pp. 14–18.

15 AWM, 3DRL/5092, Papers of Miss May Hayman, 419/11/7, 'Miss May Hayman's Last Letter before being captured by the Japanese and killed, early September 1941', to her sister Vi, August 1942.

16 Benson, *Prisoners' Base and Home Again*, p. 38.

17 NAA, A6237, Exhibit 66, dated 23 March 1943.

18 AWM, 3DRL5092, 419/11/7, Bishop of New Guinea to Mrs Waterman, 20 October 1942.

19 Wetherell (ed.), *The New Guinea Diaries of Philip Strong*, entries for 14 November 1942, pp. 136–7; 2 March 1943, p. 158; 23 March 1943, p. 167; 14 April 1943, p. 168; 27 October 1943, p. 187.

20 T. J. B. Donnelly (assistant manger) and M. H. Macfarlane (accountant) worked for Thailand Tin Mines. Keith Craigie (manager), R. Stratford (dredgemaster) and Norman Holt (accountant) worked for Straits Consolidated Ltd. For details, see NAA, A1608, 16/13/416.

21 NAA, A1066, IC 45/33/3/4/8, Reginald Stratford to Custodian of Enemy Property, 10 December 1945.

22 NAA, A1608, 16/13/416, 'Report on happenings at Pinyok, near Yala, South Siam . . .', prepared by M. H. Macfarlane, 12 January 1946.

23 NAA, A3317, 472/46, 'Resume of the experiences of M. H. Macfarlane and others in Siam from and inclusive of the 8th December 1941'.

24 This account based on a signed statement by R. A. Stratford, Moore and Cummins, all survivors of the incident who were interned in Changi, in NAA, A1066/4, IC45/20/1/7/1.

25 'Resume of the experiences of M. H. Macfarlane'.

26 NAA, A3317, 472/46, Statutory Declaration, R. A. Stratford, 15 February 1946.

27 Maureen Magness to Mrs Craigie, 26 December 1946, NAA, A1608/1, 16/13/416, Craigie, R. A.

28 This account based on a signed statement by R. A. Stratford, Moore and Cummins, all survivors of the incident who were interned in Changi, in NAA, A1066/4, IC45/20/1/7/1.

29 Rowland, 'Faithful Unto Death', p. 64.

30 The phrase the 'cultivation of hatred' is taken from Peter Gay, *The Cultivation of Hatred*, Norton, New York, 1993, and discussed in the context of total war in Jay Winter, 'Under cover of war: The Armenian genocide in the context of total war', in Jay Winter (ed.), *America and the Armenian Genocide of 1915*, Cambridge University Press, Cambridge, 2003, pp. 42–8.

31 NAA, A1461, EPCT50, War Claim Against Thailand – Geoffrey Scott-Settle.

32 NAA, B510, no. 161, Doris McCracken to Civilian Internees' Trust Fund (CITF), 7 July 1953.

33 Hank Nelson, 'The Return to Rabaul 1945', *Journal of Pacific History*, vol. 30, no. 2, 1995, p. 133.

34 *Pacific Islands Monthly*, December 1946, p. 6.

35 NAA, B510, no. 241, Hooper, George Stanley, Hooper to CITF, 15 December 1952.

36 NAA, B510, no. 326, Dimberline, Leo; B510, 209, Cherry, Robert; B510, 354, Creer, Reginald Charles; B510, 191, Ambrose, Frederick.

37 NAA, A10953, Item 6, Harry Slocombe, 'An Aussie Tramp in the Indies', War Crimes Commission [Principally] Diary of H. R. Slocombe.

38 ML, MSS 5184, Jenner, Dorothy Gordon, papers, 1921, 1938–47, microfilmed as CY Reel 2690 (Jenner Papers), Newspaper Notes, p. 7, 12 January 1942.

39 Ibid., Section 5 Notes, p. 6.

40 Gerald Horne, *Race War: White Supremacy and the Japanese Attack on the British Empire*, New York University Press, New York, 2004, pp. 80, 147.

41 NAA. B510 Box 4, no. 241, Hooper to CITF, 15 December 1952.

42 AWM, PR91/174, Papers of E. G. Henty. For biographical details on Henty, see NAA, B510, No. 308, Henty, Ernest George.

43 Jenner Papers, Newspaper Notes, p. 6, entry 25 December 1941.

44 NAA, A1066/4, IC45/55/3/4, 'Copy: Activities of Dr Surbek, International Red Cross Delegate for Sumatra'.

45 For descriptions of the different types of camps, see Despatch No. 64/45, 8 October 1945, NAA, A1066/4, IC45/55/3/4, NAA, A4144/1, 228/1945, 'Report to Australian Charge d' Affaires on Mr R. J. R. Butler's mission to Shanghai', 19 September 1945. For a complete list of missing civilians in the Territories of New Guinea, Papua and Nauru, see NAA, A518 EQ16/2/1. 'Analysis of Numbers Interned by Locations Where Interned' in 'Report on the Distribution of the Trust Fund', 14 May 1954, NAA, B512, CITF Final Report Folder [No Number], Statement A. For internees in Thailand, see NAA, A981/4, DEF537, Defence Stranded Australians, Prof. William Dancer.

46 *Parliamentary Debates*, 5th series, vol. 378, 10 March 1942, pp. 930–2.

47 Randall Gould, 'Captives of the Mikado', *Far Eastern Survey*, vol. 11, no. 11, 1 June 1942, p. 128.

48 NAA, A981, DEF 252 Part 1, Cablegram No. 176 from Australian Legation, Chungking to Department of External Affairs, 6 May 1942.

49 Horne, *Race War*, p. 7.

50 Printed paper no. F7215/391/10 in NAA, A989, 1943/460/10/1, J. H. Le Rougetel to Mr Eden, 19 October 1942.

51 Van Waterford, *Prisoners of the Japanese in World War II: Statistical History, Personal Narratives and Memorials Concerning POWs in Camps and on Hellships, Civilian Internees, Asian Slave Labourers and Others Captured in the Pacific Theater*, McFarland and Company, Jefferson NC and London, 1994, p. 232.

52 J. H. Le Rougetel to Mr Eden, 19 October 1942.

53 NAA, A981/4, DEF252 Part 1, Defence Stranded Australians, General, Far East, General, 'Stranded Australians in Enemy Territory', 23 February 1942.

54 Robert R. Wilson, 'Treatment of Civilian Alien Enemies', *American Journal of International Law*, vol. 37, no. 1, January 1943, p. 32.

55 NAA A981/4, DEF252 Part 1, Cablegram No. 78 from External Affairs Officer, London to Department of External Affairs, 11 February 1942. Charles G. Roland, 'Allied POWs, Japanese Captors and the Geneva Convention', *War & Society*, vol. 9, no. 2, October 1991, pp. 83–101.

56 Utsumi Aiko, 'Japanese Army Internment Policies for Enemy Civilians During the Asia-Pacific War', in Donald Denoon, Mark Hudson, Gavan McCormack and Tessa Morris-Suzuki (eds), *Multicultural Japan: Palaeolithic to Postmodern*, Cambridge University Press, Cambridge, 2001, pp. 174–209.

57 NAA, A981/4, DEF252 Part 1, note on file, dated 26 February 1942. NAA, A989, 1943/235/2/5/1 Defence. Stranded Australians in Far East. Representations, Memo from Department of External Affairs to Prime Minister's Department, 20 July 1943.

58 NAA, A981/4, DEF252 Part 1, telegram from Morel, International Red Cross Delegate.

59 NAA, A981/4, DEF252 Part 1, cablegram No. 2346, High Commissioner's Office, London, to Prime Minister's Department, 10 April 1942.

60 NAA, A989, 1943/235/2/5/1, Memo from Department of External Affairs to Prime Minister's Department, 20 July 1943.

61 NAA, SP109, 329/09, cablegram No. 11681, High Commissioner's Office, London, to Prime Minister's Department, 20 November 1945.

62 The evacuees from the 'Far East' arrived in the *Tatsuta Maru* on 27 August 1942 and the *Kamakura Maru* on 4 September 1942. NAA, A989, 1943/460/10/1 Japan – First

Exchange of Civilians, 'Extract from Report on the Repatriation to Australia of Party of British and Allied Officials and Non-Officials Evacuated from the Far East under the Exchange Agreement with Japan'. See also NAA, A989, 1943/235/2/5/1, Memo from Prime Minister's Department to Minister External Territories, 29 November 1943. A later cablegram gives the number as 31; see NAA, A981, JAP 117 War Records, Department of External Affairs to Dominions Office, 22 September 1942. Japan. Exchange of British and Japanese Subjects. Second Exchange.

63 The officials were Bernice Campbell, Thomas Eckersley, Montague and Mabel Ellerton, Bernard Kuskie, Frank Officer, Patrick Shaw and wife and child.

64 NAA, A989, 1943/460/10/1, Memo prepared by Secretary of State for the Dominions in response to Australian government concerns about the departure of the ship without safe conduct, Japan – First Exchange of Civilians.

65 See for example material in the file NAA, A2676, 2247 Exchange of prisoners with Japan.

66 NAA, A989, 1943/460/10/1/1, C. McLaren, Eleven Weeks in a Japanese Prison Cell, [n.d. c. 1942].

67 Copy for Prime Minister's Department Decypher to High Commissioners' Office, London, no. 4319, May 1943; E. J. Harrison to John Curtin, PM, 17 May 1943; Cablegram from High Commissioners Office, London to PM's Department, 11 June 1943, no. 5644, all in NAA, A1066/4, IC45/20/1/4/1, Protection of Australian Nationals Abroad Repatriation and Payment of Relief – Japan Nuns of 'Sacred Heart' – Japan Convents Tokio and Kobe. The interned nuns were Elizabeth Sproule, Eva McKenna, Gertrude McGrath, Ethel Timanus, Maud Stuart, Mary Foy, Avelyn Wall, Ivia Maher, Catherine Coffey, Alice Coffey, Catherine Cullen and Mary Hastings. Some of the group were interned in Tokyo at Sekiguchi and Seibo. Others were initially interned in Kobe, at Hyogo No. 2 and then moved to St Franciscus II in Nagasaki.

68 NAA, A981, JAP 117 War Records. Japan. Exchange of British and Japanese Subjects. Second Exchange Department of External Affairs to Dominions Office, 22 September 1942.

69 AWM, 3DRL/5092, Bishop of New Guinea to Mrs Waterman, 20 October 1942, Papers of Miss May Hayman.

70 The Swiss Consul at Bangkok, who regularly visited internees at that city's internment camp, slowly accrued details of the incident at Yala and passed them on. Extracted cablegrams in F. M. Forde, Acting Prime Minister to Mr Morgan MHR [Local Member of W. P, Beahen, Norman Holt's father-in-law], 30 December 1944, NAA, A1066/4, IC45/20/1/7/1. High Commissioners Office to Department of External Affairs, Cablegram I 21865, 25 May 1943, NAA, 981/4, DEF 537, Defence Stranded Australians. Professor William Dancer.

2 Race

1 ML, MSS 5184, Jenner, Dorothy Gordon, papers, 1921, 1938–47, microfilmed as CY Reel 2690 (Jenner Papers), section 4, Newspaper Notes, 30 December 1941, p. 6.

2 Ibid., section, 6, correspondence & related papers, Stanley Prisoner of War Camp.

3 ML, MSS 1425, Thomas, Gordon Papers, 'Rabaul 1942–45', p. 304.

4 Christopher Thorne, *Racial Aspects of the Far Eastern War of 1941–45*, Oxford University Press, Oxford, 1982, p. 333.

5 John Dower, *War Without Mercy: Race and Power in the Pacific War*, Pantheon Books, New York, 1986.

6 Paul Jones, '"Racial Character" and Australia and Japan in the 1930s', in Paul Jones and Pam Oliver (eds), *Changing Histories: Australia and Japan*, Monash Asia Institute, Melbourne, 2001, pp. 25–48.

7 Mark A. Stoler, 'The Second World War in U.S. History and Memory', *Diplomatic History*, vol. 25, no. 3, Summer 2001, p. 390.

8 Cinesound newsreel, *This is Japan*, cited in Prudence Torney-Parlicki, Somewhere in Asia: The Australian News-Media and Conflict in the Asia Pacific Region, 1945–1971, PhD thesis, Department of History, University of Melbourne, 1997, p. 98.

9 Thorne, *Racial Aspects of the Far Eastern War*, p. 350.

10 NAA, A3317, 472/46, Statutory Declaration, David Higgins.

11 NAA, A3317, 472/46, Statutory Declaration, Dudley Rex.

12 NAA, A1608, 16/13/416, 'Report on happenings at Pinyok, near Yala, South Siam . . .', prepared by M. H. Macfarlane, 12 January 1946.

13 NAA, A3317, 472/46, 'Resume of the experiences of M. H. Macfarlane and others in Siam from and inclusive of the 8th December 1941'.

14 Donald Denoon with Stewart Firth, Jocelyn Linnekin, Malama Meleisea and Karen Nero (eds), *The Cambridge History of the Pacific Islanders*, Cambridge University Press, Cambridge, 1997, p. 10.

15 AWM, 3DRL/5092 419/11/7, 'Miss May Hayman's Last Letter before being captured by the Japanese and killed, early September 1941', to her sister Vi, August 1942.

16 'Resume of the experiences of M. H. Macfarlane'.

17 NAA, MP742/1, 336/1/1086, War Crimes – New Britain, Statement No. 2 by Sister Marcella and Sister Editha of Bitagalip Mission, in GR3063, 'Report on Visit by DADWGS HQ First Aust Army to Rabaul'.

18 James Benson, *Prisoners' Base and Home Again: The Story of a Missionary P.O.W.*, Robert Hale, London, 1956, p. 42.

19 NAA, B510 Box 6, no. 345, Stranks, Leonard.

20 NAA, B510 Box 4, no. 205, Burton, John.

21 Stephanie Sherwood, *Growing Up as a Foreigner in Shanghai: Recollections*, Mini Publishing, Sydney, 2004, p. 69.

22 Benson, *Prisoners' Base and Home Again*, p. 61.

23 Thomas, 'Rabaul 1942–45', pp. 29, 216.

24 Hank Nelson, 'The Troops, the Town and the Battle', *Journal of Pacific History*, vol. 27, no. 2, 1992, p. 203.

25 Edward P. Wolfers, *Race Relations and Colonial Rule in Papua New Guinea*, Australia and New Zealand Book Company, Sydney, 1975, pp. 88–107.

26 Roger C. Thompson, 'Making a Mandate: The Formation of Australia's New Guinea Policies 1919–1925', *Journal of Pacific History*, vol. 25, no. 1, 1990, p. 84.

27 NAA, SP24/1, 890, Gordon Thomas, Ion Idriess to Angus & Robertson, 26 July 1946.

28 Thomas, 'Rabaul 1942–45', p. 12.

29 Ibid., p. 13.

30 Benson, *Prisoners' Base and Home Again*, p. 44.

31 AWM, 3DRL/7925, Papers of H. R. Slocombe, 4 March 1943.

32 Ibid., 11 July 1944.

33 ML, Jenner Papers, diary, 28 September 1942.

34 Thomas, 'Rabaul 1942–45', p. 36.

35 Papers of H. R. Slocombe, 4 March 1943.
36 Alice Bowman, *Not Now Tomorrow: ima nai ashita*, Daisy Press, Bangalow, NSW, 1996, pp. 113, 54.
37 Benson, *Prisoners' Base and Home Again*, p. 109.
38 Thomas, 'Rabaul 1942–45', p. 83.
39 Department of Veterans' Affairs, Australians at War Film Archive 0177, Berenice Twohill, transcript, p. 107.
40 NAA, A989, 1943/460/10/1/1, C. McLaren, Eleven Weeks in a Japanese Prison Cell [n.d. c. 1942].
41 Printed paper F 7551/867/23 contained in NAA, A989, 1943/460/10/1, Sir Robert Craigie to Mr Eden, 5 November 1942.
42 Gordon Thomas, 'How Rabaul's civilians met their fate', *Pacific Islands Monthly*, November 1945, p. 15.
43 AWM, 3DRL/6805 Papers of Theo H. Stone, Civilian Internee Changi Camp, 21 May 1942, 1 September 1942.
44 Ibid., 1 September 1942, 3 September 1942.
45 AWM, PR87/188, Papers of Harold Leslie Murray, 17 July 1944.
46 NAA, A10953/1, Item 6, War Crimes Commission. Macassar. [Principally] Diary of H. R. Slocombe.
47 NAA, A1067/1, IC46/55/2/2/5, Internees – Australians Abroad. Far East. Deaths. Three Shot at Santo Tomas Camp including B. Laycock.
48 NAA, B510 No. 176, Wong, Francis Herbert.
49 *Pacific Islands Monthly*, October 1945, p. 6: the article includes photographs of Lieutenant Colonel Chalmers and Dr B. Quin; NAA, B510 Box 1, Item 58, Harmer, Bertha Elsie.
50 Those captured on Nauru were Lieutenant Colonel F. Chalmers (administrator), Dr B. H. Quinn (government medical officer), W. H. Shugg (medical assistant) and F. Harmer and W. H. Doyle (British Phosphate Commission). See NAA, B3856, 146/1/10, Civilian Casualties Ocean Island. Six European men remained behind on Ocean Island after the British evacuated: Mr C. G. F. Cartwright (government secretary), R. W. Third (government radio operator), Lindsay Cole and H. A. Mercer (members of the staff of the British Phosphate Commission) and Father Pujebet and Brother Brummell (Catholic missionaries). See *Pacific Island Monthly*, February 1946, p. 7.
51 NAA, B510, Cole, Jessie Norine, Mrs Cole to CITF, 18 August 1957.
52 Benson, *Prisoners' Base and Home Again*, p. 62.
53 AWM, 3DRL/7925, Papers of H. R. Slocombe, 6 January 1943.
54 Ibid., 27 January 1943, 27 April 1943.
55 NAA, A373/1, 12207, 'A' Interrogation no. 1, Dr Elizabeth Gibson.
56 Roy Stanford to Violet [his sister], 27 March 1945, to Lawrence [his brother], 25 April 1945, AWM, PR86/275, Records of D. R. Stanford.
57 Dorothy Jenner, *Darlings, I've Had a Ball*, Ure Smith, Sydney, 1976, p. 209.
58 NAA, A10953/1, Item 6, War Crimes Commission. Macassar. [Principally] Diaries of H. R. Slocombe.
59 NAA, B510 Box 5, No. 266, McKechnie, George.
60 NAA, MP742/1, 336/1/1068, War Crimes – New Britain, Statement No. 18 by Mr James H. Ellis former resident of Rabaul and Prisoner of the Japanese until the time of the surrender, GR3063, 'Report on visit by DADWGS HQ First Aust Army to Rabaul'.

61 ML, Jenner Papers, section 6: Correspondence and Related Papers, Stanley Prisoner of War camp.
62 Benson, *Prisoners' Base and Home Again*, p. 62.
63 Thomas, 'Rabaul 1942–45', p. 155.
64 AWM 93, 50/2/23/209, Records of the War 1939–45, Rev. James Benson, Seizo Okada to Revd James Benson, 22 April 1946.
65 Benson, *Prisoners' Base and Home Again*, p. 123.
66 AWM, Papers of Harold Leslie Murray, 8 August 1944.
67 Department of Veterans' Affairs, Twohill, transcript, p. 17.
68 McLaren, Eleven Weeks in a Japanese Prison Cell.
69 Jenner, *Darlings, I've Had a Ball*, p. 196.
70 AWM, Papers of H. R. Slocombe, 15 December 1942 and 10 January 1943.
71 McLaren, Eleven Weeks in a Japanese Prison Cell, p. 21.
72 Bowman, *Not Now Tomorrow*, p. 115.
73 NAA, B510 Box 4, no. 241, Hooper to CITF, 22 December 1952.
74 AWM, Papers of Harold Leslie Murray, 22 July 1944.
75 Sheila Allen, *Diary of a Girl in Changi 1941–45*, Kangaroo Press, Sydney, 1994, p. 41.
76 Ibid., p. 172.
77 Jean Gittins, *Stanley: Behind Barbed Wire*, Hong Kong University Press, Hong Kong, 1982, p. 66.
78 AWM, 3DRL/5072, MacNider, Eric Diary, entry 31 July 1942.
79 NAA, B510 Box 5, No. 276, Pinkerton, Stanley Corry, including copy of letter sent by PM's office to R. C. Pinkerton [Stanley's brother] with extract of letter from Mr R. A. Gunnison.
80 NAA, A373/1, 12207, 'A' Interrogation No. I, Dr Elizabeth Gibson.
81 McLaren, Eleven Weeks in a Japanese Prison Cell, p. 2.
82 AWM, Papers of Theo H. Stone, Theo Stone to Australian Red Cross, 1 October 1945.
83 *Sun*, 20 September 1945, p. 6.
84 *Age*, 21 September 1945, p. 7.
85 ML, Jenner Papers, diary, p. 28.
86 Benson, *Prisoners' Base and Home Again*, p. 121.
87 AWM, PR000015, Papers of Jack Percival, Diary 12 July 1944.
88 Ibid., 8 February 1944.
89 NAA, A4144/1, 228/1945, A. R. Kennedy to Charge d'Affaires, Australian Legation, Chungking, 9 October 1945.

3 Community and conflict

1 'Address by His Excellency Major General Michael Jeffrey ... on the occasion of the dedication ceremony for an Australian Ex-Prisoners of War Memorial', 6 February 2004, <www.gg.gov.au/html/fset_speeches_media_vr.html>, accessed 6 September 2006, cited in Lachlan Grant, Mateship, Memory and the Australian Ex-Prisoners of War Memorial, MA thesis, School of Historical Studies, Monash University, 2005.
2 Elizabeth Head Vaughan, *Community Under Stress: An Internment Camp Culture*, Princeton University Press, Princeton, New Jersey, 1949.
3 AWM, PR 000015, Papers of Jack Percival (Percival Papers), Diary, 16 July 1944.
4 ML, MSS 1425, Gordon Thomas, 'Rabaul 1942–45', p. 21.

5 Audrey Begley-Bourke, Ian T. Begley and C. Neil Begley (comps), *Separated for Service: A Biography on the Life and Service of Colin Keith Begley and Edith May Begley, Missionaries to China and India*, Melbourne, Salvation Army, 1994, p. 74.

6 Lavinia Warner and John Sandilands, *Women Beyond the Wire: A Story of Prisoners of the Japanese 1941–45*, Michael Joseph, London, 1982, p. 14; Bernice Archer, *A Patchwork of Internment: The Internment of Western Civilians under the Japanese 1941– 45*, Routledge Curzon, London, 2004, p. 72.

7 ML, MSS 5184, Jenner, Dorothy Gordon, papers, 1921, 1938–47, microfilmed as CY Reel 2690 (Jenner Papers), Diary, 1 September 1942.

8 NAA, B510, No. 186A Westwood, Amy Beatrice.

9 Sheila Allen, *Diary of a Girl in Changi 1941–45*, Kangaroo Press, Sydney, 1994, p. 45.

10 NAA, A4144/1, 810/1945, Jean Armstrong to Mr Stokes, 7 August 1945; Begley-Bourke et al., *Separated for Service*, p. 68; Archer, *A Patchwork of Internment*, p. 80.

11 Jenner Papers, Section 5, Notes, p. 3, (original emphasis).

12 Allen, *Diary of a Girl in Changi*, p. 4; AWM, PR87/188, Papers of Harold Leslie Murray, Civilian Internee, Changi, Sime Rd, 10 July 1944; Dorothy Jenner, *Darlings, I've Had a Ball*, Ure Smith, Sydney, 1975, p. 210. See also Jenner Papers, Diary, 23 April 1942.

13 Percival Papers, Diary, 14 February 1944, 24 March 1944.

14 Archer, *A Patchwork of Internment*, p. 82.

15 Jenner, *Darlings, I've Had a Ball*, p. 210.

16 AWM, 3DRL/7925, Papers of H. R. Slocombe Civilian Internee, 19 April 1943.

17 Ibid., 29 January 1943.

18 Papers of Harold Leslie Murray, 1 August 1944, 6 August 1944.

19 Berenice Twohill, 'Prisoners of the Japanese army, Rabaul, New Britain, December 1941–August 15, 1945', *Annals: Journal of Catholic Culture*, Nov/Dec 1995, p. 44, tss in Our Lady of the Sacred Heart Provincial Archives, Kensington, New South Wales.

20 Jenner, *Darlings, I've Had a ball*, p. 210.

21 Regulations of Yangchow Civil Assembly Centre, 27 February 1943, in AWM, PR00838 Neville, Alice (Civilian Internee) Leaflet of Regulations 1943.

22 AWM, PR86/275, Records of D. R. Stanford, Roy Stanford to Violet [his sister], 6 April 1945.

23 Jenner Papers, Diary, 21 September 1942.

24 Papers of Harold Leslie Murray, 18 July 1944.

25 Roy Stanford to Violet [his sister], 6 April 1945, Records of D. R. Stanford.

26 NAA, B510, Box 4, No. 241, Hooper, George Stanley.

27 Douglas Coles to CITF, 8 February 1945, NAA, B510, No. 215, Coles, Douglas Phipps.

28 Warner and Sandilands, *Women Beyond the Wire*, p. 15.

29 Archer, *A Patchwork of Internment*.

30 Ibid., p. 80.

31 Cf ibid., p. 88.

32 NAA, B510, Box 5, No. 253, Marriott, Robert.

33 NAA, B510, Box 3, No. 169, Robertston, Annie.

34 Archer, *A Patchwork of Internment*, pp. 142, 150.

35 Begley-Bourke et al., *Separated for Service*, p. 77.

36 AWM, Papers of H. R. Slocombe, 5 January 1943.

37 *Age*, 11 September 1945.

38 Department of Veterans' Affairs, Berenice Twohill, Australians at War Film Archive 0177, transcript, p. 113.
39 Archer, *A Patchwork of Internment*, p. 131.
40 Jenner, *Darlings, I've Had a Ball*, p. 202.
41 Allen, *Diary of a Girl in Changi*, p. 77.
42 James Benson, *Prisoners' Base and Home Again: The Story of a Missionary P.O.W.*, Robert Hale, London, 1957, p. 87.
43 Ibid., p. 157.
44 Department of Veterans' Affairs, Twohill, transcript, p. 14.
45 Ibid., p. 25.
46 Benson, *Prisoners' Base and Home Again*, p. 176.
47 Ibid., p. 182.
48 Ibid., pp. 150, 149.
49 Thomas, 'Rabaul 1942–44', p. 304.
50 AWM, Papers of H. R. Slocombe 26 January 1943. The other Australians were Lieutenant Howard, a flying officer from Adelaide, and Mr Chamberlain, from Western Australia.
51 Thomas, 'Rabaul 1942–45', p. 163.
52 Percival Papers, Diary, 25 December 1944.
53 Jenner Papers, Diary, 5 September 1942.
54 Papers of Harold Leslie Murray, 15 and 9 July 1944.
55 Allen, *Diary of a Girl in Changi*, pp. 120, 69.
56 Begley-Bourke et al., *Separated for Service*, p. 75.
57 Alice Bowman, *Not Now Tomorrow: ima nai ashita*, Daisy Press, Bangalow, NSW, 1996, p. 167.
58 AWM, PR87/228, Papers of Nurse J. O. Harris – Rabaul POW.
59 AWM, 3DRL/6805, Papers of Theo H. Stone, 17 April 1942 (Changi); Jenner Papers, Diary, 24 September 1942 (Hong Kong); Percival Papers, Diary, 8 November 1944 (Santo Tomas).
60 NAA, B510, No. 186A, Westwood, Amy Beatrice.
61 AWM, 3DRL/5072, MacNider, Eric Diary, entry for 26 January 1945.
62 Ibid., see entries 29 September 1942, 14 December 1942, 29 January 1945.
63 Percival Papers, Diary, 18 May 1944.
64 Percival Papers, 30 April 1944; Papers of Harold Murray, Diary, 8 August 1944; NAA, A10953/1, 6, War Crimes Commission, Macassar [Principally] Diaries of H. R. Slocombe, 29 December 1942.
65 'Pootung' to the Editor, *Shanghai Herald*, 14 October 1945, contained in NAA, A4144/1, 228/1945.
66 Jenner Papers, Section 5, Notes, p. 24.
67 Thomas, 'Rabaul 1942–45', p. 34; Percival Papers, 1 August 1944.
68 Percival Papers, 10 May 1944.
69 Jenner Papers, Diary, 3 September 1942.
70 Summary of Reports received from Dr Laupper, Assistant-Delegate of the IRCC in Bangkok regarding . . . , the visits which accompanied by Dr Weidmann, delegate of the IRCC in Batavia, he made to the Batavia Camps, September 1945, NAA, A1066/4, IC45/55/3/4.
71 The Sacre Coeur nuns received assistance during their detention in Japan from 1944. A 65-year-old music teacher who spent the war interned at Kobe, Arthur Peacock, also received aid. See NAA, A1066/4, IC45/20/1/16.

72 NAA, B510, No. 345, Stranks, Leonard Hickson.

73 Begley-Bourke et al., *Separated for Service*, pp. 68–9.

74 Ibid., pp. 75–6.

75 Jenner Papers, Section 5, Notes.

76 See letter to his sister published in *Colac Herald*, 12 February 1943, in NAA, A4144/1, 48/1945, POW [Prisoners of War] and Internees – Goulter, Reverend O – Repatriation to Australia.

77 East Asian Residents Association to Mrs Mary Quinton, Colac, 16 March 1944, in NAA, A4144/1, 48/1945, POW [Prisoners of War] and Internees – Goulter, Reverend O – Repatriation to Australia.

78 Chungking Chancery No 51/45 to External Affairs, 17 March 1945, in NAA, A4144/1, 48/1945, POW [Prisoners of War] and Internees – Goulter, Reverend O – Repatriation to Australia.

79 Herbert W. Lennon to John Curtin, date stamped 18 July 1944, NAA, A1066/4, IC45/20/1/4/1.

4 Collaboration

1 NAA, A989, 1943/460/10/1, J. H. Le Rougetel to Mr Eden, 19 October 1942, printed paper F7215/391/10.

2 For statements of the effect of the war on the Walker family, see NAA, B510 No. 185A, Walker, Jessie Louisa, and No. 185B, Walker, George Henry.

3 ML, MSS 5184, Jenner, Dorothy Gordon, papers, 1921, 1938–47, microfilmed as CY Reel 2690 (Jenner Papers), Section 5, Notes p. 4; diary 30 and 31 July 1942.

4 Ibid., Diary, 2, 3, and 4 August 1942.

5 Murdoch to CITF, 6 February 1953, NAA, B510, No. 263, Murdoch, Douglas Athol.

6 Gerald Horne, *Race War: White Supremacy and the Japanese attack on the British Empire*, New York University Press, New York, 2004, p. 95.

7 NAA, A4144, 228/1946, A. R. Kennedy to H. Stokes, Charge d'Affaires, Australian Legation, Chungking, 25 October 1945.

8 NAA, B510, No. 263, Murdoch, Douglas Athol, Murdoch to CITF, 6 February 1953.

9 NAA, A6126/XMO, Raymond, Alan Willoughby, vol. 2, Deputy Director, Security Services Vic. to Director-Gen, Security, 17 July 1942.

10 *Shanghai Evening Post & Mercury*, vol. 65, no. 160, 6 July 1942, in NAA, A4144/1, 244/1946.

11 Copies of these articles are reproduced in NAA, A4144/1, 244/1946.

12 NAA, A4144/1, 244/1946, copy of Statement made by Alan Willoughby Raymond to Captain W. R. Blackett of the Australian Security Service on 5th December 1946.

13 Bernard Wasserstein, *Secret War in Shanghai*, Profile Books, London, 1999, p. 179.

14 NAA, A6126/XMO, Raymond, Alan Willoughby, vol. 2, Director-General Security to Director of Military Intelligence, Allied Land Force HQ, Victoria Barracks, Melbourne, 11 Feb 1943; NAA, A1066/4, IC45/94/5, Director-General of Security to Acting Secretary, Department of External Affairs, 5 October 1945.

15 NAA, A6126/XMO, Raymond, Alan Willoughby, vol. 2; report of interview with Miss Georgina Fuller, ex-internee Shanghai, Friday April 5th and Monday April 8th, 1946.

16 NAA, A4144/1, 244/1946, copy of Statement made by Alan Willoughby Raymond to Captain W. R. Blackett of the Australian Security Service on 5th December 1946.

17 NAA, A1066/4, IC 45/94/5, 'John Joseph Holland'; NAA, A6119/79, Item 718, Director, CIS to Secretary, Department of Immigration, 16 June 1948.

18 NAA, A6126/XMO, Raymond, Alan Willoughby, vol. 2, John J. Holland to Dr. J. Holland repr. in Director General, Security to Director of Military Intelligence, Allied Land Forc HQ, 11 February 1943.

19 NAA, A6126, No. 1213, McDonald, Wynette Cecilia, Bowden report on Mr H. O. Linquist, 10 September 1940.

20 NAA, A6126, No. 1213, McDonald, Wynette Cecilia, V. G. Bowden, Australian Government Trade Commissioner China, Report on Wynette Cecilia McDonald, 23 December 1940.

21 NAA, A6126, No. 1213, McDonald, Wynette Cecilia, statement of Mrs R. A. Taylor (no date) and Bowden to Colonel Jones, Director Investigation Branch, Canberra, 27 December 1940.

22 Report of interview with Miss Georgina Fuller.

23 *Daily Telegraph*, 23 February 1946, clipping in NAA, A6126, No. 1213, McDonald, Wynette Cecilia.

24 Report of interview with Miss Georgina Fuller.

25 Copy of Statement made by Alan Willoughby Raymond to Captain W. R. Blackett.

26 NAA, MP742/1, 255/2/686, Australian Internees ex Shanghai Area, 1945–6, Attachment, Statement by Miss McDonald to Captain Blackett, in Report on Shanghai Position Prior to Embarkation of Shanghai Detachment, 10 January 1946.

27 NAA, A1066/4, IC45/94/5, Captain Blackett to Secretary, Attorney-General's Department, 2 January 1946.

28 NAA, A6126/XMO, Raymond, Alan Willoughby, vol. 2, S. H. Jackson, Deputy Director of Security to Director General Security, Canberra, 31 May 1943.

29 Secret Appendix B, NAA, A6162/XMO, Raymond, Alan Willoughby, vol. 2.

30 NAA, A6126/XMO, Item 63, Security Service, Alan Willoughby Raymond, 2 February 1943.

31 Precis of Report by Australian Government Trade Commissioner in China on A. W. Raymond, in NAA, A6126/XMO, Raymond, Alan Willoughby, vol. 2; Alan Willoughby Raymond, NAA, A1066/4, IC45/94/5.

32 NAA, A6126/XMO, Item 63, Security Service, Alan Willoughby Raymond, 2 February 1943.

33 Precis of Report by Australian Government Trade Commissioner in China on A. W. Raymond.

34 Bowden report on Mr H. O. Linquist, 10 September 1940.

35 V. G. Bowden, Australian Government Trade Commissioner China, Report on Wynette Cecilia McDonald.

36 NAA, A6126, No. 1213, McDonald, Wynette Cecilia. Bowden to Colonel Jones, Director Investigation Branch, Canberra, 27 December 1940. Report of interview with Miss Georgina Fuller.

37 Report of interview with Miss Georgina Fuller.

38 V. G. Bowden, Australian Government Trade Commissioner China, Report on Wynette Cecilia McDonald.

39 NAA, A4144, 288/1946, Henry Stokes, Situation at Shanghai, 8 November 1945.
40 NAA, A6126, No. 1213, McDonald, Wynette Cecilia. F. G. Galleghan, Deputy Director to Director General, CIB, 28 February 1946.
41 NAA A367/1, C73410, De Villa, Kathleen Mary Doris. Interview with Kathleen Mary Doris de Villa by Security Services.
42 NAA, A367/1, C73410, De Villa Kathleen Mary Doris. Dr Edward de Villa and Mrs Kathleen Mary Doris de Villa, Report by Security Service, Sydney, 21 June 1945.
43 NAA, A367/1, C73410, De Villa Kathleen Mary Doris. Information to Director-General of Security, Canberra, 12 July 1945.
44 NAA, A367/1, C73410, De Villa Kathleen Mary Doris. Director-General of Security to Controller of Postal and Telegraph Censorship, 10 July 1945.
45 New South Wales Operation Report No. 1/45 13th April 1945: Mrs de Villa, NAA, A367/1, C73410, De Villa Kathleen Mary Doris.
46 NAA A367/1, C73410, De Villa Kathleen Mary Doris. Interview with Kathleen Mary Doris de Villa by Security Services.
47 Dr Edward de Villa and Mrs Kathleen Mary Doris de Villa, Security Service Report.
48 NAA, A1456/1, EPCP17. Doris de Villa to Controller of Enemy Property, 22 February 1946.
49 New South Wales Operation Report No. 2/45, 14 April 1945, Mrs de Villa, NAA, A367/1, C73410, De Villa Kathleen Mary Doris.
50 NAA, A1066/4, IC45/94/5, Secretary, Attorney-General's Department to Secretary, Department of External Affairs, 24 October 1945.
51 Clipping from *Herald* (Melbourne), 28 September 1945, in NAA, A6126/XMO, Raymond, Alan Willoughby, vol. 2.
52 NAA, A1066/4, IC45/94/5, Captain Blackett to Secretary, Attorney-General's Department, 2 January 1946.
53 NAA, A1066/4, IC45/94/5, External Affairs to Australian Legation, cablegram, 23 April 1946.
54 NAA, A1066/4, IC45/94/5, Acting Secretary, Attorney-General's Department to Secretary Department of External Affairs, 20 May 1946.
55 NAA, A6126/XMO, Raymond, Alan Willoughby, vol. 2. CIS to Sec, Dept Imm, 22 October 1948.
56 Australia, Senate 1945, *Debates*, vol. 185, 4 October 1945, p. 64–65.
57 NAA, A1066/4, IC45/94/5, Dorothy Tangney to F. M. Forde, Minister for the Army, 25 March 1946.
58 [Report – title obscured by access restrictions], NAA, A6126/XMO, Raymond, Alan Willoughby, vol. 2.
59 NAA, A1066/4, IC45/94/5, Memo for Department of the Army, 20 May 1946; NAA, A1067/1, IC46/23/2/18, Acting Director, Commonwealth Investigation Branch to Acting Secretary Department of External Affairs, 19 September 1946; Newsclipping, 'Australian on Charge of Aiding Enemy', *Herald*, 19 February 1947, in NAA, A6119/79, No. 718.
60 NAA, A6119/79, No. 718, Director of Public Prosecutions, London to Solictor-General, Commonwealth of Australia, 7 February 1947.
61 Transcript of Sentencing by Lord Chief Justice in *R v John Joseph Holland*, Old Bailey, 25 March 1947, Central Criminal Court, in NAA, A6119/79, Item 718.
62 Ibid.

5 Sex and health

1 Dorothy Jenner, *Darlings, I've Had a Ball*, Ure Smith, Sydney, 1975, p. 204.
2 ML, MSS 5184, Jenner, Dorothy Gordon, papers, 1921, 1938–47, microfilmed as CY Reel 2690 (Jenner Papers), diary, 7 August 1942.
3 Christopher Castiglia, *Bound and Determined: Captivity, Culture-Crossing and White Womanhood from Mary Rowlandson to Patty Hearst*, University of Chicago Press, Chicago, 1996; Robert C. Doyle, *Voices from Captivity: Interpreting the American POW Narrative*, University of Kansas Press, Lawrence, Kansas, 1994.
4 Amirah Inglis, *'Not a White Woman Safe': Sexual Anxiety and Politics in Port Moresby 1920–1934*, Australian National University Press, Canberra, 1974.
5 See for example 'Bushido', *Argus*, 12 March 1942.
6 ML, MSS 1425, Thomas, Gordon, Papers, 'Rabaul 1942–45', p. 75.
7 Jenner Papers, Diary, 26 December 1941.
8 Ibid., Correspondence and Related Papers, Stanley Prisoner of War Camp.
9 Department of Veterans' Affairs, Berenice Twohill, Australians at War Film Archive 0177, transcript, p. 89.
10 Alice Bowman, *Not Now Tomorrow: ima nai ashita*, Daisy Press, Bangalow, NSW, 1996, p. 55.
11 Jenner, *Darlings, I've Had a Ball*, p. 206.
12 Jenner Papers, Diary, 26 December 1941.
13 Bernice Archer, *A Patchwork of Internment: The Internment of Western Civilians under the Japanese 1941–45*, London, Routledge Curzon, 2004, p. 41; Lynn Z. Bloom, 'Escaping Voices: Women's South Pacific Internment Diaries and Memoirs', *Mosaic*, vol. 23, no. 3, 1990, p. 108.
14 Betty Jeffrey, *White Coolies*, Angus & Roberston, Sydney, 1954, and Jessie Simons, *While History Passed: The Story of the Australian Nurses who were Prisoners of the Japanese for Three and a Half Years*, William Heinemann, Melbourne, 1954.
15 Jenner Papers, Diary 3, 11 July and 7 August 1942.
16 Sheila Allen, *Diary of a Girl in Changi 1941–45*, Kangaroo Press, Sydney, 1994, p. 167.
17 Ibid., p. 94.
18 Shirley Fenton Huie, *The Forgotten Ones: Women and Children Under Nippon*, Angus & Robertson, Sydney, 1992.
19 See also Bart van Poelgeest, 'Oosters stille dwang: Tewerkgesteld in de Japanse bordelen van Nederlands-Indie' [Eastern Silent Force: Employed in Japanese Brothels in the Dutch East Indies], org. published in *NRC Handelslad*, 8 August 1992, repr. In *ICODO Info*, vol. 93, no. 3, pp. 13–21. Esther Captain criticises van Poelgeest's approach as being overly reliant on 'official' documents and insufficiently interested in the testimony of survivors themselves. She suggests that the figure is an arbitrary one in 'Spreken over gedwongen prostitutie en zwijgen over verkrachtingen: Bronnengebruik in een zaak over Japanse legerbordelen in Nederlands Indie', *ICODO Info*, vol. 94, no. 1, pp. 37–48. Translations from Dutch by Loes Westerbeek.
20 Jan Ruff-O'Herne, *50 Years of Silence*, Tom Thompson Editions, Sydney, 1994.
21 Christina Twomey, 'Australian Nurse POWs: Gender, War and Captivity', *Australian Historical Studies*, vol. 36, no. 124, October 2004, 255–74.
22 For the trial of Washio Awochi for 'Enforced Prostitution as a War Crime', for 'having forced Dutch women to practice prostitution', see Case no. 76, UN War Crimes

Commission, *Law Reports of Trials of War Criminals*, vol. 13, HMSO for the UN War Crimes Commission, London, 1949, pp. 122–5.

23 Ruff-O'Herne, *50 Years of Silence*.

24 Thomas, 'Rabaul 1942–45', p. 36.

25 Watanabe Kazuko, 'Militarism, Colonialism and the Trafficking of Women: "Comfort Women" Forced into Sexual Labour for Japanese Soldiers', in Joe Moore (ed.), *The Other Japan: Conflict, Compromise and Resistance since 1945*, M E Sharpe, New York, 1997, pp. 305–19; George Hicks, *The Comfort Women: Sex Slaves of the Japanese Imperial Forces*, Allen & Unwin, Sydney, 1995; Yuki Tanaka, *Japan's comfort women: Sexual slavery and prostitution during World War II and the US Occupation*, Routledge, London, 2002.

26 AWM, PR87/188, Papers of Harold Leslie Murray, Civilian Internee, Changi, Sime Road, 1 August 1944.

27 Jenner Papers, Diary, 11 July 1942.

28 Sister Mary Hastings, Memories of Internment, MSS. Sacre Coeur Provincial Office, Tokyo, Japan.

29 AWM, PR00015, Papers of Jack Percival (Percival Papers), 1 and 2 February 1944.

30 Ibid., 25 March 1944 and 11 May 1944.

31 Jenner, *Darlings, I've Had a Ball*, p. 199.

32 Percival Papers, 11 May 1944.

33 Stephanie Sherwood, *Growing Up as a Foreigner in Shanghai: Recollections*, Mini Publishing, Sydney, 2004, p. 89.

34 NAA, 1068/7, IC 47/100/2/3. Witnesses were William and Zena Preston. Married on 20 December 1942, Pamela Marie, born 7 May 1943, and Frank Raoul, born 26 March 1945, and Marie Preston at Santo Tomas.

35 Archer, *A Patchwork of Internment*, p. 137.

36 NAA, B510, 207, Buttfield, Lionel Frank.

37 Oral history interview with Mrs Nelma Davies, 1999, tapes in author's possession.

38 Archer, *A Patchwork of Internment*, p. 140.

39 Jean Gittins, *Stanley: Behind Barbed Wire*, Hong Kong University Press, Hong Kong, 1982, p. 62.

40 Audrey Begley-Bourke, Ian T. Begley and C. Neil Begley (comps), *Separated for Service: A Biography on the Life and Service of Colin Keith Begley and Edith May Begley, Missionaries to China and India*, Melbourne, Salvation Army, 1994, p. 76.

41 AWM, PR85/342, Letter of Molly Jefferson, Civilian Internee, Molly Jefferson to Frank's Aunt Nell, Murla, Isabel, Nurah, 9 March 1945.

42 *Sydney Morning Herald*, 24 September 1945, p. 4.

43 NAA, B510, No. 353, Ossendryver née Blair, Roma Winsome.

44 AWM, PR86/275, Records of D. R. Stanford, Roy Stanford to Violet [his sister], 27 March 1945.

45 Allen, *Diary of a Girl in Changi*, p. 74.

46 NAA, B510, No. 336, Kirwan, William Thomas.

47 Percival Papers, 2 May 1944, 27 November 1944, 26 April 1944.

48 Ibid., 10 July 1944.

49 Papers of H. R. Slocombe, 19 March 1943 and 5 April 1943.

50 Thomas, 'Rabaul 1942–45', p. 35.

51 AWM, 3DRL/6805, Papers of Theo H. Stone, Civilian Internee Changi Camp, 9 July 1942.

52 Begley-Bourke et al., *Separated for Service*, p. 75.
53 Papers of Theo H. Stone, Minutes of Camp Executive Committee Meeting, 9 April 1942.
54 Papers of Harold Leslie Murray, 1 August 1944.
55 Percival Papers, 25 February 1944.
56 Hastings, Memories of Internment.
57 Records of D. R. Stanford.
58 Percival Papers, 26 February 1944, 29 September 1944, 21 November 1944, 1 December 1922, 12 September 1944.
59 Letter of Molly Jefferson, 9 March 1945.
60 NAA, B512, CITF Final Report Folder [No Number], Statement A. Statistics created from Analysis of Numbers Interned by Locations Where Interned, in Report on the Distribution of the Trust Fund, 14 May 1954.
61 NAA, B510, No. 148, Evans, Edith Evelyn, and No. 149, Evans, Lily.
62 NAA, A373/1, 12207, 'A' Interrogation no. 1, Dr Elizabeth Gibson.
63 NAA, A1067, IC46/55/2/2/5, George W. Laycock to Minister of Foreign Affairs, Australia, 8 January 1946.
64 Hobart *Mercury*, 14 September 1945, p. 3.
65 Percival Papers, 25 March 1944.
66 Archer, *A Patchwork of Internment*, p. 67.
67 Thomas, 'Rabaul 1942–45', p. 20.
68 Stephen Garton, *The Cost of War: Australians Return*, Oxford University Press, Melbourne, 1996, pp. 208–27.
69 Papers of Theo H. Stone, 17 April 1942.
70 Internews, 12 May 1942, in Percival Papers.
71 Papers of H. R. Slocombe, 5 March 1943.
72 Jenner, *Darlings, I've Had a Ball*, p. 193.
73 Letter from Jack Percival to Henderson, 14 February 1945, cited in Gavin Souter, *Company of Heralds: A Century and a half of Australian Publishing by John Fairfax Limited and its predecessors, 1831–1981*, Melbourne University Press, Melbourne, 1981, p. 225.
74 Bloom, 'Till Death Do us Part', p. 78.
75 Shirley Hazzard, *The Great Fire*, Virago, London, 2003, p. 127.
76 Archer, *A Patchwork of Internment*, pp. 69, 109.
77 Thomas, 'Rabaul 1942–45', p. 28.
78 James Benson, *Prisoners' Base and Home Again: The Story of a Missionary P.O.W.*, Robert Hale, London, 1957, p. 88.
79 Papers of Harold Leslie Murray, 1 August 1944.
80 Papers of Theo H. Stone, 9 July 1942.
81 Benson, *Prisoners' Base and Home Again*, p. 141.
82 Both stories reported in *Pacific Islands Monthly*, November 1945, p. 39.
83 Thomas, 'Rabaul 1942–45', p. 158.
84 Jenner, *Darlings, I've Had a Ball*, p. 206.
85 Allen, *Diary of a Girl in Changi*, pp. 171, 173.
86 Ibid., pp. 111, 133.
87 C. McLaren, Eleven Weeks in a Japanese Prison Cell, n.d. c. 1942, p. 17.
88 NAA, B2455, Thomas E L G, Thomas Edward Lewellyn Gordon, SERN 6890, Medical Report on an Invalid, 3 August 1918, AIF Depot, UK; Medical Report on an Invalid, 18 June 1919, Sydney.

89 NAA, B510, No. 294, Thomas, Edward Llewellyn Gordon, Doctor's certificate re Gordon Thomas, signed Ivor Thomas, 1 April 1953.
90 Papers of H. R. Slocombe, 16 April 1943, 18 February 1943, 9 January 1943.
91 Papers of Harold Murray, Sunday 6 August 1944.
92 Percival Papers, 23 December 1944.
93 NAA, A1066, IC45/55/3/11/17.

6 Liberation

1 James Benson, *Prisoners' Base and Home Again: The Story of a Missionary P.O.W.*, Robert Hale, London, 1957, p. 166.
2 Our Lady of the Sacred Heart Provincial Archives, Kensington, NSW, Sister Catherine O'Sullivan, New Britain: The Evacuation from Ramale on the signing of the Armistice, 13 September 1945, Historical Material [F.C.]: Missionary Experiences During Pacific War 1944–1987. Ramale Camp.
3 Jean Gittins, *Stanley: Behind Barbed Wire*, Hong Kong University Press, Hong Kong, 1982, p. 48.
4 AWM, PR 86/275, Records of D. R. Stanford, Roy Stanford to Violet [his sister], 6 April 1945.
5 AWM, PR000/015, Papers of Jack Percival (Percival Papers), 25 September 1944.
6 NAA, B510, Box 6, No. 351, Rex, Dudley Richmond.
7 NAA, B510, No. 318, Neples, Eileen Ellis, Affadavit signed by Raymond H. Cameron, ex-internee and fellow crew member *Nankin*, 10 April 1948.
8 Sacre Coeur Provincial Office, Tokyo, Japan, Sister Mary Hastings, Memories of Internment, MSS.
9 Alice Bowman, *Not Now Tomorrow: ima nai ashita*, Daisy Press, Bangalow, 1996, p. 187.
10 Sacre Coeur Provincial Office, Tokyo, Japan, Sister Reggie McKenna to Estelle, Nagasaki Internment Camp, 12 September 1945, TSS.
11 Hastings, Memories of Internment.
12 Bowman, *Not Now Tomorrow*, pp. 187, 201.
13 NAA, SP300/3, Item 305/2, Box 4.
14 AWM, PR85/342, Letter of Molly Jefferson, Civilian Internee Molly Jefferson to her husband's aunts, 9 March 1945, Jefferson Papers.
15 AWM, Photograph No. 118701, 14 September 1945.
16 ML, MSS 1425, Thomas, Gordon, Papers. 'Rabaul 1942–45', p. 306.
17 Department of Veterans' Affairs, Berenice Twohill, Australians at War Film Archive 0177, transcript, p. 29.
18 Our Lady of the Sacred Heart Provincial Archive, O'Sullivan, New Britain: The evacuation from Ramale on the signing of the Armistice.
19 *Age*, 11 September 1945.
20 *Age*, 15 September 1945, p. 3.
21 Thomas, 'Rabaul 1942–45', pp. 309–10.
22 Our Lady of the Sacred Heart Provincial Archive, O'Sullivan, 'New Britain: The evacuation from Ramale on the signing of the Armistice'.
23 *Sydney Morning Herald*, 24 September 1945, p. 4; *Sun*, Melbourne, 19 September 1945, p. 2.
24 *Sun*, Melbourne, 10 September 1945, p. 2.
25 *Sun*, Melbourne, 20 September 1945, p. 6, and 10 September 1945, p. 2.

26 Christina Twomey, 'Australian Nurse POWs: Gender, War and Captivity', *Australian Historical Studies*, vol. 36, no. 124, pp. 255–74.

27 *West Australian*, 11 October 1945, p. 6.

28 Margaret Clarence, *Yield Not to the Wind*, Management Development Publishers, Sydney, 1982, p. 134.

29 Abigail Solomon-Godeau, *Photography at the Dock: Essays on Photographic Histories, Institutions and Practices*, University of Minnesota Press, Minneapolis, 1991.

30 AWM, Film F01438, *Civilian Internees and Dockyards Singapore*.

31 *West Australian*, 11 October 1945, p. 4.

32 *Herald* (Melbourne), 21 September 1945, p. 5.

33 Percival Papers, 23 December 1944.

34 Audrey Begley-Bourke, Ian T. Begley and C. Neil Begley (comps), *Separated for Service: A Biography on the Life and Service of Colin Keith Begley and Edith May Begley, Missionaries to China and India*, Melbourne, Salvation Army, 1994, p. 79.

35 NAA, A4144/1, 228/1945, R. Butler to Officer, Chargé d'Affaires, Chungking, 24 September 1945.

36 NAA, A1066/4, IC45/55/3/4, Despatch No. 64/45, Officer to Acting Minister for External Affairs, 8 October 1945.

37 NAA, MP742/1, 282/1/731, Secretary-General, Australian Red Cross Society to Prime Minister, 16 February 1945.

38 Ibid.

39 NAA, MP742/1, 282/1/731, The Relationship of the Society to the Government: For Submission to the Prime Minister, 1 March 1945.

40 Ibid.

41 NAA, A1066/4, IC45/48/9, Report of Standing Conference POW and CI (Far East), 22 March 1945.

42 NAA, MP742/1, 282/1/731, Red Cross Relief for Liberated Prisoners of War and Civilian Internees in Japanese Hands, submitted to Minister of Army and officials of Department of External Affairs, 28 February 1945.

43 NAA, MP11/4/1, Item 1, J. M. Fraser, Acting Minister for the Army to John Curtin, Prime Minister, 14 March 1945, and John Curtin, PM to J. M. Fraser, Acting Minister for the Army, 15 March 1945.

44 NAA, MP742/1, 282/1/731, Red Cross Relief for Liberated Prisoners of War and Civilian Internees in Japanese Hands.

45 Ibid., p. 2.

46 Ibid.

47 NAA, A5954/69, Item 673/4, Teleprinter Message No. M. 970, C-in-C [Blamey] to Minister for Army, 15 March 1945.

48 NAA, A1066/4, IC45/48/9, Report of Standing Conference POW and CI (Far East), 22 March 1945.

49 NAA, A4144/1, 810/1945, Officer to A. G. C. Ogden, British Embassy, Chungking, 5 September 1945.

50 NAA, A4144/1, 228/1945, Statement made by Mr Keith Officer, 3 October 1945.

51 NAA, A4144/1, 288/1945, Report to Australian Chargé d'Affaires on Mr Butler's Mission to Shanghai, 14 September 1945.

52 NAA, A4144/1, 228/1945, Report to Australian Chargé d' Affaires on Mr R. J. R. Butler's mission to Shanghai, 19 September 1945.

53 NAA, A4144/1, 810/1945, Jean Amstrong to Mr Stokes, 7 [September] 1945.

54 NAA, A4144, 228/1946, Kennedy to Stokes, 30 October 1945.

55 NAA, A4144/1, 810/1945, Telegram No. 186, Department of External Affairs to Chungking, 5 September 1945.
56 NAA, MP742/1, 255/2/834, Australian Legation to HQ AMF – Melbourne, 27 November 1945.
57 NAA, A1066/4, IC45/55/3/4, Despatch No. 64/45, Officer to Acting Minister for External Affairs, 8 October 1945.
58 Ibid.
59 NAA, A4144/1, 288/1945, A. R. Kennedy to Chargé d'Affaires, Australian Legation, Chungking, 9 October 1945.
60 Dorothy Jenner, *Darlings, I've Had a Ball*, Ure Smith, Sydney, 1975, p. 217.
61 NAA, A4144/1, 810/1945, Department of External Affairs to Chancery, Australian Legation, Chungking, 17 September 1945; and Telegram No. 258.
62 NAA, A4144/1, 228/1945, contains copy of 41-line telegram; and Telegram No. 281, Officer to External Affairs, 25 September 1945.
63 NAA, A4144/1, 228/1945, A. R. Kennedy to Australian Legation, Chungking, 19 October 1945.
64 NAA, A1066/4, IC45/20/1/4/1, Mother McGuinness to PM, 2 October 1945; Mark Sheldon to PM, 13 August 1945; PM to Mother McGuinness, 1 November 1945.
65 NAA, A4144/1, 810/1945, Secret Cipher Signal from Aust Mission SEAC to Keith Officer, 14 September 1945.
66 NAA, A4144/1, 810/1945, Telegram No 187, Department of External Affairs to Chungking, 6 September 1945.
67 NAA, MP742/1, 255/2/686, Report on Shanghai Position Prior to Embarkation of Shanghai Detachment, 10 January 1946.
68 Ibid.
69 NAA, MP742/1, 255/2/686, Report by Major W. H. Jackson of 3 Aust PW Contact and Enquiry Unit on Position regarding evacuation of Aust. Internees from SHANGHAI, 9 October 1945.
70 NAA, MP742/1, 255/2/686, Australian Internees Ex Shanghai Area, 1945–6, Report on Shanghai Position Prior to Embarkation of Shanghai Detachment, 10 January 1946.
71 NAA, MP742/1, 255/2/834, Australian Legation to HQ AMF – Melbourne, 27 November 1945.
72 NAA, MP742/1, 255/2/686, Report on Shanghai Position Prior to Embarkation of Shanghai Detachment, 10 January 1946.
73 NAA, MP742/1, 255/2/834, Australian Legation to HQ AMF – Melbourne, 27 November 1945.
74 Stephanie Sherwood, *Growing up as a Foreigner in Shanghai: Recollections*, Mini Publishing, Sydney, 2004, p. 4.
75 Fernandez details from NAA, MP742/1, 255/2/686, Australian Civilian Internees at St Luke's 16 October 1945, in J. Jackson to LHQ, Melbourne, 23 October 1945; NAA, B510, No. 229, Fernandez, Sybil.
76 For details on the Turnbulls see NAA, MP742/1, 255/2/686; A1068/7, IC47/20/1/11/14.
77 Mischenko/Marshall details from NAA, MP742/1, 255/2/686, Australian Civilian Internees at St Luke's 16 October 1945, in J. Jackson to LHQ, Melbourne, 23 October 1945; NAA, B510, No. 254 Marshall, William, and No. 255, Marshall, Vera.
78 NAA, A6126/XMO, Item 63, Alan Raymond – Collaborator.
79 NAA, A4144/1, 288/1945, Statement made by Mr Keith Officer, 3 October 1945.

80 NAA, A1066/4, IC45/94/5, Australian Legation, Chungking to Department of External Affairs, 2 December 1945, Secret Cablegram.
81 NAA, A4144, 228/1946, Henry Stokes to A. R. Kennedy, 22 October 1945.
82 NAA, A4144/1, 288/1945, A. R. Kennedy to Australian Legation, Chungking, 16 October 1945.

7 Homecoming

1   NAA, A1379/1, EPJ1108, Merritt (Mrs) Mary Bertha, Mrs Mary Merritt to Minister for Information, 4 June 1945.
2   NAA, A1379/1, EPJ1107, Merritt, Frank Leslie, Frank Merritt to Treasurer, undated.
3   'High Charge for Repatriation', *Age*, 17 May 1945.
4   NAA, A1379/1, EPJ1108 Merritt (Mrs) Mary Bertha, Treasurer to Minister for Information, 12 June 1945; NAA, A1838/300, I451/1/2. Internees. Far East. Expenditure.
5   NAA, A5954/69, Item 673/4, Cablegram No. 219, Australian Legation, Washington to Department External Affairs, received 1st March, 1945; Teleprinter Message from Secretary, Department of External Affairs to Secretary, Department of the Army, 27 February 1945.
6   NAA, A5954/69, Item 673/4, Cablegram No. 316, Department of External Affairs to Australian Legation, Washington, 3 March 1945, containing text of message sent from Prime Minister to General MacArthur; and Douglas MacArthur to John Curtin, 4 March 1945.
7   NAA, A1838/300, I451/1/1/2, Internees. Far East. Expenditure. British Consulate General, Manila to Department of External Affairs, 15 May 1945.
8   The 316 consisted of 53 Australians, 16 NZ, 183 from the UK, 59 Dutch nationals, 4 Americans and 1 Pole. Details in NAA, MP742/1, 282/1/731, Australian Red Cross Society: Civilian Evacuees from the Philippines.
9   NAA, A1066/4, IC 45/55/1/2, Part 1, Acting Consul-General, British Consulate-General, Philippines, to Principal Secretary of State, Foreign Affairs, 15 May 1945, copied for Department of External Affairs, 25 May 1945.
10 NAA, MP742/1, 255/2/685, Message from His Royal Highness the Governor-General [Duke of Gloucester] and the Duchess of Gloucester to British and Allied internees released from Japanese Prison Camps, Manila.
11 Ninety, including twenty-seven children, went to Mount Victoria. NAA, MP742/1, 282/1/731, Australian Red Cross Society: Civilian Evacuees from the Philippines, encl. in J. Newman Morris to Prime Minister, 14 April 1945.
12 Ibid.
13 NAA, A1066/4, IC 45/55/1/2, Part 1, J. S. Collings, Minister for the Interior, to John Curtin, Prime Minister, 28 April 1945.
14 NAA, MP742/1, 255/2/685, F. H. Berryman, Lieutenant General Chief of Staff to LHQ, 25 March 1945, Australian, New Zealand, United Kingdom and Dutch Internees Recovered from the Japanese.
15 NAA, A1838/300, I451/1/2, Civilian Internees in SEAC Area, 27 August 1945.
16 NAA, A1066/4, IC45/48/9, Report of Standing Conference POW and CI (Far East), 5 July 1945.
17 NAA, B3856, 144/2/13, ADV LHQ ADM INSTR 62: Reception of PW and Civilians Recovered from the Enemy after Cessation of Hostilities.

18 NAA, A5954/69, Item 673/4, Minister for Interior to Acting Prime Minister, 16 May 1945.
19 NAA, MP742/1, 282/1/731, Australian Red Cross Society: Civilian Evacuees from the Philippines.
20 NAA, MP729/8, 44/431/4, Minutes of Conference Held at Victoria Barracks, Melbourne, Wednesday, 6th June 1945, Regarding Civilians Recovered from Japanese Hands.
21 Ibid.
22 NAA, B3856, 144/2/15, Cablegram Dept EA to Australian High Commissioner, New Dehli, 28 August 1945.
23 NAA, A1838/1, I451/2/1, Cable, Dept Army to Dept EA, 27 September 1945 and Cable, Dept Army to PM's Dept and Dept EA, 5 October 1945.
24 NAA, A437/1, 46/6/79, Ag Sec. Dept Immigration to Collector of Customs (Brisbane, Sydney, Fremantle) and Immigration and Passports Officer, Melbourne, 10 September 1945.
25 NAA, A437/1, 46/6/79; A1066/4, IC45/49/5/1, Correspondence, June 1945, Circular Memo No. 45/37, Security Service Canberra to all state Deputy Directors, File note, 31 October 1945, Cable from Longfield Lloyd, 2 November 1945, Dept of Immigration to Dept. External Affairs, 20 August 1945.
26 The conferences were held in Sydney (7–9 May 1945), Canberra (11 May 1945) and Melbourne (6 June 1945). NAA, A1066/4, IC45/48/9, Report of Standing Conference POW and CI (Far East), 22 March 1945.
27 NAA, A1379/1, EPJ669, Dorothy Hood to Delegate of Controller of Enemy Property, 18 May 1946.
28 NAA, A1066/4, IC45/48/9, Report of Standing Conference POW and CI (Far East), 5 July 1945.
29 NAA, A659/1, 45/1/2451, Australian Civilian Ex-Internees from Far East. Policy re Subsistence Payments, and Medical, Dental and Optical Treatment. Policy statement dated 24 May 1945; NAA, MP11/4, Box 1, Director General Department of Social Services to all State Deputy Commissioners, 20 December 1945.
30 NAA, MP11/4, Box 1, Director General Department of Social Services to Acting Minister, 24 September 1945; Director General, Department of Social Services to all State Deputy Commissioners, 17 and 30 October 1945; DG DSS to all SDC SS, 17 October 1945.
31 NAA, A884/9, A1070, Acting Director General Department of Social Services to Secretary, Department of Treasury, 12 June 1946.
32 Margaret Clarence, *Yield Not to the Wind*, Management Development Publishers, Sydney, 1982, pp. 134–5.
33 Personal communication, Jean Langmead, 1999.
34 *Age*, 21 September 1945, p. 7.
35 NAA, A1068/1, 16/13/416, Craige R. A., R. A. Stratford to Mrs Craigie, 31 October 1945.
36 NAA, A1068/1, 16/13/416, Craige R. A., Mrs Craigie to Prime Minister, 3 December 1946.
37 NAA, B510/1, No. 40, Evensen, Lilian Muriel.
38 Reverend Kentish was aboard the HMAS *Patricia Cam*. NAA, MP151/1, 429/201/919, Violent Kentish to Editor, *Leader* Newspaper, Perth, 9 February 1946.
39 NAA, MP151/1, 429/201/919, Mrs Kentish to Hon. N. Makin, 30 September 1945.

40 NAA, MP151/1, 429/201/919, AMF Minute Paper 336/1/711. Rev L. N. Kentish –
    Captured by Japanese, 17 September 1946.
41 Gordon Thomas, 'How Rabaul's Civilians Met their Fate', *Pacific Islands Monthly*,
    November 1945, p. 17.
42 *Pacific Islands Monthly*, vol. xvi, no. 3, 16 October 1945, p. 9.
43 See Hank Nelson, 'The Troops, The Town and The Battle', *Journal of Pacific History*, vol. 27, no. 2, 1992, pp. 198–216; and 'The Return to Rabaul 1945', *Journal of Pacific History*, vol. 30, no. 2, 1995, pp. 131–53. For the impact on families see
    Margaret Reeson, *A Very Long War: The Families Who Waited*, Melbourne,
    Melbourne University Press, 2000.
44 NAA, B510/1, No. 8, Bowman, Edith May.
45 *Pacific Islands Monthly*, vol. xvi, no. 3, 16 October 1945, p. 3.
46 NAA, B510/1, No. 12, Bruckshaw, Mona, Mrs Bruckshaw to CITF, 13 August 1953;
    NAA, B510/1, No. 43, Forsyth, Gladys, Mrs Forsyth to CITF, 8 April 1953.
47 *Pacific Islands Monthly*, vol. xvi, no. 3, 16 October 1945, p. 9.
48 See obituary for Hogan in *Pacific Islands Monthly*, December 1945, p. 8. Obituary
    for Page in *Pacific Islands Monthly*, February 1946, p. 81.
49 NAA, A1066/4, IC 45/20/1/16, Secretary, Department of External Affairs to
    Official Secretary, Office of the Australian High Commission, London, 11 December 1945.
50 NAA, A1068, IC47/20/1/8/5, see, for example, London Tin Corporation, which
    paid the full amount owed by Charles Hughes Johnston and his three children, and
    Henry D. Higgins; NAA, A1068/7, IC47/20/1/6/9 for details on the Sacre Coeur
    nuns; NAA, A1838/1, 1520/2/82; A1838/1, 1520/2/83; A1838, 1520/2/79.
51 NAA, A1838, 1520/2/6, Director of Social Service, ARCS to Department External
    Affairs, 28 March 1947, Department of Social Security to Department of External
    Affairs, 6 April 1949. See also NAA, B510, No. 227, Farmer, Violet Stella.
52 NAA, A1838/299, 1520/2/34, Uroe to Secretary, Department of External Affairs,
    4 June 1950.
53 NAA, A1838/299, 1520/2/95, Roope to External Affairs, 15 January 1949.
54 NAA, A1838/299, 1520/2/95, Deputy Director, CIS, Sydney to Director, CIS 23
    August 1949.
55 NAA, A1838/299, 1520/2/35, Whitgob to Secretary External Affairs, 23 February
    1951, Whitgob to Secretary External Affairs, 12 January 1950.
56 NAA, A4144/1, 48/1945, A. L. Goulter to Prime Minister, 7 June 1950.
57 NAA, A1838/299, 1520/2/52.
58 Ross in NAA, A367/1, C91985, Bergmann, Evelyn et al.
59 NAA, A1838/299, 1520/2/25.
60 The missionaries were the Reverends L. A. McArthur, W. L. I. Linggood, W. D.
    Oakes, H. J. Pearson, J. W. Poole, H. B. Shelton, T. N. Simpson, J. Trevitt, S. C.
    Beazley, E. W. Pearce. For obituaries see *The Spectator and Methodist Chronicle*,
    28 November 1945, p. 773.
61 Ibid., December 5, 1945, pp. 794, 1.
62 Leaflets and flyers in George Ellis Archives, Salvation Army Heritage Centre,
    Melbourne, Personnel Folder: Walker, George and Mrs Jessie.

8 Legacy

1 NAA, B510, No. 334, Gwen Kirwan to Secretary, Civilian Internees Trust Fund
   (CITF), 25 August 1957.

2 Cathy Caruth, 'Trauma and Experience: Introduction' to Cathy Caruth (ed.), *Trauma: Explorations in Memory*, Johns Hopkins University Press, Baltimore, Maryland, 1995, p. 4. Broad agreement on the symptoms of trauma has not led to consensus in theorisations of it among psychoanalysts or cultural critics interested in applying psychoanalytic models. Debate has centred on whether the origins of trauma are located within or outside the psyche. Dominick LaCapra is adamant that there is in fact an important distinction to be drawn between structural trauma and historical trauma. Everyone experiences structural trauma – 'in terms of the separation from the (m)other . . . the entry to language . . . and so forth' – he insists, but historical trauma is specific and 'not everyone is entitled to the subject-position associated with it'. Dominick LaCapra, 'Trauma, Absence, Loss', *Critical Enquiry*, Summer 1999, vol. 25, issue 4, online version, paragraphs 33, 34 and 35, <http://find.galegroup.com.ezproxy.lib.monash.edu.au/itx/infomark.do?&content Set=IAC-Documents&type=retrieve&tabID=T002&prodId=EAIM&docId= A55721730&source=gale&userGroupName=monash&version=1.0>, accessed 27 September 2006. LaCapra's work has been centrally concerned with the Holocaust, but his insights can be applied usefully to the experiences of civilian internees of the Japanese. They too – in their wartime experiences of detention, neglect and, in some cases, physical abuse – experienced a set of circumstances that amount to historically specific trauma.

3 Caruth, 'Trauma and Experience', pp. 4–5.

4 Eve ten Brummelaar, *You Can't Eat Grass*, Image DTP and Printing, Sydney, 1996, p. 80.

5 Caruth, 'Trauma and Experience', p. 5.

6 ten Brummelaar, *You Can't Eat Grass*, p. 81.

7 Dori Laub, 'Truth and Testimony: The Process and the Struggle', in Caruth (ed.), *Trauma*, p. 64.

8 Bessel A. Van Der Kilk and Onno van der Hart, 'The Intrusive Past: The Flexibility of Memory and the Engraving of Trauma', in Caruth (ed.), *Trauma*, p. 176.

9 NAA, Series B512, 52/68, Press Release, [no number], 8 December 1952, by Acting Prime Minister (Fadden), Civilian Internees Trust Fund. The fund was established under Section 13 F (3) of the *Trading with the Enemy Act 1939–1957*.

10 NAA, Series B512/1, Box No. 1, CITF. Final Report: Covering the Operations of the Trust 1952–1962, 29 October 1962, TS.

11 NAA, B510, No. 281.

12 NAA, B510, No. 296, Mrs R. T. to CITF, 11 August 1953.

13 Jean Gittins, *Stanley: Behind Barbed Wire*, Hong Kong University Press, Hong Kong, 1982, p. ix.

14 NAA, B510, No. 255.

15 NAA, B510, No. 259.

16 NAA, B510, No. 196.

17 NAA, B510, No. 286, E. R. to Professor Bland, MHR, 21 December 1953.

18 NAA, B510, No. 268, C. J. to CITF, 9 February 1953.

19 NAA, B510, No. 184.

20 NAA, B510, No. 256.

21 NAA, B510, No. 229.

22 NAA, B510, No. 329.

23 NAA, B510, No. 290, Dr W. L. Kirkwood, Statement 24 January 1953.

24 NAA, B510, No. 337, Kevin W. Priddis, 22 March 1957.

25 NAA, B510, No. 337, Mrs Lovett to CITF, 21 June 1961.
26 NAA, B510, No. 245, A. I. to CITF, 17 February 1953.
27 AWM, PR87/188, Papers of Harold Leslie Murray, Civilian Internee, Changi, Sime Road, Diary, 17 August 1944; and NAA, B510, No. 264.
28 AWM, PR00846 Canning, Zena: Papers, Jimmie Canning to Zena Canning, 6 December 1945.
29 Ibid.
30 NAA, B510/1, No. 29. See also the case of Rosemary Pearce, born 2 January 1942, daughter of Methodist Missionary Ernest Pearce: NAA, B510/1, No. 27; NAA, B510, No. 25, Mrs Coomber to Sec CITF, 7 September 1957; NAA, B510/1, No. 37; NAA, B510/1, No. 70, Klopp, Nellie, Mrs Klopp to CITF, 8 September 1957. Nellie Simpson was remarried, to Albert Edward Klopp, in 1948.
31 NAA, B510/3, No. 154, Mrs Hurst to CITF, 13 March 1953.
32 NAA, 4144/1, 228/1946, Albert G. Quark, Sgt, Army Inspection Staff NSWS to Secretary, Department of External Affairs, 19 November 1945 and Department of Immigration to Albert Quark, 7 November 1945.
33 NAA, B510, No. 172, Mrs Valma Cherlin to CITF, 25 September 1957.
34 James Benson, *Prisoners' Base and Home Again: The Story of a Missionary P.O.W.*, Robert Hale, London, 1957, p. 7.
35 *War Cry*, 12 November 1949, p. 4.
36 'Missionary Warrior', *War Cry*, 13 June 1970, p. 7.
37 NAA, B510, No. 204.
38 NAA, B510, No. 226.
39 NAA, B510, No. 346.
40 NAA, B510/3, No. 185A, Walker, Jessie Louisa, J. L. Walker to Secretary, POW Trust Fund.
41 NAA, B510, No. 350.
42 NAA, B510, No. 334, Kirwan, Gwen, Mrs Kirwan to CITF, 25 August 1957.
43 Ian Begley, personal communication, 17 December 2003.
44 NAA, B510, No. 193, Armstrong, Ada Jane, Jean Armstrong to Secretary CITF, 22 January 1953.
45 NAA, A367/1, C9448, C. B. Campbell, Investigator to Deputy Director, Brisbane, 16 February 1953.
46 *Sydney Morning Herald*, February 1945, newsclipping in AWM, PR000015, Papers of Jack Percival (Percival Papers).
47 See newsclippings in Percival Papers.
48 Percival cited in Pat Burgess, *Warco: Australian Reporters at War*, William Heinemann, Melbourne, 1986, pp. 95–6.
49 Letter from Percival to Henderson, 14 February 1945, cited in Gavin Souter, *Company of Heralds: A Century and a half of Australian Publishing by John Fairfax Limited and its predecessors, 1831–1981*, Melbourne University Press, Melbourne, 1981, p. 226.
50 Dorothy Jenner, *Darlings, I've Had a Ball*, Ure Smith, Sydney, 1975, p. 234.
51 NAA, B510, No. 218, Conn, Herbert Robert, Herbert Conn to CITF, 14 February 1957.
52 NAA, B510, No. 328, Grimpel, Alexander; NAA, B510, No. 335, Kirwan, Herbert.
53 NAA, B510, No. 199, Blaikie, Walter Hislop, Mr Blaikie to CITF, 20 August 1957.
54 NAA, B510, No. 236, Greig, Allister, Allister Greig to CITF, 29 December 1952.

55 Jenner, *Darlings, I've Had a Ball*, p. 217 and caption accompanying photograph opposite p. 236.
56 NAA, B510, No. 301, Warren, Samuel John, Samuel Warren to CITF, 25 February 1953.
57 NAA, B510, No. 310, Hope, James Wallace.
58 NAA, B510/6, No. 308, Henty, Ernest, Mr Henty to CITF, 9 August 1953.
59 NAA, B510, No. 262 Morcombe, Brian Moody. See also NAA, B510, No. 251, Lee, Hubert.
60 NAA, B510, No. 221, Crocker, Herbert Jago.
61 NAA, A1461, EPCT 32, Claim against the Siam Government – M. H. Macfarlane.
62 NAA, B510, No. 181, M. W-L. to CITF, 10 June 1953.
63 NAA, B510, No. 258, Draft of a Letter to Mrs M. contained in PM's Department to Mr J. Kelly, Private Secretary to the Treasurer, 12 December 1952.
64 NAA, B510, No. 237, Hall, Frederick.
65 Alice Bowman, *Not Now Tomorrow: ima nai ashita*, Daisy Press, Bangalow, 1996, p. 229.
66 NAA, B510, Box 1, No. 68, Hosking, Lorna, Re Mrs Davies, Fullarton SA in Mrs Hosking to CITF, 21 August 1952.
67 NAA, A1838/1, 1452/2/30, W. Beahan to F. M. Daly, MHR, 10 August 1947.
68 Ibid.
69 NAA, A1066/4, IC 45/20/1/7/1, W. P. Beahan to Chas A. Morgan MHR, 8 November 1945.
70 Joy Damousi, *Living With the Aftermath: Trauma, Nostalgia and Grief in Post-war Australia*, Cambridge University Press, Cambridge, 2001, p. 3.
71 NAA, B510, No. 223, Dodwell, Joan, Mrs Dodwell to CITF, 27 February 1953.
72 NAA, B510, No. 223, Dodwell, Joan, Mrs Dodwell to CITF, 28 August 1957.

9 Compensation

1 NAA, A518/1, 16/3/279, Bignell, Kathleen, Mrs Kathleen Bignell, MBE to Prime Minister, 19 February 1948.
2 NAA, A518/1, 16/3/279, Bignell, Kathleen, Mrs Bignell to Secretary, External Territories, 16 January 1946.
3 Ibid.
4 NAA, A518/1, 16/3/279, Bignell, Kathleen, Secretary, External Affairs to Mrs Bignell, 4 July 1946.
5 NAA, MP742/1, 164/1/464, Kathleen Bignell to Brigadier Wrigley, 19 October [1945].
6 NAA, B510, No. 198, Bignell, K. D. and NAA, B512, 53/157.
7 NAA, B510, No. 286, Russell, Eva, Mrs Eva Russell to Professor F. A. Bland, 21 December 1953; NAA, B510, No. 229, Fernandez, Sybil, Mrs Sybil Fernandez to Secretary, CITF, 21 January 1953; NAA, B510, No. 207, Buttfield, Lionel Frank, Supporting statement of Lionel Buttfield; NAA, B510, No. 339, Macmaster, John Dunlop.
8 Stephen Garton, 'War and masculinity in twentieth-century Australia', *Journal of Australian Studies*, no. 56, 1998, p. 90.
9 John Bodnar, 'Pierre Nora, National Memory and Democracy: a review', *Journal of American History*, vol. 87, no. 3, December 2000, p. 959.

10 AWM, 54, 391/13/50, J. Edmonds-Wilson, Recommendation for Decoration, 20 September 1945.

11 NAA, A463/61, 59/3864, Maj-Gen, ADM COMD FIRST ARMY to HQ AMF, 12 January 1946; and Secretary, Department of Army to Secretary, Department of Prime Minister, 6 February 1946.

12 NAA, A463/61, 59/3864, Minister for the Army to the Minister for Defence, 26 October 1949.

13 NAA, A463/61, 59/3864, Matron D. Maye–Honour.

14 NAA, B510, No. 30, Maye, Dorothy Mary, Maye to CITF, 28 July 1953. OBE noted in Alice Bowman, *Not Now Tomorrow: ima mai ashita*, Daisy Press, Bangalow, 1996, p. 231.

15 NAA, B510/6, No. 322, Brodie, John.

16 NAA, B510/6, No. 323, Bryant, John Clarence.

17 NAA, A1379/1, EPJ 669, Mrs Hood to Delegate of Controllers of Enemy Property, 21 April 1946.

18 NAA, A1461, ECPCT50, War Claim Against Thailand – Geoffrey Scott-Settle, Mrs Scott-Settle to L. H. Rowling, Treasury, 26 February 1949.

19 NAA, B510, No. 335, Kirwan, Herbert.

20 NAA, B510, No. 334, Mrs Gwen Kirwan to CITF, 25 August 1959.

21 NAA, B510, No. 334, Secretary, CITF to Mrs Gwen Kirwan, 11 September 1959.

22 NAA, B510, Box 6, No. 352, Coats, Claude, Claude Coats to CITF, 9 December 1956.

23 NAA, B510, Box 4, No. 209 Cherry, Robert, Robert Cherry to CITF, 27 August 1952.

24 NAA, B510, No. 221 Crocker, Herbert Jago, Crocker to CITF, 6 March 1953.

25 NAA, B510, Box 4, No. 209 Cherry, Robert.

26 NAA, B510, Box 4, No. 221, Crocker, Herbert; NAA, B510, No. 218, Conn, Herbert Robert.

27 NAA, B510, Box 4, No 221, Crocker, Herbert, Marjorie Crocker to CITF, 9 September 1957.

28 NAA, B510, Box 6, No. 347, Wardell, John Ignatius; NAA, B510, No. 323, Bryant, John Clarence, John Bryant to Robert Joshua, MP, Ballarat, 16 March 1952 and forwarded to CITF.

29 NAA, B510, Box 6, No. 340, Salmon, Frank Wesley.

30 NAA, A1608/1, BB20/1/1, Return of Civilian and POW from Pacific Territories, Papua New Guinea – Captured Civilians, Statement by Prime Minister, 26 May 1947. See also NAA, B512 52/67, Secretary, Department of External Affairs to Brigadier A. S. Blackburn, VC, Chairman CITF, 19 August 1952.

31 The legislation, the *Veterans' Entitlement Act* 1986, states in section 5c that 'eligible civilians' are those who were resident in the Australian External Territories of Papua and New Guinea. It should be noted, however, that all former civilian internees were entitled to receive the $25 000 compensation payment made available to former prisoners of the Japanese in 2001, regardless of their location when captured; *Compensation (Japanese Internment) Act 2001*.

32 NAA, A1457/1, EPCCH46, Grimpel to CEP, 8 January 1952; NAA, A1457/1, EPCCH46, Delegate Controller Enemy Property to Mr Grimpel, 26 September 1951.

33 NAA, A1461, EPCT50, 'Article VIII' of Peace Treaty with Siam repr. in Delegate of the Controller of Enemy Property to G. Scott-Settle, 30 July 1947.

34 NAA, A1066, IC45/33/3/4/3.
35 NAA, A1461, EPCT50, Mrs Scott-Settle to L. H. Rowling, Delegate of the Controller of Enemy Property, 24 July 1951.
36 NAA, B512, 52/68, Press release, no number, 8 December 1952, by Acting Prime Minister (Fadden), Civilian Internees Trust Fund.
37 *Herald*, 20 January 1953, clipping in NAA, B512, 52/68.
38 NAA, B512, CITF Final Report Folder [no number], A. H. Body for Acting Secretary External Affairs to Sec, PM's Department, 17 March 1953.
39 NAA, B512, CITF Final Report Folder [no number], Brigadier A. S. Blackburn, Chairman CITF to Secretary, Prime Minister's Department, 6 May 1953.
40 NAA, B510, No. 339, Macmaster, John Dunlop.
41 NAA, B512, CITF Final Report Folder [no number], M. C. Timbs, Secretary Prime Minister's Department to Brigadier Blackburn, CITF, 26 May 1953.
42 NAA, B510, No. 323, Bryant, John Clarence, John Bryant to CITF, 17 January 1953.
43 NAA, B510, No. 200, Blanchard, Mary Mrs, Mrs Reuben to CITF, 30 January 1953.
44 NAA, B510, Box 3, No. 197, Benson, Rev. Canon, James Benson to CITF, 7 February 1953.
45 NAA, B510, No. 348, Whalan, Clive, Clive Whalan to CITF, 18 February 1953.
46 NAA, B510, No. 236, Greig, Allister Thomas.
47 NAA, B510, No. 298, Townsend, Cyril John. Eileen Townsend to CITF, n.d.
48 NAA, B510, No. 324, Cloake, Richard John, R. J. Cloake to CITF, 23 January 1953.
49 NAA, B510, No. 345, Stranks, Leonard, Leonard Stranks to CITF, 30 September 1957.
50 NAA, B510, No. 229, Fernandez, Sybil, Sybil Fernandez to CITF, 21 January 1953.
51 NAA, B510, No. 43, Forsyth, Gladys, Mrs Forsyth to CITF, 8 April 1953.
52 NAA, B510, No. 68, Hosking, Lorna.
53 NAA, B510, No. 257, Merritt, Frank.
54 NAA, B510, No. 12, Bruckshaw, Mona, Mona Bruckshaw to CITF, 13 August 1953.
55 NAA B510, No. 5, Banks, Lily Eva.
56 NAA, B510, No. 347, Wardell, John, John Wardell to CITF, 9 September 1957.
57 NAA, B510, No. 357, Evans, James Edward, Secretary CITF to Department of Treasury, 16 February 1962: 'In the CITF minutes of 14th October 1953 para 4(i) it states "all applicants who suffer from a permanent disability referable to internment, be allocated a grant from the Fund without regard to the applicants financial status"'.
58 NAA, B510, No. 162, McKenzie Hall, Grace Gillian, Mrs McKenzie Hall to CITF, 9 April 1953.
59 NAA, B510, No. 54, Greenwood, Edna; and NAA, B510, No. 347, Wardell, John, John Wardell to CITF, 9 September 1957.
60 NAA, B510, No. 186, Westwood, Amy, Mrs Westwood to Sec., CITF, 20 January 1954.
61 NAA, B510, No. 296, Thompson, Robina, Mrs Robina Thompson to Sec., CITF, 27 February 1953.
62 NAA, B510, No. 229, Fernandez, Sybil, Sybil Fernandez to Sec., CITF, 18 June 1953.
63 NAA, B510, No. 284, Roope, Robert Lionel, Robert Roope to Sec., CITF, 23 December 1952. See also NAA, B510, No. 273, O'Neill, Thomas.

64 NAA, B510, No. 181, Wahlstrom-Lewis, Marie Hilda, M. H. Lewis to Sec., CITF, 10 June 1953 and 22 February 1954.
65 NAA, B510, No. 329, Hood, Dorothy, Dorothy Hood to Sec., CITF, July 1957.
66 NAA, B510, No. 293, Taylor, Ruby Alicia, Ruby Taylor to Sec., CITF, 27 August 1957.
67 NAA, B512, CITF Final Report Folder [no number], Colonel Arthur Spowers to Prime Minister, 14 May 1962.
68 NAA, B512, Chairman CITF, Brigadier A. S. Blackburn to Secretary, Prime Minister's Department.
69 NAA, B510, Box 5, No. 266, McKechnie George.
70 NAA, B512, CITF Final Report Folder [no number], I. M. Reid, Treasury to Withers, Secretary CITF, 4 May 1962.
71 NAA, B510, No. 221, Crocker, Herbert, Sec., CITF to Mrs Crocker, 11 December 1963.
72 NAA, B510, No. 221, Crocker, Herbert, Crocker to CITF, 15 September 1957.
73 NAA, B510, No. 223, Dodwell, Joan, Mrs Joan Dodwell (née Walker) to CITF, 27 February 1953.
74 NAA, B510, No. 229, Fernandez, Sybil, Mrs Sybil Fernandez to Sec., CITF, 21 January 1953.
75 NAA, A518/1, 16/3/279, Bignell, Kathleen, Mrs Bignell to Department of External Affairs, 9 June 1946.

Conclusion

1 Jay Winter, 'Forms of kinship and remembrance in the aftermath of the Great War', in Jay Winter and Emmanuel Sivan (eds), *War and Remembrance in the Twentieth Century*, Cambridge University Press, Cambridge, 2000, p. 41.
2 Ibid.
3 Cited in Gerald Horne, *Race War: White Supremacy and the Japanese Attack on the British Empire*, New York University Press, New York, 2004, p. 3.
4 Jill Bennett and Rosanne Kennedy describe the Holocaust as 'central to American memorial culture' in 'Introduction', Jill Bennett and Roseanne Kennedy (eds), *World Memory: Personal Trajectories in Global Time*, Palgrave Macmillan, New York, 2003, p. 1.
5 *Mercury*, 14 September 1945, p. 3.
6 ML MSS, Gordon, Thomas, Papers. Thomas, 'Rabaul 1942–45', p. 109.
7 In the postwar years there has been continued speculation in some circles that instead of perishing aboard the *Montevideo Maru*, most of its passengers were in fact massacred before they left the island. While acknowledging the pain and loss of relatives, several eminent historians have conducted detailed research and concluded that the majority of New Guinea's prewar white community did indeed die aboard that ship. The rumours were given renewed life in 1960 when Reverend Leo Scharmach, the Bishop of Rabaul who had been interned during the war, published his memoirs and suggested that the story of the *Montevideo Maru* was most likely a fabrication. See his *This Crowd Beats Us All*, Surry Hills, NSW: Catholic Press Newspaper Company, 1960, pp. 30–1. For refutations of these allegations see Hank Nelson, 'The Return to Rabaul 1945', *Journal of Pacific History*, vol. 30, no. 2, 1995, p. 152, and A. J. Sweeting, 'Montevideo Maru: Myth or Merchantman', in Theo Aerts (ed.), *The Martyrs of New Guinea: 333 Missionary Lives Lost*

During World War II, University of Papua New Guinea Press, Port Moresby, 1994, pp. 186–90.

8 Hank Nelson considers it 'the greatest single disaster suffered by Australians in World War II': 'The Return to Rabaul', p. 151.

9 The number usually cited is four men: Gordon Thomas, James Ellis, George McKechnie and Alfred Creswick. I have also included James Benson. The nuns were from the order of Our Lady of the Sacred Heart.

10 NAA, A989, 1943/235/2/5/1, I. G. Mcdonald, Hon Sec New Guinea Women's Club to Hon E. J. Ward, Minister for External Territories, 22 October 1943.

11 *Compensation (Japanese Internment) Act 2001*.

12 *Canberra Times*, 7 August 1999, p. 6.

13 *Pacific Islands Monthly*, no. 3, 16 October 1945, p. 4.

14 *Pacific Islands Monthly*, July 1946, p. 28.

15 Scott Macwilliam, 'Papua New Guinea in the 1940s: Empire and Legend', in David Lowe (ed.), *Australia and the End of Empires: The Impact of Decolonisation in Australia's Near North 1945–65*, Deakin University Press, Geelong, 1996, pp. 25–42. Some argue more forcefully for the intention of colonial reform. See Huntley Wright, 'Protecting the National Interest: The Labor Government and the Reform of Australia's Colonial Policy, 1942–45', *Labour History*, no. 2, May 2002, pp. 65–79. See also Donald Denoon with Stewart Firth, Jocelyn Linneking, Malama Meleisea and Karen Nero (eds), *The Cambridge History of the Pacific Islanders*, Cambridge University Press, Cambridge, 1997, pp. 319–22.

16 Ian Begley, personal communication with author, 17 December 2003. Mr Begley and I began corresponding after I spoke on an Australian radio station about my interest in researching the history of civilian internment.

17 NAA, B510, No. 258, Merritt, Mary, Mary Merritt to CITF, 15 January 1953.

BIBLIOGRAPHY

Primary sources

Australian War Memorial

3DRL/5072   MacNider, Eric Diary
3DRL/5092   Papers of Miss May Hayman, Anglican Missionary in New Guinea
3DRL/6805   Papers of Theo H. Stone, Civilian Internee Changi Camp
3DRL/7925   Papers of H. R. Slocombe, Civilian Internee

Film F01438   *Civilian Internees and Dockyards Singapore*

PR000015   Papers of Jack Percival
PR00838   Neville, Alice (Civilian Internee) Leaflet of Regulations 1943
PR00846   Canning, Zena: Papers
PR85/342   Letter of Molly Jefferson, Civilian Internee
PR 86/275   Records of D. R. Stanford
PR87/188   Papers of Harold Leslie Murray, Civilian Internee, Changi, Sime Rd
PR87/228   Papers of Nurse J. O. Harris – Rabaul POW
PR91/174   Papers of E. G. Henty

AWM 54   Written Records, 1939–45 War
AWM 93   Australian War Memorial Registry Files, First Series

Photographs
AWM Photograph No. 118701, 14 September 1945

National Archives of Australia

2 Echelon, Army Headquarters
B3856, Correspondence Files, 1942–54,

Australian Broadcasting Corporation, Head Office
SP300/3, War Correspondents' talk scripts, general wartime scripts and related correspondence, 1939–47

Australian Imperial Force Base Records Office
B13/0, 1934/7225, Merritt
B2455, First Australian Imperial Force Personnel Dossiers, 1914–1920

Australian Legation, Republic of China
A4144, Correspondence Files, 1941–49

Australian Security Intelligence Organisation, Central Office
A6119, Personal Files, alpha-numeric series, 1915–
A6126, Microfilm copies of personal and subject files, 1920–

Australian War Crimes Commission [II]
A10953 Unnumbered Files of the Commission of Inquiry on War Crimes Committed by Enemy Subjects Against Australians and Others.

Civilian Internees Trust Fund Trustees – Secretary
B510, Application forms for grants and associated documents, 1952–62
B512, Correspondence Files, 1952–61.

Commission of Inquiry into Japanese Atrocities
A6237, Exhibits of the Commission of Inquiry into Japanese Forces Atrocities, 1942–44

Controller of Enemy Property
A1379, Correspondence Files, Japan, 1939–66
A1456, Correspondence Files, Philippines Islands, 1942–55
A1457, Correspondence Files, China, 1939–1958
A1461, Correspondence Files, Thailand, 1942–45

Department of Army, Central Office
MP729/8, Secret Correspondence Files, 1937–60
MP742/1, General and Civil Staff Correspondence Files and Army personnel files, 1920–1956.

Department of Defence [III], Central Office
A5954, The Shedden Collection, 1901–71.

Department of External Affairs [II], Central Office
A981, Correspondence Files, 1921–70
A989, Correspondence Files, 1927–45
A1066, Correspondence Files, 1919–65
A1067, Correspondence Files, 1942–53
A1068, Correspondence Files, 1933–71
A1838, Correspondence Files, 1914–1993

Department of External Affairs, London
A3317, Correspondence Files, 1944–47

Department of External Territories [I], Central Office
A518, Correspondence Files, 1899–1983.

Department of Immigration, Central Office
A437, Correspondence Files, 1923–57

Department of Interior [II], Central Office
A659, Correspondence Files, Class 1, 1892–1970.

Department of Social Services, Central Office
A884, Correspondence Files, 1909–74
MP11/4, Miscellaneous Correspondence Relating to Civilian Internees

Investigation Branch, General Office, Melbourne and Canberra
A367, Correspondence Files 1916–53
A373, Correspondence Files, 1923–56

Navy Office [IV], Department of Navy [II]
MP151, Policy files relating to all aspects of the Department's activities.

Prime Minister's Department
A463, Correspondence Files, 1903–
A1608, Correspondence Files, 1914–50

War Cabinet Secretariat
A2676, War Cabinet Minutes Without Agenda Items, 1939–46

War Damage Commission
SP24/1, War Damage Commission Claim files, reference maps and photographs

Mitchell Library, Sydney

ML MSS 1425 Thomas, Gordon Papers
ML MSS 5184 Jenner, Dorothy Gordon, papers, 1921, 1938–47 Microfilmed
as CY Reel 2690

Private archives

Our Lady of the Sacred Heart Provincial Archives, Kensington, NSW

'Historical Material [F.C.]: Missionary Experiences During Pacific War
1944–1987. Ramale Camp'
Sister Mary Flavia [Catherine O'Sullivan], 'New Britain: The Evacuation
from Ramale on the Signing of the Armistice', 13 September 1945
Twohill, Berenice, 'Prisoners of the Japanese Army, Rabaul, New Britain,
December 1941–August 15, 1945', *Annals: Journal of Catholic Culture*,
Nov/Dec 1995, transcript.

Sacre Coeur Provincial Office, Tokyo, Japan

> Sr Mary Hastings, Memories of Internment, MSS
> Sr Regina McKenna, correspondence, MSS

Salvation Army Heritage Centre, Melbourne, Victoria.
George Ellis Archives

Newspapers and journals

Age
American Journal of International Law
Argus
Canberra Times
Far Eastern Survey
Herald (Melbourne)
Mercury (Hobart)
Pacific Islands Monthly
Spectator and Methodist Chronicle
Sun
Sydney Morning Herald
War Cry
West Australian

Official publications

Commonwealth Parliamentary Debates

Parliamentary Debates (England)

UN War Crimes Commission, Law Reports of Trials of War Criminals, vol. 13, HMSO for the UN War Crimes Commission, London, 1949

Memoirs

Allen, Sheila, Diary of a Girl in Changi 1941–45, Kangaroo Press, Sydney, 1994

Begley, Neil, An Australian's Childhood in China under the Japanese, Kangaroo Press, Sydney, 1995

Begley–Bourke, Audrey, Ian T. Begley and C. Neil Begley (comps), Separated for Service: A Biography on the Life and Service of Colin Keith Begley and Edith May Begley, Missionaries to China and India, Salvation Army, Melbourne, 1994

Benson, James, Prisoner's Base and Home Again: The Story of a Missionary P.O.W., Robert Hale, London, 1957

Binks, E., Through Japanese Hands for Three Years 1942–45, Richard Whelvell Ltd, Bolton, 1946

Bowman, Alice, Not Now Tomorrow: ima nai ashita, Bangalow, NSW, Daisy Press, 1996

Gittins, Jean, Stanley: Behind Barbed Wire, Hong Kong University Press, Hong Kong, 1982

Jeffrey, Betty, White Coolies, Angus & Robertson, Sydney, 1954

Jenner, Dorothy, Darlings, I've Had a Ball [by] Andrea; as told to Trish Sheppard, Ure Smith, Sydney, 1975

Ruff-O'Herne, Jan, *50 Years of Silence*, Tom Thompson Editions, Sydney, 1994

Scharmach, Leo, *This Crowd Beats Us All*, Catholic Press Newspaper Company, Sydney, 1960

Sherwood, Stephanie, *Growing Up as a Foreigner in Shanghai: Recollections*, Mini Publishing, Sydney, 2004

Simons, Jessie, *While History Passed: The Story of the Australian Nurses who were Prisoners of the Japanese for Three and a Half Years*, William Heinemann, Melbourne, 1954

ten Brummelaar, Eve, *You Can't Eat Grass*, Image DTP and Printing, Sydney, 1996

Vaughan, Elizabeth Head, *Community Under Stress: An Internment Camp Culture*, Princeton University Press, Princeton, New Jersey, 1949

Wetherell, David (ed.), *The New Guinea Diaries of Philip Strong 1936–1945*, Macmillan, Melbourne, 1981

Department of Veterans' Affairs

Australians At War Film Archive
www.australiansatwarfilmarchive.gov.au/aawfa
Archive No. 0177, Berenice Twohill

Secondary works

Adam-Smith, Patsy, *Australian Prisoners of War: From Gallipoli to Korea*, Viking, Melbourne, 1992

Aiko, Utsumi, 'Japanese Army Internment Policies for Enemy Civilians During the Asia–Pacific War', in Donald Denoon, Mark Hudson, Gavan McCormack and Tessa Morris-Suzuki (eds), *Multicultural Japan: Palaeolithic to Postmodern*, Cambridge University Press, Cambridge, 2001, pp. 174–209

Archer, Bernice, *A Patchwork of Internment: The Internment of Western Civilians under the Japanese 1941–45*, Routledge Curzon, London, 2004

— '"A Low-Key Affair": Memories of Civilian Internment in the Far East 1942–1945', in Martin Evans and Ken Lunn (eds), *War and Memory in the Twentieth Century*, Berg, Oxford, 1997, pp. 45–58

Bassett, Jan, *Guns and Brooches: Australian Army Nursing from the Boer War to the Gulf War*, Oxford University Press, Melbourne, 1992

Beaumont, Joan, *Gull Force: Survival and Leadership in Captivity, 1941–45*, Allen & Unwin, Sydney, 1988

Bennett, Jill and Rosanne Kennedy (eds), *World Memory: Personal Trajectories in Global Time*, Palgrave Macmillan, New York, 2003

Bevege, Margaret, *Behind Barbed Wire: Internment in Australia During World War Two*, University of Queensland Press, Brisbane, 1993

Bloom, Lynn Z., 'Till Death Do Us Part: Men and Women's Interpretations of Wartime Internment', *Women's Studies International Forum*, vol. 10, no. 1, 1987, pp. 75–83

— 'Escaping Voices: Women's South Pacific Internment Diaries and Memoirs', *Mosaic*, vol. 23, no. 3, 1990

Bodnar, John, 'Pierre Nora, National Memory and Democracy: a review', *Journal of American History*, vol. 87, no. 3, December 2000, p. 959

Brooks, Margaret, 'Passive in War? Women Internees in the Far East, 1942–45', in Sharon Macdonald, Pat Holden and Shirley Ardener (eds), *Images of Women in Peace and War: Cross-Cultural and Historical Perspectives*, Macmillan Education, London, 1987, pp. 166–78

Bunbury, Bill, *Rabbits and Spaghetti: Captives and Comrades, Australians, Italians and the War 1939–1945*, Fremantle Arts Centre Press, Perth, 1995

Burgess, Pat, *Warco: Australian Reporters at War*, William Heinemann, Melbourne, 1986

Captain, Esther, 'The Gendered Process of Remembering War Experiences: Memories about the Second World War in the Dutch East Indies', *European Journal of Women's Studies*, vol. 4, 1997, pp. 389–95

— 'Spreken over gedwongen prostitutie en zwijgen over verkrachtingen: Bronnengebruik in een zaak over Japanse legerbordelen in Nederlands Indie', *ICODO Info*, vol. 94, no.1, pp. 37–48

Caruth, Cathy (ed.), *Trauma: Explorations in Memory*, John Hopkins University Press, Baltimore, 1995

Castiglia, Christopher, *Bound and Determined: Captivity, Culture-Crossing and White Womanhood from Mary Rowlandson to Patty Hearst*, University of Chicago Press, Chicago, 1996

Clarence, Margaret, *Yield Not to the Wind*, Management Development Publishers, Sydney, 1982

Cogan, Frances B., *Captured: The Japanese Internment of American Civilians in the Philippines, 1941–45*, University of Georgia Press, Athens, Georgia, 2000

Cooke, Miriam, 'WO-Man: Retelling the War Myth', in Miriam Cooke and Angela Woollacott (eds), *Gendering War Talk*, Princeton University Press, Princeton, New Jersey, 1993, pp. 117–204

Damousi, Joy, *Living With the Aftermath: Trauma, Nostalgia and Grief in Post-war Australia*, Cambridge University Press, Cambridge, 2001

Damousi, Joy and Marilyn Lake (eds), *Gender & War: Australians at War in the Twentieth Century*, Cambridge University Press, Cambridge, 1995

Denoon, Donald with Stewart Firth, Jocelyn Linnekin, Malama Meleisea and Karen Nero (eds), *The Cambridge History of the Pacific Islanders*, Cambridge University Press, Cambridge, 1997

Dower, John, *War Without Mercy: Race and Power in the Pacific War*, Pantheon Books, New York, 1986

Doyle, Robert C., *Voices from Captivity: Interpreting the American POW Narrative*, Lawrence, Kansas, University of Kansas Press, 1994

Dutton, David, *One of Us? A Century of Australian Citizenship*, Sydney, UNSW Press, 2002

Elkner, Cate et al., *Enemy Aliens: The Internment of Italian Migrants in Australia in World War Two*, Connor Court Publishing, Bacchus Marsh, 2005

Garton, Stephen, 'War and masculinity in twentieth-century Australia', *Journal of Australian Studies*, no. 56, 1998, p. 90

— *The Cost of War: Australians Return*, Oxford University Press, Melbourne, 1996

Gay, Peter, *The Cultivation of Hatred*, Norton, New York, 1993

Gerster, Robin, *Big-Noting: The Heroic Theme in Australian War Writing*, Melbourne University Press, Melbourne, 1987

Gould, Randall, 'Captives of the Mikado', *Far Eastern Survey*, vol. 11, no. 11, 1 June 1942, p. 128

Griffin-Foley, Bridget, 'First Lady of the Airwaves', *Eureka Street*, June 2005

Hartendorp, A. V. H., *The Japanese Occupation of the Philippines*, Bookmark, Manila, 1967

Hasluck, Paul, *The Government and the People 1942–45*, Australian War Memorial, Series IV, Vol. II, Canberra, 1970

247

Hazzard, Shirley, *The Great Fire*, Virago, London, 2003

Hicks, George, *The Comfort Women: Sex Slaves of the Japanese Imperial Forces*, Allen & Unwin, St Leonards, 1995

Higgonet, Margaret Randoph, Jane Jenson, Sonya Michel and Margaret Collins Weitz (eds), *Behind the Lines: Gender and the Two World Wars*, Yale University Press, New Haven, Connecticut, 1987

Horne, Gerald, *Race War: White Supremacy and the Japanese Attack on the British Empire*, New York University Press, New York, 2004

Huie, Shirley Fenton, *The Forgotten Ones: Women and Children Under Nippon*, Angus & Robertson, Sydney, 1992

Inglis, Amirah, *'Not a White Woman Safe': Sexual Anxiety and Politics in Port Moresby 1920–1934*, ANU Press, Canberra, 1974

Inglis, K. S., 'War, Race and Loyalty in New Guinea, 1939–45', in University of Papua and New Guinea and Research School of Pacific Studies, Australian National University, *The History of Melanesia*, Canberra, 1969, pp. 503–27

Jones, Paul, '"Racial Character" and Australia and Japan in the 1930s', in Paul Jones and Pam Oliver (eds), *Changing Histories: Australia and Japan*, Monash Asia Institute, Melbourne, 2001 pp. 25–48

Kaminski, Theresa, *Prisoners in Paradise: American women in the wartime South Pacific*, University Press of Kansas, Lawrence, Kansas, 2000

Kaukas, Anthony, 'Images from Loveday: internment in South Australia, 1939–45', *Journal of the Historical Society of South Australia*, no. 29, 2001, pp. 47–57

Kazuko, Watanabe, 'Militarism, Colonialism and the Trafficking of Women: "Comfort Women" Forced into Sexual Labour for Japanese Soldiers', in Joe Moore (ed.), *The Other Japan: Conflict, Compromise and Resistance since 1945*, M. E. Sharpe, New York, 1997, pp. 305–19

Kennedy, Joseph, *British Civilians and the Japanese War in Malaya and Singapore, 1941–45*, Macmillan, London, 1987

Kenny, Catherine, *Captives: Australian Army Nurses in Japanese Prison Camps*, University of Queensland Press, Brisbane, 1986

Kochan, Miriam, *Britain's Internees in the Second World War*, Macmillan, London, 1983

LaCapra, Dominick, 'Trauma, Absence, Loss', *Critical Enquiry*, 25:4, Summer 1999; online at <http://find.galegroup.com.ezproxy.lib.monash.edu.au/itx/infomark.do?&contentSet=IAC-Documents&type=retrieve&tabID=T002&prodId=EAIM&docId=A55721730&source=gale&userGroupName=monash&version=1.0>, accessed 27 September 2006

Lake, Marilyn and Damousi, Joy, 'Warfare, History and Gender', in Joy Damousi and Marilyn Lake (eds), *Gender and War: Australians at War in the Twentieth Century*, Cambridge University Press, Cambridge, 1995, pp. 1–20

Mackay, Ross, 'The War Years: Methodists in Papua and New Guinea, 1942–1945', *Journal of Pacific History*, vol. 27, no. 1, 1992, pp. 29–43

McKernan, Michael, *This Pain Never Ends: The Pain of Separation and Return*, University of Queensland Press, Brisbane, 2001

Macwilliam, Scott, 'Papua New Guinea in the 1940s: Empire and Legend', in David Lowe (ed.), *Australia and the End of Empires: The Impact of Decolonisation in Australia's Near North 1945–65*, Deakin University Press, Geelong, 1996, pp. 25–42

Matthews, Tony, 'Missionary Martyrs: Second World War 1939–45', *Wartime*, no. 21, 2003, pp. 13–15

Nagata, Yuriko, *Unwanted Aliens: Japanese Internment in Australia*, University of Queensland Press, Brisbane, 1996

Nelson, Hank, 'The Return to Rabaul, 1945', *Journal of Pacific History*, vol. 30, no. 2, 1995, pp. 131–53

— 'Measuring the Railway: From Individual Lives to National History', in Gavan McCormack and Hank Nelson (eds), *The Burma-Thailand Railway: Memory and History*, Allen & Unwin, Sydney, 1993, pp. 10–26

— 'The Troops, The Town and the Battle: Rabaul 1942', *Journal of Pacific History*, vol. 27, no. 2, 1992, pp. 198–216

— *P.O.W.: Prisoners of War – Australians Under Nippon*, ABC Enterprises, Sydney, 1985

Neumann, Klaus, 'A Doubtful Character: Wolf Klaphake', <www.uncommonlives.naa.gov.au>, accessed 30 November 2005

Reed, Liz, *Bigger Than Gallipoli: War, History and Memory in Australia*, University of Western Australia Press, Perth, 2004

Reeson, Margaret, *A Very Long War: The Families Who Waited*, Melbourne University Press, Melbourne, 2000

Roland, Charles G., 'Allied POWs, Japanese Captors and the Geneva Convention', *War & Society*, 9:2, October 1991, pp. 83–101

Rowland, E. C., 'Faithful Unto Death', in Theo Aerts (ed.), *The Martyrs of Papua New Guinea: 333 Missionary Lives Lost During World War II*, Papua New Guinea Press, Port Moresby, 1994, pp. 55–7

Saunders, Kay and Roger Daniels (eds), *Alien Justice: Wartime Internment in Australia and North America*, UQP, Brisbane, 2000

Saunders, Kay and Helen Taylor, 'The enemy within? The Process of internment of enemy aliens in Queensland 1939–45', *Australian Journal of Politics and History*, vol. 34, no. 1, 1988, pp. 16–27

Scharmach, Leo, *This Crowd Beats Us All*, Catholic Press Newspaper Company, Sydney, 1960

Solomon-Godeau, Abigail, *Photography at the Dock: Essays on Photographic Histories, Institutions and Practices*, University of Minnesota Press, Minneapolis, 1991

Sontag, Susan, *Regarding the Pain of Others*, Penguin, London, 2003

Souter, Gavin, *Company of Heralds: A century and a half of Australian Publishing by John Fairfax Limited and its predecessors, 1831–1981*, Melbourne University Press, Melbourne, 1981

Stanley, Peter, 'He's (not) coming south: the invasion that wasn't', in Steve Bullard and Tamura Keiko (eds), *From a Hostile Shore: Australia and Japan at War in New Guinea*, Australia–Japan Research Project, Australian War Memorial, Canberra, 2004, pp. 3–57

Stoler, Mark A., 'The Second World War in U.S. History and Memory', *Diplomatic History*, vol. 25, no. 3, Summer 2001, p. 390

Summerfield, Penny, 'Gender and War in the Twentieth Century', *International History Review*, vol. xix, no. 1, February 1997, pp. 3–15

Sweeting, A. J., 'Civilian Wartime Experience in the Territories of Papua and New Guinea', in Paul Hasluck, (ed.), *The Government and the People, 1942–45, Australia in the War of 1939–45*, Series IV, Vol. II, Australian War Memorial, 1970, Canberra, pp. 668–708

— 'Montevideo Maru: Myth or Merchantman', in Theo Aerts (ed.), *The Martyrs of New Guinea: 333 Missionary Lives Lost During World War II*, University of Papua New Guinea Press, Port Moresby, 1994, pp. 186–190

Tanaka, Yuki, *Japan's comfort women: Sexual slavery and prostitution during World War II and the US Occupation*, Routledge, London, 2002

Thomas, Gordon, 'How Rabaul's civilians met their fate', *Pacific Islands Monthly*, November 1945, p. 15

Thompson, Roger C., 'Making a Mandate: The Formation of Australia's New Guinea Policies 1919–25', *Journal of Pacific History*, vol. 25, no. 1, 1990, pp. 68–84

Thorne, Christopher, *Allies of a Kind: The United States, Britain and the War Against Japan 1941–45*, Hamish Hamilton, London, 1978

— *Racial Aspects of the Far Eastern War of 1941–45*, Oxford University Press, Oxford, 1982

Torney-Parlicki, Prudence, '"Unpublishable Scoops: Australian Journalists as Prisoners of the Japanese 1941–5', *Journal of Australian Studies*, no. 66, 2000, pp. 180–9

— Somewhere in Asia: The Australian News-Media and Conflict in the Asia Pacific Region, 1945–1971, PhD thesis, Department of History, University of Melbourne, 1997

Twomey, Christina, 'Australian Nurse POWs: Gender, War and Captivity', *Australian Historical Studies*, vol. 36, no. 124, October 2004, pp. 255–74

van Poelgeest, Bart, 'Oosters stille dwang: Tewerkgesteld in de Japanse bordelen van Nederlands-Indie', *ICODO Info*, vol. 93, no. 3, pp. 13–21

Van Velden, D., *De Japanse Interneringskampen voor burgers gedurende de tweede wereldoorlog*, J. B. Wolters, Groningen, 1963

Waiko, John Dademo, *A Short History of Papua New Guinea*, Oxford University Press, Melbourne, 1993

Walker, Alan S., *Medical Services of the R.A.N. and R.A.A.F. With a Section on Women in the Army Medical Service*, Australian War Memorial, Canberra, 1961

Warner, Lavinia and John Sandilands, *Women Beyond the Wire: A Story of Prisoners of the Japanese 1941–45*, Michael Joseph, London, 1982

Wasserstein, Bernard, *Secret War in Shanghai*, Profile Books, London, 1999

Watanabe, Kazuko, 'Militarism, Colonialism and the Trafficking of Women: "Comfort Women" Forced into Sexual Labour for Japanese Soldiers', in Joe Moore (ed.), *The Other Japan: Conflict, Compromise and Resistance since 1945*, New York, M. E. Sharpe, 1997, pp. 305–19

Waterford, Van, *Prisoners of the Japanese in World War II: Statistical History, Personal Narratives and Memorials Concerning POWs in Camps and on Hellships, Civilian Internees, Asian Slave Labourers and Others Captured in the Pacific Theater*, McFarland and Company, Jefferson NC and London, 1994

Wigmore, Lionel, *Australia in the War of 1939–45, Series One: Army, Volume IV: The Japanese Thrust*, [1957], Australian War Memorial, Canberra, 1968

Willson, Robert, 'A Canberra nurse who became a martyr', Anglican Historical Society Journal, no. 14, October 1992, pp. 37–41

Wilson, Robert R., 'Treatment of Civilian Alien Enemies', *American Journal of International Law*, vol. 37, no. 1, January 1943, p. 32

Winter, Christine, 'The long arm of the Third Reich: internment of New Guinea Germans in Tatura', *Journal of Pacific History*, vol. 38, no. 1, June 2003, pp. 85–108

Winter, Jay, 'Forms of kinship and remembrance in the aftermath of the Great War', in Jay Winter and Emmanuel Sivan (eds), *War and Remembrance in the Twentieth Century*, Cambridge University Press, Cambridge, 2000, pp. 40–60

— 'Under cover of war: The Armenian genocide in the context of total war', in Jay Winter (ed.), *America and the Armenian Genocide of 1915*, Cambridge University Press, Cambridge, 2003, pp. 42–8

Wolfers, Edward P., *Race Relations and Colonial Rule in Papua New Guinea*, Australia and New Zealand Book Company, Sydney, 1975

Wright, Huntley, 'Protecting the National Interest: The Labor Government and the Reform of Australia's Colonial Policy, 1942–45', *Labour History*, No. 2, May 2002, pp. 65–79

INDEX